D1426915

# HUNGARY

## A SHORT HISTORY

## NORMAN STONE

**P**

**PROFILE BOOKS**

For Anil Seal

First published in Great Britain in 2019 by
Profile Books Ltd
3 Holford Yard
Bevin Way
London WC1X 9HD
*www.profilebooks.com*

A CIP catalogue record for this book is available from the British Library.

ISBN 978 1 78816 050 6
eISBN 978 1 78283 448 9

Typeset in Caslon by MacGuru Ltd

Printed and bound in Great Britain by Clays Ltd, Elcograf S.p.A.

# Contents

# Maps and illustrations

# Preface

I n the last sixty years Hungary has made world news on three occasions – in 1956, 1989 and 2015 – and her present Prime Minister, Viktor Orbán, explains this quite simply: the Austrian border. The first two occasions concerned the Soviet Union, whose army had occupied Hungary in 1945 and forced her into the Communist world. The same might have happened to Austria – Vienna had also fallen to the Russians – but the western Allies had taken most of the country, and in 1955 the Russians withdrew. They recognised Austria as a neutral state, and she began to prosper. The Hungarians would gladly have followed that example, and next year they rebelled, making headlines. For ten days there was an illusion of freedom, but Soviet tanks crushed Budapest. Two hundred thousand Hungarians managed to escape to the west. In 1989 came another headline moment. By then, the Soviet grip had relaxed, and you were not automatically shot or blown up if you went to Austria (although one unfortunate East German somehow provoked a guard and was killed on 21 August). People from other countries of the Soviet bloc could legally go to Hungary, and thousands of East Germans went there on holiday. In 1989 word got out that they would not be stopped if they crossed into Austria. The Hungarian opposition organised a Pan-European picnic, and six hundred people just crossed the border, followed by thousands and thousands in August. The Communist East German state, which had a smell of brown coal, a stupidity of sloganeering and a bullying frontier system all its own, was hopelessly discredited, and the shock to the Communist system was such that the most famous part of the Iron Curtain, the Berlin Wall, was breached, and East Germany collapsed, followed by other Communist states.

These two moments of Austro-Hungarian history had to do with the decline of Communism. But in the summer of 2015 came another headline moment, when hundreds of thousands of refugees or migrants from the Middle East trudged into Hungary, making for the Austrian border. They were doing this because the German Chancellor, Angela Merkel, had invited them. She did not ask the Hungarians' opinion. Overwhelmed by (mostly) young men trudging through from Serbia, Viktor Orbán famously put up a razor-wire fence to keep them out until they could be registered. Official Europe howled with rage, and the Austrian Chancellor, according to a Reuters report, likened Orbán's refugee policies to Nazi deportations – not an obvious comparison. Orbán vigorously defended himself; later on, he said that many places in western Europe had become unrecognisable – he could have mentioned Brussels – and that in fifteen years' time an adolescent born then would ask how this could have happened. No one had voted for it. And he also knew what he was talking about. For Hungary this was a matter of national survival. Her southern border is porous, the countryside flat, an invitation to invasion.

Hungary had already had a Moslem occupation, lasting a century and a half, under the Ottoman Turks. The Turks themselves in modern times have been quite popular in Hungary, for reasons that will be looked into, and in any case, after a good century of westernising reform, are tolerably prosperous, with no compelling reason to migrate. But the back areas of the old Ottoman Empire are on the move – North Africa, the Sudan, Syria and Iraq – and the Hungarians fear being overwhelmed. Their country is not rich. Being a member of the European Union has not been an unmixed blessing: agriculture has not flourished as it should have done (you can see the difference when you cross the Austrian border), and Austrian banks acquired a reputation for rapacity in dealings with rents and mortgages in Hungary. Freedom of movement in Europe is no doubt a good thing, but it has also meant that more than half a million young Hungarians emigrated, mainly to Austria, Britain and Germany, and the national health system will take time to recover. Viktor Orbán stands up for himself, and now has an international reputation that few leaders of small countries have matched.

The most recent (and best) English-language history of Hungary, by Bryan Cartledge, is called *The Will to Survive*, and that title sums it up. Hungary's survival is indeed strange. The Magyars – their name for themselves – descended on Europe as one of several central Asian tribal federations, called 'hordes' (in Turkish, *ordu*; 'Hungary' comes from 'On ogur', meaning 'ten arrows' in old Turkish, and may have something to do with 'Hun'), and that is where their language comes from. All other such hordes vanished (or almost: there are remnants, such as the Turkish Gagauz – 'Kara oguz' – in Moldova and the Hungarian Csángó in Rumania) as they assimilated with peoples whom they had subjected: the originally Turkish Bulgars became Orthodox and spoke Slavonic. The Hungarians became Christian, but kept their language, and Hungary became a great state in the Middle Ages. Then, after 1526, she succumbed to German-Austrian Habsburg imperialists and Ottoman Turkish imperialists: for well over a century she was a battleground between two world empires. But she was not cut off from Europe, and joined in European movements: the Reformation in particular. The Turks did not bother with Christian divisions, which they could not understand: they only wanted tribute from non-Moslems, and even discouraged conversion to Islam. This gave Hungary her peculiar character, because the Turks prevented the Habsburgs from carrying through the Catholicising and Germanising programme that they implemented by force elsewhere, especially in the Czech lands, and in the eastern part of the country there was an independent principality, Transylvania, under Turkish protection. It is a spectacular part of the world, a land of forests and high mountains, and if you define Europe's borders in terms of Gothic cathedrals, it is indeed on the edge. There Calvinism, with its ferocious devotion to education, survived in strength, the only place in Europe east of Switzerland where this happened. In the nineteenth century Calvinists played a dominant role in the Hungarian revival.

When the Austrians and their allies in the Papal-inspired Holy League finally won the Turkish wars at the start of the eighteenth century, Hungary was taken over by the Habsburg dynasty, and the title of a good book on this period (by János Barta) is *In the Shadow of the Double-Headed Eagle*, an allusion to the Imperial symbol. There is more than an echo of that term today, as the country is absorbed into the European Union. German and other settlers arrived, and only one third of the country could count as Magyar. The Habsburgs fomented and collaborated with a great aristocracy, and much of the Hungarian nobility, Esterházys and Pálffys especially, went along with this. The towns, such as they were, often used German. However, Hungary always had her separate constitution, and in the later eighteenth century there was a national revival. She clawed her way back, and the language was launched again. A period of reform and revolution followed, and in 1867 the Habsburgs recognised Hungary's right to run her own affairs. She did so very effectively, and modern Budapest is the monument to that era, which went on until 1914. There is another religious theme here: the very large Jewish presence. Jews got on better in Budapest than almost anywhere else in Europe at the time, and a theory went the rounds that they were not really Jews and that they were descended from the Khazars, a Turkish people whose rulers had adopted Judaism because they disliked the Christian attitude to sex and the Moslem attitude to alcohol. Arthur Koestler wrote a book to this effect (*The Thirteenth Tribe*, 1976), although its conclusions are not widely shared. True, Zionism was born here, but the chief Jewish periodical *Equality* editorialised that 'There is only one name for

Zionism in Hungary – treason'. The Budapest Jews contributed an immense amount, from Hollywood to the atomic bomb, and Arthur Koestler's memoirs show their spirit.

Hungary had a good nineteenth century and then a horrible twentieth: murderous defeat in the First World War, a Communist episode in 1919, truncation, by two-thirds, of the country at the Treaty of Trianon in 1920, then another world war, a Nazi occupation and a Soviet one, until finally, on 23 October 1989, she became a parliamentary republic, and the Russians agreed to go. I was there in the Parliament that day, sent by Max Hastings for *The Daily Telegraph*. Fat-faced men with piggy eyes voted for their own extinction as deputies, having made certain of a good sinecure with which to escape; but outside, it was moving to see how people somehow walked differently after the declaration had been made in the Parliament. Hungarians had at last had some good news. True, the end of Communism was ragged and unsatisfactory, but Hungary was able to rejoin the west. The European Union no doubt has its failings, but being able to travel without restriction through almost all areas of the old Habsburg Monarchy is an undoubted plus. In the old days you might have to endure long hold-ups at borders, and the train journey from Vienna to Budapest took eight hours (as against just over three today).

My own qualifications for writing about this go back some way – now, over fifty years. As a very young man I had got interested in the Habsburg Monarchy, especially its army, and in 1962 I asked the British Council if there were any scholarships to Austria. No, came the answer, but as things had turned out, they had just had an enquiry from Hungary about whether British students might be interested in a Hungarian language course – the British Council paying the train fare, the Hungarians doing the rest. I now know that this was a small part of a Moscow-inspired programme of détente, and we had a good welcome. The steam train from the Westbahnhof in Vienna took a long time, with customs and security checks at Hegyeshalom, and you arrived at a dark and dingy

Keleti (Eastern) Station in a Budapest that was also dark and dingy, the buildings still marked with bullet holes from the siege of 1945 and the rebellion of 1956. The Castle was a ruin, and the Elisabeth Bridge had not been reconstructed; there were empty spaces, like bomb sites in post-war London, where the Ritz and the Hungaria hotels had stood. We were put up, rather grandly, in the Astoria (still, mercifully, as it was) and the Grand Hotel on the Margaret Island, also nowadays largely as it used to be. The language course was in Debrecen, at the University, which had monumental buildings, opened, with his usual bad timing, by the last Habsburg Emperor, Karl, in October 1918. We stayed in a spartan agricultural college, and my best friends there were East Germans and Poles. The Hungarians we met were very good – well read, with excellent and humorous English, and I made some progress, though not much, with the language. I went again in 1963, and then had a great stroke of luck. Early in 1964 I got involved in a crazy enterprise to smuggle someone's fiancé out to Austria via Slovakia. We were caught on the border, but my timing had been fortuitous. Three months earlier, and I would have had nine years in a camp. Three months later, I would have been quietly expelled. As things were, I spent three months in prison while the authorities scratched their heads, and I shared the cell with a Transylvanian gypsy who did wonders for my Hungarian.

Back at Cambridge in 1965, I battled on with it for a while, but it was difficult. I had been powerfully affected at the time by A. J. P. Taylor's *Habsburg Monarchy, 1809–1918*, a wonderful essay, and Taylor had taken some of his views from his friend the 'Red Count' Michael Károlyi, whom he described as a saint; and besides, the great British authority was R. W. Seton-Watson, who denounced the Hungarians' treatment of their minorities, who then made up half of the country. In any case, someone said that central Europe was a subject for either the very young or the old man, and I was no longer very young. I had gone to Vienna for three years, working as a graduate student in the war archives, and I can remember thinking, when I got back to Cambridge, it is either Germany or Russia. I moved on to Russian history, wrote about the eastern front of the First World War and came back to Hungarian history only in the early 1980s, when, as part of the Fontana *History of Europe*, I had the volume covering 1878–1919 to write. By then I had a better appreciation of what old Hungary had achieved, and was no longer starry-eyed about minority nationalism, having had the dismal experience of seeing Transylvania under nationalist-Communist rule in 1982, when you got impetigo from filthy hotel pillows and food poisoning even in hard-currency restaurants. Hungary was much better than Rumania, and I started going back to the country in 1985, when it was already changing fast. I went with a small team from Channel 4 to prospect for a programme about it, and by then Budapest was already involved in a sort of post-Communism that had its surreal side. We were taken through the sleety hills of Buda to an Institute of International Relations for a breakfast meeting. Arriving at one of those grand villas, we encountered treble-locked wrought-iron gates, behind which an enormous dog was howling hatred. A heavily upholstered maid in a white pinny came out, silenced the dog with a chop to its neck, and let us in. We were met by the director, a trade-union war-horse with no languages, and his assistant, a pasty-faced overweight young man who, on my enquiry as to his purpose in this life, answered, in an accent that reminded me of a lorry crunching over gravel, that he did the theory of inter-national relations – but not the theory, the theory of the theory. Before he could go on, we were heartened by the clink of glasses upon bottles, as the maid came back in with the very welcome breakfast nip. By then everyone, but everyone, was cynical about Communism, and was looking for the exit. I was drawn more and more to the country, as were many people with foreign passports, some of whom were taken in by 'reform Communism' much more than the natives were. In Oxford there were well-intentioned sem-inars on the subject, at which a tubby Hungarian in a shiny brown suit would lorry-gravel his way through a lecture on 'market reform in a socialist economy', would meet with a thoughtful response and be discovered next day spending his expenses on female underwear in Marks & Spencer. Such people were quite well placed to take over when Communism collapsed in 1989, and official Europe also found it easy enough to go on working with them. The present-day popularity of Viktor Orbán has something to do with this.

I hope with the present book to set out the main lines of Hungary's modern past, since 1848. The Hungarians have been obsessed with their own history, and a great deal has been written – not easy, because for so much of the time you have to refer to other people's history, whether Austrian, Czech, or German. I have used most of these books, but as this one is designed for an English-speaking readership, I have not formally referred to them all. In any case, since there has been a huge and important Hungarian emigration to the west, the English-speaking reader is even rather spoiled for classic books, and I begin my list of sources and recommended reading with some of them.

I have had useful help from many Hungarians and Budapest residents in the course of trying to make sense of modern Hungary. The Foundation for Civic Hungary supported the initial work, and I am grateful to Mária Schmidt for her support. Áron Mathé, editing the manuscript, has helpfully kept a foot on the brake when it comes to my generalisations. George Schöpflin, late of the LSE and now of the European Parliament, has been a constant encouragement, and I have had much sympathetic help from Tom Barcsay, Mark Odescalchi and Pista Pálffy. The London Library also deserves special recognition for the richness of its collection and the helpfulness of its staff. The late Professor Mihály Szegedy-Maszák was wonderful on literature, and introduced me to a Hungarian art form, malicious gossip. The late Gavin Stamp, an old student and friend, was hugely helpful about Hungarian architecture: as enthusiastic about it as he was about Victorian Glasgow. Bálint Varga has kept me going with suggestions as to reading, and I owe much to his supervisor, the late György Granasztói, as also to the former

Hungarian ambassador in Ankara, János Hóvári. At Oxford in the later 1980s many Hungarian students appeared, and I took an interest in them, which has been well rewarded, because several, including Viktor Orbán and Zsolt Németh (whose brother took me to Transylvania), have gone on to great things. It remains for me to thank Paul Forty and Matthew Taylor for their patient and professional editing, my son Rupert Stone for being my target reader and Sebahattin Kanat for general and generous assistance. I should also like to acknowledge the great help I have had from the rector of my university, Bilkent in Ankara, for 'sabbatical leave'.

Hungary is now a small country, but she is, as D. H. Lawrence said of Balzac, a gigantic dwarf, with an interest far beyond her size and the remoteness of her language. All in all, I am very grateful for the strange fate that caused me to be involved with Hungary all those years ago.

# CHAPTER I

# The Setting

T here is a landmark monument to Great Britain in the middle of Budapest: the Chain Bridge, over the Danube. It was designed in 1839 by an Englishman, William Clark (who also designed Hammersmith Bridge in London), and was put up by Scotsmen under the direction of Adam Clark; it was finished in 1849. It was, for the time, an engineering marvel, suspended over the broad Danube, and was the first permanent link between Buda, the old royal capital of Hungary on the hilly right bank of the Danube, and Pest, on the left bank, where barges were unloaded and the great Hungarian plain started. Pest was developing quite briskly, with a university, a national theatre and a museum, but at the time Hungary was in the backwoods of Europe, and the British arrived to construct bridges, drains and railways (and, on the Pest side of the Chain Bridge, an elaborate Lloyd's Insurance building, the Gresham Palace, now the Four Seasons Hotel). The Chain Bridge amounted to a statement that Hungary was about to be modernised, and for a time the tolls collected from people crossing it constituted a good part of the town's income. In the next generation Pest was a vast building site, and was planned by a body similar to the London Metropolitan Board of Works, its sewage sorted out by the board's chief engineer,

Joseph Bazalgette.[1] At that time London counted as Europe's most go-ahead city, defeating cholera well before any other and, with the 'Tube', pioneering the underground railway. In 1904 a final homage to Great Britain was opened in Budapest: the enormous Parliament, the inspiration of which was the Palace of Westminster, though it outdoes the work of Charles Barry and Augustus Pugin in historicising theatricality and sort-of-Gothic evocations of central Asia.

England was something of a model for Hungary in the mid-nineteenth century, and much was made of the historical parallels. There was an old two-chamber Parliament, called the Diet, from the Latin word for 'food allowance': in modern parlance, 'expenses'. It had had its equivalent of Magna Carta, although the Hungarian version (1222) was mostly designed to lessen the big nobles' power over the lesser ones. There was also a Hungarian equivalent of the landed gentry, the squires, who had given headaches to English kings, and there was a great aristocracy, some of it of medieval origin; some magnates saw themselves as Whigs, defending the nation against a tyrannical monarch. (In 1840 they already had their own grand club in Pest, the National, which was set up in conscious imitation of British examples, where horse-racing and politics were central concerns.) But the parallels with Britain did not really work, for there was precious little of a middle class, let alone a City of London.

Around 1530 Hungary fell to foreigners.

This happened quite suddenly. In the Middle Ages Hungary had counted as a Great Power, and fought Venice for control of the Adriatic; her kings in 1102 also became kings of Croatia and Dalmatia, whose power ranged from Bulgaria to the Czech lands and even Poland. That in itself was anomalous, for the Hungarians (they called themselves Magyars) were not originally European. They had arrived in Europe from central Asia in the later tenth century, in what might be called the last barbarian invasion, and for a time they, good horse-archers, terrified Europe. (The name Hungary may have something to do with 'Hun', and Attila became a popular first name.) They had come from central Asia, and their language has grammatical parallels with Turkish; the Byzantines called an eleventh-century king 'Prince of Turkey'. All other such central Asian invaders were absorbed in the end by the host places: the Bulgarians, originally Turkish-speaking, adopted Orthodoxy and Slavonic, and other incomers, such as the Jazygs or Cumans, leave a trace only in place-names (in Hungary, anything containing 'Jász' or 'Kun'). But the Hungarians set up a powerful kingdom that adopted Christianity early on, the language survived, and it was the local Slavs who assimilated. In the era of the Renaissance, Hungary flourished, but something went wrong: over-mighty barons, peasant revolts and, on the Balkan doorstep, the Ottoman Turks. In 1526 the battle of Mohács found a badly led Hungarian army facing more than twice its numbers, with professional janissaries and first-rate artillery. The king himself was killed. From then until the end of the seventeenth century Hungary dissolved into three parts.

The largest part, the flat land east of the Danube, of which Buda was the chief town, was taken by the Ottoman Turks. They had, historically, a bad image: if a town resisted them, it was severely punished, but Hungarian legend and literature remembers many episodes of resistance: the wine Bull's Blood, *bikavér*, drunk during a siege of the northern town of Eger, is supposed to have strengthened the defenders so that the Turks were amazed by its alleged qualities (though in this case the episode was invented by a later poet). On the other hand, when the Turks took over Balkan places, they were often supported by the Orthodox, whose chief enemy was Catholicism, and for the first generation or two they operated a functioning state. However, it was a war-zone for much of the time, and agriculture in the Central Plain, the *Alföld*, was primitive, the great river Tisza creating malaria-ridden swamps. Hungarians were caught 'between two heathens in one homeland'. Around 1600, probably because of the great price inflation and climate change that afflicted southern Europe as a whole in the later sixteenth century, the great empire of Süleyman the Magnificent entered a slow decline. It was exposed on too many fronts, especially the Persian one, and its inventiveness waned. Maps and telescopes had, of course, been essential for navigation, but these disappeared, as the religious authorities said that searching the secrets of the stars was blasphemy, that God sent earthquakes as punishment. The then Sultan, exhausted by his harem – another fateful invention of the late sixteenth century – gave way, and the telescopes vanished from their tower in Beşiktaş. The Turkish navy from then on was not much of a threat to anybody. The Ottomans also lost control of their forests, which in Hungary, as in central Anatolia, were destroyed by goats and by peasants cutting down trees incontinently. When the Habsburgs took Ottoman Hungary in the course of a quarter-century war around the turn of the seventeenth and eighteenth centuries, it was a war zone, depopulated and primitively farmed. But a large part of the Hungarian population had much more time for the Turks than for the Habsburgs, whose ways they feared.

The Habsburgs had the smallest part of divided Hungary. The slain king left no direct heirs, and his dynasty died out; the crown was taken by his sister's husband, Ferdinand of Habsburg, the German Emperor. With that, Hungary's fate became entwined with that of Germany. In the sixteenth century the Habsburg dynasty saved at least western and northern Hungary from the Turks, lands that modern Hungary has mainly lost (they are now in Austria or Slovakia or the Ukraine), and the price was loss of independence. Ferdinand, whose base was Austrian, was German Emperor, and the Habsburg family at the time, by a set of unique twists, ran Spain, much of Italy, the Netherlands and Spanish America. The Austrian branch of the family had inherited various archduchies, which now largely make up the territory of modern Austria, and it also – though with less secure title – ruled Bohemia, the Czech lands, sometimes calling Prague the capital, rather than Vienna. Hungary therefore became part of the Habsburg Empire, and the relationship between Czech Prague, German Vienna and

Hungarian Budapest is a main theme in what follows. There were, of course, many other peoples – called 'nationalities' – in the Empire (in 1914 mobilisation posters went up in fifteen languages, including Yiddish).

By 1610 the Habsburg Empire had become a spearhead of the Catholic Counter-Reformation, and the Thirty Years War (1618–48) tore Germany apart, leaving, in the exhausted end, a mainly Catholic south and a mainly Protestant north. The Habsburgs applied a sort of formula. The Church acquired enormous lands and power, still reflected in the giant monasteries that you can see at Klosterneuburg or Melk, on a bend in the Austrian Danube above Vienna, and in Prague. The Jesuit Order cleverly converted local aristocrats, and the Habsburgs rewarded their collaborators. They had to retake the Czech lands from Protestants, whose lands they seized, and the great Bohemian families were often German in origin – the Schwarzenbergs, for instance, who had ninety-nine castles. One more, and they would have had to supply an army for the Emperor. Their crest shows, apart from the double-headed imperial eagle, a raven, pecking the eyes out of a dead janissary, for in the seventeenth century these noble families were heavily involved in Turkish wars as well as German ones, and were given preferential treatment when it came to land grants. The Habsburg part of Hungary received something of the same formula, and grand aristocratic families did well, the grandest being the Esterházys and the Pálffys: big estates, worked by serfs who were required to do the lords' bidding. The Church also had preferential treatment, and a Counter-Reformation got under way: three dozen Protestant pastors with their families were marched to the galleys in Naples, from where they were rescued by a Dutch expedition. In Italy and Spain the Counter-Reformation encouraged, as Indro Montanelli says, 'monstrous inequalities', recreating 'a feudal-type society in which the closed caste of privileged ecclesiastics and laymen towered over the rest'.[2]

But there were severe limits as to what could be done through the Church Militant. The Protestants in Hungary had a safe haven.

Protestantism was stamped out almost everywhere, except in pockets, between Switzerland and eastern Hungary, of which the Principality of Transylvania was the chief part. In the Turkish-occupied central areas (the largest third of the country) it survived, chiefly because the Turks mainly just occupied the towns, and anyway were as bewildered by Christian divisions as Christians are bewildered by Moslem ones. A Turk could make no more sense of disputes as to whether Jesus Christ was a Real Presence at Communion (the Catholic idea) or not (a Protestant idea, though with disputed modifications), just as Christians can hardly understand the difference between Sunni and Shia Islam (something to do with whether the Prophet's son-in-law should have succeeded him in the seventh century). In their part of Hungary the Turks were quite indifferent, and when Protestants and Catholics asked the Pasha of Buda to mediate as to which had the right to a church, he just accorded the nave to the one and the choir to the other.[3] But these now weird-seeming quarrels were symbols of much deeper differences, affecting even the architecture, and especially the schools.[4] Protestants were literate, reading the Bible in their native languages. The Catholic upper classes, Jesuit-trained, were also literate, but not their serfs. A Catholic church was an elaborate affair, all baroque whorls, cherubs, gilded statuary, with a crowd of beggars outside. Monks ran the pawnshops as charitable institutions, and these are known in France or Italy as 'Mounts of Piety'. The Protestant churches were plainer, and the Calvinist version was a grim box, with another grim box attached, marked 'school'; begging was severely discouraged, and pawnshops (or 'pledge houses') were run by pawnbrokers of uncharitable disposition. Calvin himself, at Geneva, just removed the children of the poor from their parents and put them into a school.[5] His followers at Amsterdam invented the workhouse, where the lazy were put in a cellar that gradually filled up with water. They were given a pump to save themselves from drowning, and thereby to learn the work ethic. Hungarian Calvinism was very demanding: Péter Bornemisza gave two-hour sermons in the later sixteenth century, and there were only biblical holidays, as distinct from the Catholics' innumerable saints' days; music – unaccompanied voice – was only gingerly permitted.[6] By 1621, in the era when, under the sovereign Gábor Bethlen, Transylvania counted as a European Power (and as such was represented at the Peace of Westphalia in 1648), there were court schools in Gyulafehérvár and Sárospatak, taking in so many peasant boys that the nobles complained.[7] But it can be said of Protestantism that through education and sobriety it offered a way out of serfdom. The Turks had a very bad press (unjustly: the area was a war zone), and did nothing to prevent the decay of old buildings (which were anyway in decay as Hungarian kings lost control), but in central Hungary Protestantism did survive, and the main books on the subject (Zoványi and Murdock) hardly mention the Turks at all. What the Turks did do was to protect Transylvania from the Habsburgs. The great Counter-Reformation figure Cardinal Pázmány gave the game away when he said 'It is only the existence of a Prince of Transylvania that makes Vienna respect us'.[8]

Transylvania has the most romantic name in Europe and deserves that. In the seventeenth century it was an independent principality, three times the size of today's Belgium, with a very varied and sometimes spectacular landscape of mountain and forest. Its population was mixed, for it lay on the border of Rome and Byzantium. Hungarian conquerors had taken Transylvania early on, and to develop it, in the twelfth century, they had brought in German settlers, called 'Saxons' – at the time, a widely used name for Germans. Later, German miners were introduced into another area in the north-east, known as the Zips, where their towns survive in some splendour. Germans (some were from the Netherlands) understood land drainage, agriculture and mining, and they built well. They had seven castle towns, and their name for the country was Siebenbürgen: superb early modern places, frozen in a sort of aspic by the economic stagnation that set in around 1600 (as was the case with the equally superb towns of the *romantische Strasse* south of Würzburg, which with one exception were spared Allied bombing in 1945). In time these Saxons, with their German connections, became Lutheran, and their village churches survive: to protect themselves against Tatar raiders, they were made into small fortresses where the population could take refuge and the Saxon towns had special statutes that guaranteed them protection from feudal exactions. They flourished. The chief one, Kronstadt (in Hungarian Brassó, and nowadays Braşov), sat in the south-eastern corner of the Transylvanian Alps, at the head of the Türkenschanz (Predeal) Pass, and was well connected for trade, as was the other substantial town, Hermannstadt (Nagyszeben, now Sibiu), within easy reach of the Rotenturm Pass. To the north-east of their main area was Székler country, where a people very similar to the Magyars lived. And after the turn of the twelfth and thirteenth centuries Hungarian monks revealed the existence of another population, whom they called Vlachs, or Wallachians. These are what we now call the Rumanians, living mainly in the mountainous areas, and driving sheep. They were Orthodox, and spoke a language with many Latin elements (*pîne* – *panis* in Latin – is 'bread', and *cîne* – *canis* – is 'dog').

When the Turks took over Hungary, they recognised the ruler of Transylvania as autonomous – their vassal, paying tribute, but otherwise left alone. Many Transylvanians made considerable careers with the Ottomans – Urban, the designer of the great gun that bombarded Constantinople in 1453, and Ibrahim Muteferrika, the bringer to Turkey of the printing press – and in these circumstances the Counter-Reformation was kept at bay. With a Transylvanian hinterland Calvinism spread to neighbouring parts of Hungary: Debrecen was its chief town, but it had counterparts in today's eastern Slovakia and in the Sub-Carpathian Ukraine, where there are Hungarian minorities to this day. Calvinism was relatively egalitarian: there was no clerical bureaucracy or hierarchy, and it flourished mainly in provincial places – Scotland, Switzerland, Massachusetts – where resentment reigned against the fancy cosmopolitan world to the south. It took over a large part of Transylvania, and there the Hungarian language survived, for religious books abounded. This area produced a great revolt against the Habsburgs: that of Prince Ferenc Rákóczi, himself nominally Catholic, which came to an end only in 1711, with the treaty of Szatmár. Here, at last, wisdom prevailed. The Hungarians stopped their rebellion, accepting Habsburg rule, and the Habsburgs undertook to tolerate Protestantism. There would be no confiscation of land. The treaty itself was agreed between two grandees: one a Count Károlyi, on the Protestant side, the other a Count Pálffy, for the Habsburgs. Poor Rákóczi took refuge with the Turks, as other Hungarians were to do much later on, and his followers spread around the armies of Europe, bringing the concept of the 'hussar' to light cavalry.

By then the Turks had mostly left Hungary. They were defeated when, in 1683, they besieged Vienna (their camels could only carry light cannon-balls, ineffective against the city walls) and a Habsburg reconquest occurred – finally sorted out with the Peace of Passarowitz in 1718. At this point Hungary might simply have gone under, as Bohemia had done: Germanised, Catholicised. However, this did not happen, in part because of a dynastic accident. Emperor Charles VI did not have a male heir, and wanted his daughter Maria Theresa to succeed him, against the dynastic rules. In 1723 the Diet accepted this, in other words recognising that Hungary belonged, together with the other Habsburg lands, in rather than to the Habsburg Monarchy, but her separate character was recognised. Independence-minded Hungarians could ever afterwards cite this arrangement, known as the Pragmatic Sanction, in their defence. In 1740 the Hungarians accepted Maria Theresa as Queen. One result of all of this was that Hungary preserved her ancient, crazy-paving constitution, whereas the Bohemian equivalent had been abolished. A parliament – the Diet – assembled in Pozsony (now Bratislava), the then capital, and represented the aristocracy and clergy, in two chambers. There was one for the magnates and the greater clergy and one for the lesser nobility, of whom there were a great many, some owning hardly more than an orchard, but with serfs attached.

The lesser nobles, many of them Protestant, had entrenched power in the counties, where they administered justice (for a fee) and elected the local administrative head. They resisted taxation, from which they were exempt provided they supplied an army when required. It was rarely raised, and consisted of village bad-hats with ancient weaponry. Since the Empire could not raise taxes without their consent – rarely given – the only recourse was to set up a customs barrier between Hungary and the rest of the imperial lands and collect a tariff on goods coming out of Hungary: generally wine or scrawny cattle.

Maria Theresa took a long view of such problems. She encouraged the grand families to come to Vienna, to the Theresianum military school for young noblemen, and to attend her Court. Many of them happily adopted Austro-German styles, forgot Hungarian and served as army officers: a Count Hadik (from the Erdődy family) led a force of hussars who briefly occupied Berlin in the Seven Years War (1756–63). These aristocrats, though of ancient origin, were not as rich as the Bohemian ones, as Bohemia was much richer than Hungary, and they could not build residences in Vienna to rival the Kinsky or Lobkowitz or Schönborn or Schwarzenberg Palaces: only the Pálffys, Esterházys and the two princely families of Italian origin, Odescalchi and Pallavicini, could keep up, and to do so needed considerable favours at Court. But there were severe limits to Maria Theresa's success, and the lesser nobles, especially where Calvinist, obstructed imperial rule. Provincial lawyers, citing obsolete and tyrannical law books at great length in broken Latin, greatly irritated the Austrians, who were nevertheless helpless without some collaboration. So much for the carrot.

Vienna did have two big sticks to wield. In the first place, the country was being de-Magyarised. In 1711 it was sparsely populated, and the reality in the eighteenth century was mass migration, of German settlers, of Serbs (or Vlachs, as the Rumanians were then known, or Armenians). In their hundreds of thousands, German peasants came down the Danube to take over empty land in southern Hungary and in the Banat, a very fertile region now on the Serbian–Hungarian–Rumanian border. They were known as Swabians, since they had started off from south-western Germany, and were generally, unlike the Transylvanian Saxons, Catholic. (The chief town in the Banat, Temesvár – today Timişoara – has a fine centre, with baroque buildings that make it a little Vienna.) More land was handed over to the army: 13,000 square miles, mainly in southern Slav territory, and called the Military Frontier. There soldiers were given land confiscated from the nobles to farm when they were not fighting the Turks. (These soldiers, generally known in history as 'Croats', were more often than not Orthodox, coming from Serbia, but most were Vlach – i.e., proto-Rumanian – and the law governing this arrangement, in 1630, was called *Statuta Valachorum*. But they were under the Serbian Patriarch and so became Serbs, and an essential element in the Austrian army.) Because of all this, the Hungarian share of the population dropped from a half to one-third, and even then a good part of that third did not count as part of 'the political nation'. They were serfs, and this was the Habsburgs' other stick. The business of serfdom was obviously wrong, in economics and equity alike. Maria Theresa decreed (by 'urbarial patent', the technical term) that serfs' compulsory labour should be limited. This put the Diet on the defensive. She died in 1780, and her successor, her son Joseph II, was impatient with his mother's patience. He despised much of the Counter-Reformation world, regarded the Hungarian Constitution as obsolete nonsense and refused to take an oath to respect it. He pushed through reforms that the Pope and the aristocracy greatly resented: Protestants and Jews were emancipated, and at the end, by 1790, so were the serfs. With this, Joseph touched on the greatest problem of modern Hungary: the vast inequality of landholding. It was a largely peasant country, and the peasants often farmed with primitive methods. Most were serfs, under a landlord's control and required to work at his behest. Maria Theresa had tried to limit their exploitation to three days' labour in the week (but in Catholic Europe there were also a great many saints' days, which counted as Sundays). Joseph went much further and freed them outright, hoping to create a class of loyal Habsburg subjects to displace the nobles, who refused to pay taxes and who controlled local government.

But serf emancipation was exceedingly difficult. The serf owners were also responsible for public order, communications, army recruitment and justice: remove them, and a state civil service would have to take over, for which neither the money nor the human resources existed. In fact, serf emancipation really succeeded only where it was unnecessary. (Serfdom ceased to be a reality in England in late medieval times, because peasants could get money and pay a rent to buy their freedom, but it was only formally done away with in 1922, whereas slavery, for which the common law made no provision, had gone long before, with the Mansfield judgement, in 1772. On English soil one man could not 'own' another.) If, under formal feudalism, a class of yeoman farmers had already developed, with heritable land, then serfdom would not involve endless wrangling as to landlord compensation and peasant entitlements, a problem that Joseph II immediately encountered. In other matters he also blundered, out of good intentions. He could not understand why people persisted with languages that had no real use: why not just use German? The educational system, for its time enlightened, was accordingly adapted, and Hungarians were encouraged to use it. It had something of a reverse effect, and by 1788 Ferenc Kazinczy (yet another Protestant from eastern Hungary, educated at Sárospatak) was translating *Hamlet* into Hungarian, inventing words where appropriate ones did not exist. He was imprisoned for a time, though for sedition rather than crimes against linguistics. Joseph II made too many enemies all at once, and had not thought things through. By 1790 there was uproar throughout his lands, and he died disillusioned. It is fair to say that no subsequent Habsburg ever attempted such rationalism, except perhaps Crown Prince Rudolf, who was educated by *Deutschliberal* professors of economics and killed himself in tawdry circumstances almost a century after Joseph II's death. The Habsburg Empire did not encourage rationalism.

However, the Enlightenment had won many of its battles. No one was now burned for heresy, and the monarchy ceased to be of Divine Right: it became part of the state. But the Enlightenment split in the 1780s. Part went on as if there were pie-chart solutions and statistical answers to everything, ignoring poetry. Part recognised that this was not the case, and took up romanticism, known in Scotland as 'sensibility', and here the national languages came in. The German philosopher Herder said that language – even Latvian (he knew the Protestant Baltic) – was soul. The French Revolution gave a model for this, since it was so strongly identified with French nationalism, and of most continental countries you can say, like a famous German historian, starting his volumes on Germany, 'In the Beginning was Napoleon'. So it was, even in remote Hungary. The Habsburg Empire fought the French Revolution and Napoleon for a good quarter of a century, on and off, lost many battles and won in the end, in 1814. Ideas of romantic nationalism reached Hungary, and so also, for once, did some money. In the Napoleonic Wars, landowners in western Hungary ('Transdanubia') profited from the disruption of other suppliers in Austria, and made some progress with grain and cattle. Pest began to develop as a river port. Aristocrats read, travelled and, when the Napoleonic Wars ended, in 1815, were ready for conscious modernisation. The 'reform generation' got going.

Count István Széchenyi was its greatest figure, and it was he who brought the British engineers to put up the Chain Bridge. But there was a vastly important educational side: Hungary needed a literate population, and that meant developing the national language. A pioneer in this was György Bessenyei, who as a subaltern in Maria Theresa's Hungarian Guard was resentful that French and German had developed so far and resolved, with a few collaborators, mainly in Transylvania (he was a Calvinist), to re-create a Hungarian literature, first publishing a play, with the Empress's support, in 1772. Now, a generation later, as higher education got going in Pest, more people looked at the language and wondered as to its possibilities. At the time the towns, such as they were, mainly used German, and Buda was known as 'Ofen' (a smaller part to the north, now Óbuda, was called Altofen) because it was dominated by German artisans. But, in a process that mystified the Austrians, a linguistic revival took place – one not confined to the obscure and resentful Protestant clergymen in the back of beyond. Why not just get on in German? Hungarian was a difficult language, because it was not Indo-European, and the complications are daunting. For instance, each verb has two possible endings, depending on whether it is followed by a 'the', and apart from subjunctives, there are many complications: 'can' and 'cause to' as well as reflexives are added to the verb, complete with vowel changes. Very few foreigners not exposed to it in childhood can quite get this right, even if they can manage the utterly unfamiliar-looking words. Hungarian had not died out, and grammars of it appeared on and off, but it was rarely printed and there was no agreed spelling; words for modern things just did not exist, and the Diet used Latin while the aristocracy used German at home. Provincial Protestants launched a revival, and a decisive moment came in 1825, when the Academy of Sciences was established. It set up a linguistic research section, and had a won-derful time inventing thousands of words, having rummaged through old texts or listened to old gaffers.[9] The English have been very fortunate, and (with maybe a Dutch exception) unique, in never having had to go through a similar process. The language emerged as commercial exchange in Gothic grunts, and then the Norman French added their Latin contribution. There was no Academy of Sciences to lay down the law. In the Hundred Years War some monk tried to suppress the Latin French, and rendered the book title 'Remorse of Conscience' as 'Agenbyte of Inwit'. The English intelligentsia have their faults, but no one has ever accused them of lacking in humour. A shout of laughter went up over the Inns of Court, and language reform has never been taken seriously ever since, leaving us with 'enough', 'plough' and 'although'. Other peoples have not had it so easy, and in Hungarian scholars got to work. The sounds – central Asian, as with Turkish – are not altogether easy to render in Latin letters, and odd ways out were found. 'Gy', for instance, would have been 'dj' (in English) but is slightly different. (The Turks, who had a good look at the Hungarian example when they launched their own linguistic reform in the 1920s, render it with a 'c' and replace our 'c' with 'k' or 's'.) One sometimes comic aspect of this is that, to find a word for something modern, people reached for one or other of these German Lego words – *Einbildungskraft* (imagination) is *képzelőerő*, 'capacity to put pictures inside', and there are endless similar cases. This includes idioms: in German you do not 'call' an election, you write it out, and so also in Hungarian (*válazstásokat kiírni, ki-* being *aus* and *írni, schreiben*). Theodor Herzl, pioneer of Zionism, was born in Budapest, but when Hebrew was suggested as the language, a great many people regarded it as hopelessly antiquated and would have preferred German; there were riots in the Jerusalem schools. His example must have been Hungarian, for the Jews went over to Hungarian in the 1860s quite suddenly. The process was saved from pedants and grammarians by the poets, Mihály Csokonai the pioneer (and yet another Calvinist, though he was expelled from Debrecen College for bad behaviour), Mihály Vörösmarty, János Arany and Sándor Petőfi: reciting them was inspiring.

Historians and novelists got to work on the national past. Where did the Magyars come from? By the mid-eighteenth century it was clear enough that the language had much in common with Turkish, but what about further east? One Sándor Csoma Kőrösi (1784–1842) set out to explore. He was born into a poor family from a village in Transylvania, worked his way with manual labour through the Calvinist College at Nagyenyed (a sort of miniature Debrecen) and then got a scholarship to Göttingen, in Hanover, where Oriental languages were taught. In 1770 János Sajnovics (a Transylvanian, but this time Catholic) wrote a pioneering book on the similarities between Hungarian and Lappish,[10] and in 1819 Csoma went east to find out more, suspecting some link with the Uyghurs, an ancient Turkic people living in western China. He had very little money and had to travel via the Black Sea to Alexandria and Beirut on ships at risk from the Plague. He reached Tibet, and wrote the first English–Tibetan dictionary; he was honoured by the academic society of Bengal, and has a statue there; in time he was made a Japanese Buddhist saint. The romanticism extended to music, where the presiding genius is Franz Liszt. He was born on the Austro-Hungarian border (in 1811) to a German family, and he never really mastered Hungarian. But he was a child prodigy as a pianist and (first in Vienna, then in France) made his reputation among the romantics for impossible-to-play pyrotechnics; quite soon he picked up Hungarian nationalism and placed it on the European cultural map, touring everywhere, including Constantinople.

But beyond the romanticism, serious thought was going on as to reality. István Széchenyi was the great patron, and he knew the west. How do you make Hungary, with its multifarious and mainly peasant population, into a modern nation? Here, for any thinking aristocrat, the model was British or – for historical fiction, given Sir Walter Scott – Scottish. At the time, England – as it was universally known on the Continent – counted as the model of progress. The British had produced a miracle, a country with old institutions but without polit-ical oppression; they had a monarchy, an Established Church and an aristocracy, which elsewhere counted as blocks on progress, yet the British had the most go-ahead economy in the world, accounting for half of its trade and most of the inventions. The British might even claim to have set up the first nation-state, with the Union, in 1707, of England and Scotland, where there was a national language, without much room for minority languages such as Welsh (if you spoke it in the playground at school, you were beaten, and the great men of the Edinburgh Enlightenment tried hard to suppress Scotticisms[11]). That national language has gone on to become the world's universally used medium. Széchenyi, in remote Hungary, looked at the example, and so did any thinking Hungarian, contrasting British ways with the system that prevailed in central Europe. How do you get there – Parliament, banks, industrial revolution, railways, telegraphs, steamships and deep stability? In Hungary a backward economy and stick-in-the-mud politics reinforced each other. There was, however, much that could be done by well-off and well-intentioned men such as Széchenyi himself, and others could see that, with improvements in communication, there was money to be made. In Hungary, after 1825 reform was in the air.

Szechényi's economic projects had been ambitious: steamships on Lake Balaton, the draining of the mosquito-ridden marshes of the River Tisza and, especially, the removal of obstacles to navigation on the Danube. If opened to steam-driven traffic, it could do wonders for the commerce that Széchenyi wanted, because from its Delta mouths on the Black Sea at Galatz (Galaţi) or Constanţa, goods from central Europe could reach the promising Ottoman market (at the time, more important than even Russia), but the river changed course, meandered through swamp and at the Iron Gates, roughly on the Serbian–Hungarian–Rumanian border, ran into a great block. Here, between huge cliffs, the river became shallow, over a bed strewn with rocks and boulders. The Romans, with their genius, had hacked out a passageway for portage – i.e., the manual handling of cargo along the river's impassable stretch – but that would never do for steamships, and the Hungarians worked at this, though the work was not completed for another generation. There is a superb English account of this period, John Paget's two-volume *Hungary and Transylvania* (1839).[12] One of the two great men of the era, Count Gyula Andrássy, made his entry into politics in 1847, when, aged twenty-five, he addressed a local council in Zemplén on behalf of a company then just setting out to put steamships on the River Tisza. It was he who, as Prime Minister, brought experts from the London Board of Works to construct the canalisation of Pest. In his speech in Zemplén he made the point that, in the end, government action would be necessary to clear all formal obstacles (grotesquely surviving property rights etc.) and guarantee the financial outlay. With this, he touched on the central problem. There could be no proper politics without a proper economy, and vice versa. It would take strong government to break the vicious circle, but the Habsburg Monarchy was not supplying that.

In 1815, after the defeat of Napoleon, Austria was the main winner, in terms of territory. She had inherited much of the Holy Roman Empire of the German nation, an ancient institution that Napoleon had abolished in 1806; and the Habsburg dynasty, ruling Austria, could look back on five centuries of glory. The list of titles of Emperor Franz I contained some fifty items, the second of which was 'apostolic King of Hungary' – half of his lands – and the last 'Lord of Trieste', a port that was his commercial windpipe to the Mediterranean. The final item was 'Increaser of the Empire' (*Mehrer des Reichs*), and in that, Emperor Franz had done well. He ruled northern Italy – Milan and Venice – and ran much of the rest through the Pope or small states run by relatives. He also had the overlordship of a German Confederation, though he did not rule directly. And he had hereditary lands, stretching from Bregenz on Lake Constance, taking in the old Czech Kingdom of Bohemia as well as that of Hungary. This was the very antithesis of the national principle, and the Habsburgs had built it up through well-judged marriages, well-chosen alliances, Papal blessing and lucky wars. The army was at the centre of their Empire, and Austria was a Great Power. She also solved, or shelved, problems that Europe would rather not face, the solution of which, in the twentieth century, involved wars and massacres or 'ethnic cleansing'. In 1815 she was left in a dominant position. Her chief statesman, Clemens von Metternich, lent his name to a system that, in later years, was much respected by Henry Kissinger. Its essence was: change nothing, because any change will just lead to worse. Austria was backed by Russia, which was then even more military-reactionary, and in 1815 a Holy Alliance had been proclaimed, to include Prussia, which ran northern Germany. These three had taken over almost all of Poland, and had an interest in keeping her down. More generally, they had an interest in stopping revolution, secularism and separatist nationalism. The British and French were not interested, but at least the peace was kept, uniquely in European history, for forty years, and there was civil peace in central Europe, a part of the world that was soon to supply one explosion after another. The Habsburgs were slightly bewildered that their subjects would not simply use German, but they were not intolerant of young people's interest in native languages. Emperor Leopold II, Joseph II's brighter brother, set up a Chair of Czech at Prague University, and the police did not stop periodicals smudgily printing Slovene or Croat poets, who were seen as harmless, quaint. In Hungary many of the towns, such as they were, were dominated by German-speakers, but the use of Hungarian grew as printing and education spread, and Metternich, with a Hungarian wife, Melanie Zichy, did not discourage it. Late in 1847 the Emperor Ferdinand, Franz's son, somewhat feeble in mind and a cat's-paw in Metternich's hands, opened an elected assembly with three sentences of Habsburg-pronounced Hungarian.

True, the Empire counted as Catholic-reactionary in progressive, western eyes. The poets disapproved: Thomas Hardy wrote of 1815, 'Earth's wormy dynasties re-robe', and in *Childe Harold* Byron was scathing: 'an Emperor tramples where an Emperor knelt' (in this case Venice); Victor Hugo's *La légende des siècles* said of one of the Habsburg principalities in Italy that 'Modène étranglée râle sous son archiduc' ('throttled Modena is in death-agonies under her Archduke'). All of it exaggerated, as happens with poets – as a class, only just after actors in preposterous politics – but it was certainly true that in western liberal eyes the Habsburg Empire stood condemned. It had inherited Counter-Reformation ways of doing things, and these were at odds with the political economy that Great Britain was pioneering. The Catholic Church was enormously powerful, and it had huge estates. These were meant to pay for its educational and charitable activities, and they were generally speaking not well managed. John Paget, an acute British observer, was appalled when he visited a private estate in the Banat that was utterly undeveloped because a Croat bishop a hundred miles away had rights over the inheritances. But the Church's lands were held in entail, meaning that they could not be sold. This also meant that they could not attract credit and therefore often remained under-developed, much to the disadvantage of agriculture. The same applied to aristocratic estates, and in any case 'usury' was forbidden by law. All of this offended against British ideas of political economy. In Austria the bureaucracy, the army and the nobility were in charge. The censorship was absurd, and the playwright Grillparzer came under fire for referring to the 'little Cossack horses', as if the Tsar had horses that were anything other than large. There were representative bodies, as the nobility of a particular archduchy or province were invited to discuss local matters, but their remit was limited and in any case these bodies' composition was not representative of the nationality as a whole. Except in Hungary. Elsewhere in their empire, particularly in the Czech lands, the Habsburgs had stamped out proto-parliamentary bodies in the name of absolutism and Counter-Reformation. They had not quite managed to do the same in Hungary, and there they had had to come to terms with men they saw as provincial troublemakers: obstinate backwoodsmen tangling everything up in dog-Latin legal flim-flam – what the French called *avocasserie* – in defence of obsolete privileges.

Emperor Franz could have bypassed the Diet, and after 1815 could maybe even have scrapped the Constitution altogether. It was complicated, because although king-in-parliament was supposed to be the rule, especially as regards taxation, in practice the Crown had income of its own, through tariffs, mines and estates, which it could sell off. Again, though local government was supposedly autonomous, the Crown could appoint a Lord-Lieutenant who could, if need be, call on the army to keep in check the squires who operated local government, including justice, communications and recruitment for the army. They appointed the officials who ran these things, including the Deputy Lord-Lieutenant. Voting was confined to men with a claim to noble status – i.e., exemption from taxes in return for contributing to any war effort – and since Hungary was on a fighting frontier, there were many families (5 per cent) with noble status, some with almost no land, others with a small estate worked by a few serfs. In these circumstances power was the only local industry, and for the counties' administration voting (which was open) intimidation was frequent. The counties sent two delegates each to the Lower House of the Diet, and the towns, such as they were, had, altogether, one vote. The Upper House (the 'Table of Magnates') had the higher aristocracy and the senior clergymen. Any government measure needed difficult negotiation, and after 1815 the government was not popular. It had declared bankruptcy in 1811, and did so again in 1816 because it had spent fabulously on the Congress of Vienna. This meant defrauding bond-holders. After 1811 the Diet was not convoked until 1825, when some effort was made to sort out finance. The trouble was that Hungary could not be run without the counties, but they in turn made impossible government of the sort the reformers wanted. After 1825 the reformers, with Széchenyi at their head, worked away. In 1830 he astonished the Diet by addressing it in Hungarian (it was not brilliant), and by 1844 the language had been declared official, replacing Latin. This at once made for problems in Croatia, since Latin had at least been an international language. The decree only went through the Croat Diet because so much weight was deployed there by 'Magyarised' noblemen – Pejácsevich, Somssich, Grassalkovich and many other names ending in a Slavonic '-ich' or '-ics'. This marked the start of what was to become a fatal problem. Otherwise, the reformers, conscientiously reading progressive tomes on economics, prison reform, education and insurance in their sometimes splendid libraries (the Andrássy one largely survives at Homonna Castle in eastern Slovakia), did their homework, and some of them were outstanding, particularly Baron József Eötvös, who in 1837, at the age of twenty-four, wrote a study of poverty in Ireland. But this was all pipe-dreaming so long as there was no proper government to advance the cause.

And in the 1830s and 1840s the Habsburg government indeed did little. The Emperor, after 1834, was mentally deficient; matters were run by a sort of regency council, consisting of three old men – a frivolous archduke, a lazy Bohemian magnate and Metternich. He was by now tired, had seen it all and held to two great truths: that the monarchy's existence really depended on outside factors, especially the link with Russia, and that a war would ruin everything. In 1834, when old Emperor Franz died, Austria could get away with this. In 1833, at Münchengrätz in Bohemia, Metternich met the Tsar and the King of Prussia, all agreeing that 'revolution' must be stopped. Just before the meeting, the old Bourbon dynasty had been thrown out of France, Belgium and Greece had become independent and there had been a revolt in Russian Poland. The three rulers agreed to co-operate, in particular to preserve the Ottoman Empire from further uprisings (and in 1833, with the Treaty of Hünkiar Iskelesi, the Tsar not only sent troops to Constantinople to protect the Sultan from French-backed rebels in Syria but also agreed to be his patron).

This was no doubt heroic reaction. But in the thirty years after 1815 the business of government became much more complicated because the inventions of the west, especially the British, took effect. The most obvious was the railway, but the electric telegraph and printing advances allowed for the emergence of books, newspapers and public opinion. These defeated the censors, for books could be published in Leipzig or Hamburg and smuggled into the Austrian lands. Széchenyi's *Credit*, of 1830, a denunciation of the entail system and, in its way, perceived as a defence of 'usury', was looked at by the censors with suspicion, but nothing could prevent the spread of its ideas, as the author argued for a great expansion of commerce. Besides, medical knowledge also advanced, and death rates were cut in Vienna, where a Dr Semmelweis from Budapest worked out how to stop women from dying after childbirth.[13] Populations grew, and myriads of young men, some with an education, looked for work. The 1840s saw a set of misfortunes which, owing to the existence of the electric telegraph, might even be seen as the first worldwide economic crisis – bad harvests, and then a financial collapse to do with the discovery of gold mines in California, news reported at once by telegraph to London, where the gold standard was suspended. Western Europe was in ferment, a moment at which the dying was not dead and the living was yet unborn. The finances of the Austrian Empire were in trouble, and a special arrangement was made as regards Jewish bankers, who were freed from tiresome restrictions if they could stump up. A sign of the revolutions to come was that the universities were in turmoil. A rising in Sicily sparked the whole trouble, in January 1848. The self-confidence of the old order began to fade, and even Metternich wanted to call an Austrian States-General to discuss what should be done, because even now it was clear enough that there would be terrible trouble if the Empire went. In France, in February 1848, the buds came early on the trees, and the discontents all merged to overthrow the government of King Louis Philippe, an old man who grabbed his wallet and his wife (in that order) and trundled off to England. A Republic was proclaimed. One after another, Vienna, Budapest, Berlin, Munich and Milan experienced upheavals. This was 1848, supposedly 'the spring-time of peoples'.

Archduchess Sophie intrigued against old Metternich and intended to put her very young son Franz Joseph on the throne to replace Ferdinand (he was not beyond remarking, much later on, that it had not been necessary to make him abdicate in order to lose so many battles and provinces). She encouraged the liberals to demonstrate, and they did so on 13 March, the day on which the Assembly of Lower Austrian nobility was supposed to convene in the Herrengasse ('Lords Street'), just next to the Imperial Palace, the Hofburg. Having surreptitiously fomented trouble, Sophie then tried to stop it once she had achieved her aim, the fall of Metternich, and instead she provoked revolt. Bearded students and ruffians overwhelmed the police – more of a night watch – and the liberals got their wish, a parliament. On 15 March the same occurred in

Budapest as well. The Diet was in session in Pozsony, still, in 1847, full of reform projects but divided as to how to proceed. The reformers, especially Eötvös, meant to centralise the administration, more or less as Napoleon had done – restricting the powers of the counties or even abolishing them, as fetid little pools. But the conservatives defended them, as they could dominate many of them. But they were joined by a group of nationalist and proto-democratic radicals, who saw them as bedrocks for the Hungarian independence movement. The leader of these was Lajos Kossuth. He was himself of noble origin, a Lutheran, from northern Hungary (the name is obviously Slovak), and he started out as a lawyer, delegated to attend the Diet. He recorded its proceedings, but did so in such a way as to over-represent the radicals' role. Of these there were a few, despite the voting system, and they had noisy support in Pest. Joseph II had set up what we would now call a technical university in 1782, and engineers did not have much time for Catholic conservatism. There was another university, Pest, which inevitably produced lawyers. At the time Pest was developing as a proto-capital, with a café culture, and although censorship prevailed, it could hardly catch reports of Diet proceedings. For 'sedition' Kossuth was nevertheless imprisoned in 1839 for three years, but he was released early and went back to journalism, widely read in the cafés. A year in prison embitters, and Kossuth hated the Habsburgs, as Rákóczi had done: they had wrecked the country with immigrants and Counter-Reformation. He got himself elected, and his oratory was mesmeric. He raised subjects that were taboo – the creation of a Hungarian customs barrier to block Austrian goods, and abolition of the tariff border on the Austrian side. His allies spoke wildly against non-Hungarian inhabitants, and poets drove the students wild with enthusiasm. In response, the Austrians, and conservative Hungarians, came up with some liberalisation, allowing a free press and preparing for a reform of the counties to admit greater representation of the towns; the various laws discriminating against non-Catholics were now widely ignored (Moslems were never included in them, for the sake of Turkish trade), and by December 1847 there was a sensible con-servative programme in place, providing for gradual change. The central problems concerned the emancipation of serfs and reform of the counties, neither of which, without money, would be man-ageable. Kossuth, supporting the counties, was not helpful as regards abolition of the serfs' forced labour days, because so many small serf owners were entrenched in the counties that he defended. His oratory swept the board just the same. The Diet was in session, discussing a finance bill, when the March revolution broke out in Vienna, and Kossuth took the opportunity to say that finance would always be the mess that it was until constitutional rights were set out; his speech was broadcast in Vienna, inspiring the crowd invad-ing the Lower Austrian Estates in the Herrengasse. On 15 March the Emperor gave way in haste to the Hungarian demands – press freedom and an end to feudalism, and a parliamentary government under Count Lajos Batthyány. Students (with the poet Sándor Petőfi well to the fore) generally took the lead, and laws were passed to set up an elected national parliament.

The Hungarian revolution, of course, occurred in a European context. Liberalism and constitutions were in the air, and so, in Italy and Germany, was a movement for national unification. In France a Second Republic was proclaimed and universal male suffrage instituted; a great Romantic poet, Lamartine, took centre-stage. The Austrian army abandoned Milan to nationalist rebels, and the German question was posed when, on 18 March, there was a rising in Berlin. One reason for Metternich's willingness to concede something to the liberals was Austria's competition with Prussia, for she had made considerable industrial progress, and she had established a free trade area, the *Zollverein*, from which Austria was excluded. It was to get a parliament of sorts, where joint economic subjects were discussed and laws passed. Metternich needed to show that Austria was not the antiquated tyranny that she appeared to be, and was prepared even to summon an Estates-General to discuss reform. He also badly needed money, and Hungary would have to be part of the process. In what followed Kossuth went too far, but he did so for intelligible reasons, calculating that the Habsburg dynasty would be evicted. In Frankfurt a German parliament came into existence and by October was voting to take in the Austrian Germans, which would mean the end of the Habsburg Monarchy altogether. An independent Hungary could easily fit in with this (as events twenty years later were to show). The Habsburgs themselves panicked, agreed to everything and then, in fear for their lives, retreated to pious and provincial Innsbruck, the first seat, centuries before, of their family.

There they listened to reactionary advisers and waited, in effect, for the revolutionaries to fall apart, as indeed they did. The new Vienna parliament proclaimed peasant emancipation and then found that the peasantry were in the main conservative, controlled by their priests. The soldiers remained loyal, and the Italian nationalists were defeated by a general of genius, Joseph Radetzky. A new and energetic adviser, Prince Felix Schwarzenberg, took over, playing with moderate constitutionalists and then scrapping the constitution in 1850. In Prague there was unrest when a Slav Congress met, attended by the anarchist Mikhail Bakunin (it deliberated in German), but it was put down early on, in June, by the army under Schwarzenberg's brother-in-law Prince Windisch-Grätz. The remarkable feature of these months was that the army held out: as Marx wrote of similar events in Paris, 'the uniform is the national costume of the peasant'. In September there was a rising in Vienna, when a mob protested against the despatch of troops to Hungary, and lynched the War Minister, Count Latour. Windisch-Grätz moved methodically on Vienna and crushed the rebellion. This was the end of the Austrian troubles, and Windisch-Grätz, now with reinforcements from Italy, could move against Hungary.

There the revolution was to last much longer. It divided into three phases: the period of Austrian collapse, to April, next the period of recovery, to October, and then the war with Hungary, which went on until August 1849. In the first period a parliamentary government was established in Pest, which was the new capital, and it produced a set of laws along liberal lines, though it did not specify the terms on which the serfs were to be freed of feudal burdens. It set about organising an army, the Honvéd, or Home Defence (force), and since Emperor Ferdinand had recognised the new government, its officers, generally drawn from the imperial army, took an oath of loyalty to Hungary. So many of them were not Hungarian at all that the new army was, for much of the time, commanded in German. But a great problem was brewing up. Hungary was not even half Hungarian at this stage. There were other nationalities – Germans, Rumanians (the largest minority) as well as Slovaks, Serbs and Croats – and they, some more vehemently than others, wanted rights: education in their own language, for instance. The Croats, with the part-Orthodox Military Frontier, were strongly Catholic and looked to Vienna, not Budapest: a military commander there, Jelačić, attacked Hungary, and so did the Serbs on the Banat, under their Patriarch's influence. The Rumanians of Transylvania also produced a rebellion, and there were massacres of Hungarians. But Jelačić was seen off in the Hungarians' first victory, at Pákozd, in September, and the Honvéd crossed the Austrian border, with a view to helping the Vienna revolutionaries. They were defeated around Schwechat, today's airport, and Windisch-Grätz promised retribution. But he sent a new commander to Buda, a Count Lamberg, with orders to find a peaceful way out if possible. A mob dragged him out of his carriage as he crossed the bridge, and lynched him.

Thereafter the temperature rose on both sides, and the moderates – Batthyány in particular, but also the architects of the eventual settlement, Ferenc Deák and József Eötvös – withdrew from affairs. It was now Kossuth who made the running, buoyed up by the belief that a united Germany would soon emerge. Far from everyone shared his convictions, but he inspired, and also terrified. After months of military vicissitudes, in which the Hungarians made a spectacular comeback, Kossuth, on 14 April 1849, declared the House of Habsburg, having committed terrible crimes, deposed. At that point came a decisive moment. Tsar Nicholas I felt strongly that he must support the old order in central Europe, for fear of revolution elsewhere, particularly in Poland, and in May 1849 his forces intervened. This was too much for the Hungarians, and in August 1849 they capitulated, with the armistice of Világos. Kossuth and thousands of followers made their way to the Turkish border, where they were given asylum. The descendants of several of them went on to distinguished careers in Turkey, and a leader of the army, Bem, even became governor of Aleppo. Kossuth himself stayed in western Turkey for two not very happy years before being taken to Britain and then the United States, where he received a rapturous welcome.

The damage done to Russia's reputation (and, of course, to Austria's) had much to do with the outbreak of the Crimean War in 1853–4, and with the subsequent unification of Italy (1859–61), which was largely a creation of British Liberals and French Bonapartists. Austria in 1849 was under the control of vengeful reactionaries, but this time not stupid ones. Prince Felix Schwarzenberg took over, with a plan to force the Hungarians to accept imperial rule. He abolished the constitution. Habsburg absolutism was back. Prince Felix was advised (rightly) that clemency would be in order. He said, 'Yes, but some hanging first'. Thirteen generals were hanged at Arad (now in Rumania) on 6 October 1849. On the same day Lajos Batthyány, who as Prime Minister had tried desperately to bridge the gap, was shot in the barracks of Pest, a spot marked today with an eternal flame (the *mecsés*, located close to a Calvinist and a Unitarian Church, and not far from the Parliament). Yet the Austrians had a very strong case indeed. They ruined it: Hungary would never quite forgive them this stupid vindictiveness – what a British Prime Minister (Asquith) described as 'Austrian crassness'. Public opinion in Great Britain looked on, aghast, and when the time came welcomed Italian unification as a relief from the tyranny of the Habsburgs. But for the moment the Austrians would have a chance to show that they could modernise Hungary. A revolutionary decade followed.

# CHAPTER 2

# Absolutism and Compromise

O n the Gellért Hill in Buda there is a long, low fortress, the Citadella, and its guns in 1850 pointed through the embrasures at Pest. The castle of Buda had itself survived a long siege and was now occupied by stern military governors – first Prince Windisch-Grätz and then Baron von Haynau, a man who had made himself a ferocious reputation in the pacification of Brescia, in Italy. Haynau, the son by morganatic marriage of a Grand Duke of Hessen-Kassel,[1] just said that the Hungarians had been rebelling for centuries and had been treated far too leniently. The Tsar himself begged Franz Joseph to show mercy, and Palmerston in Britain said that vindictiveness would be wrong-headed against people whose bravery had caught the imagination of the world. Austrian rule was vindictive, as martial law was proclaimed, and restrictions proliferated; informers were rumoured to be everywhere, and foreigners were kept out. (Even in 1854 only five British visas were issued, one of them to an Andrássy governess who was kept waiting for weeks in a Vienna hotel, and kept a fascinating diary.) Revolutionary beards were forbidden; Verdi's *Ballo in maschera* was allowed only if its central character, the assassinated Gustavus III of Sweden, remained alive.[2] There was a purge even of senior medical professors in the Academy of Sciences, including paediatricians who had happened to deal with Hungarian wounded.

And the Austrians behaved stupidly into the bargain. The Emperor had after all, as King of Hungary, accepted the April Laws, under which the transferred officers in Hungary swore loyalty to him as King of Hungary and therefore took orders from the government in Pest. They had fought in the Hungarian army, and were now being punished for not being disobedient. A Chancellor of Transylvania was absurdly imprisoned in the fortress of Theresienstadt, and poor Batthyány died in a barracks at Pest, in a street now named after the moon (*hold*) but not so long ago, in an even more absurd occupation, after a Mr and Mrs Rosenberg, whom the Americans condemned as Communist spies. There were 120 other executions, some of them of prominent men, and the silver plate of General Kiss was declared the legitimate plunder of General Haynau. Fifty thousand soldiers were sent off to serve in horrible conditions in Italy or Bohemia, and 1,200 convicted officers served their sentences in chains. Haynau, an obvious embarrassment, was got rid of in 1850, but he left a long-lasting poison (and oddly enough ended his days in Hungary, as an estate owner). Schwarzenberg and the rising star of absolutism, Alexander Bach, who was Minister of the Interior, started off very harshly in Hungary. They had other things to think of, and in their eyes Hungarian obstructiveness was simply hindering their German strategy. Prince Felix Schwarzenberg had plans for a Greater Germany, under the Habsburg dynasty, which would also rule its own non-German lands. Any answer to the Hungarian problem would therefore depend on what happened in Germany. Everyone knew that German unification was coming, in one form or another.

Its shape had been learnedly discussed by (mostly) liberal-minded delegates, many of them professors, at a parliament in Frankfurt in 1848. There were about forty more or less sovereign German states, some of them merely picturesque nuisances, and the two Great Powers were Protestant Prussia and Catholic Austria.

Austria, historically, had the better claim to run Germany, and in comparison with the Habsburgs the Hohenzollerns counted as dowdy provincials. Friedrich Wilhelm IV of Prussia was a hysterical romantic, who went mad, and his successor, Wilhelm I, when giving a dinner, made sure that the wine was poured meanly, before himself re-corking the bottle, marking on the outside the level of the remaining wine so that the servants would not have a go at it. On the other hand, Prussia was already quite substantially industrialised, because in 1815 she had been given the Grand Duchy of Berg, latterly known as the Ruhr, with the largest coal and iron deposits in Europe. (Much later, Chancellor Adenauer teased a British enquirer, Noel Annan, as to what had been the worst mistake in their handling of Germany: his answer was that they had let Prussia at the Congress of Vienna take Berg, because the industry of the west became associated with the militarism of Berlin, to fatal effect.) Of course, Prussia was in a sense weakened by this divided character, as urban Rhineland liberals could hardly co-operate with the reactionary landowners who ran things east of the River Elbe. Schwarzenberg planned to unify Germany on Austrian terms, starting with a huge free trade area from the Baltic to the Adriatic. It would, of course, be dominated by Catholics, its capital in Vienna, but this time round the Catholics would show that they could be good liberals in terms of administration and economic matters – they would get rid of Emperor Franz's interfering paternalism and come to terms with capitalism. (Aristocrats complained to Bismarck about Schwarzenberg's 'clique of Jews'.[3]) Schwarzenberg had made Emperor Ferdinand abdicate and replaced him with an eighteen-year-old nephew, Franz Joseph, son of the scheming Archduchess Sophie, and Schwarzenberg would find him easy to control. By now, as a democratic age got under way, dynasties needed glamour, and Franz Joseph was married off soon enough to a Bavarian cousin, Elisabeth, who had chocolate-box qualities. As her superb biographer Brigitte Hamann notes, she was a figure remarkably similar to Diana, Princess of Wales, and had been chosen for similar reasons: she simpered for Austria. In 1849 a new constitution was decreed, and then itself suspended in December 1851. Given these great concerns, Hungary was an irritating side-show. She should be made to supply recruits and taxes for Schwarzenberg's German project, and she too should be reformed, getting modernisation from above. In 1850 she was in effect abolished.

The Lands of the Crown of St Stephen – the historic term for a Hungary then three times larger than today's country – had formed a unity of sorts before the arrival of the Turks, and they were now split up. Transylvania, together with areas known as the *Partium* (roughly east of Debrecen) which had sometimes been with Hungary, was under separate administration. An attempt was made to turn particular nationality areas into separate administrative units, and these nationalities thought that their loyalty to the Empire would be acknowledged. Not so: their local assemblies were closed down, and a Hungarian exile, Ferenc Pulszky, delivered an early version of a Hungarian art form, defeated satire, when he told them that what Hungary had received as a punishment they were getting as a reward. Croatia, which had been under the King of Hungary since 1102, was split off. The same applied to the mostly Serb Voivodina and the partly Serb and partly Rumanian region called Serbian Vojvodina and Banat of Temesvár. A further sub-stantial piece of land was the Military Frontier, where soldiers, generally southern Slav, had been commissioned, with land, to hold off marauding Turks. It remained in existence, though it now had no real function. The old, autonomous and gentry-dominated local county administration was abolished, for in Austrian eyes (and not theirs alone) it was corrupt and backward.

Hungary was divided into five military districts, and travel between them was subject to permits. Hotel registration was strictly applied (in untranslatable bureaucratese, *Meldewesen*), and you were forbidden to entertain strangers in the evening. A state of siege – martial law – prevailed,[4] and prominent politicians, even those opposed to Kossuth, such as Ferenc Deák or József Eötvös, retired to domestic or foreign exile. Old Hungary had not really known a modern administration. Its place had been taken by semi-feudal officials, and not too many of them: they ran justice along with everything else, as lay magistrates. There was now a regular bureaucracy, collecting new and Austrian taxes, and running state monopolies (e.g., a lottery and tobacco administration). The new administrators were nicknamed 'Bach Hussars'. Alexander Bach, the Imperial Minister of the Interior, was a liberal who had initially rebelled in 1848, but who now saw that Schwarzenberg's top-down methods could bring about modernisation more effectively than waffling democrats could ever do. He recruited officials, mainly Czech, to run Hungary, and put them into a weird uniform to take charge of taxes and recruiting. The Austrian Civil Code now replaced the old Hungarian law, which had been administered locally, by the gentry serf owners according to their whims (and with a rake-off or two along the way). At least in the old system people had known each other; the new one was operated by 'judicial officials' who knew no one and were anyway boycotted. Much of all this had been tried by Joseph II in the 1780s, and it had been a failure. But he had taken on the Church as well. Schwarzenberg enlisted it as an ally, and a new Concordat in 1855 gave it considerable power over education, in which 'anything that conflicts with the Catholic Faith may not appear in the curriculum'. It was awarded 700,000 acres of land, and the Jesuits, whose activities had been banned by Maria Theresa, came back in full force. Tithes were increased and made compulsory. There was some discrimination against Protestants, and the Debrecen Reformed College had to send its students to take their examinations in the Premonstratensian High School in Nagyvárad, a day's journey away, because the bulk of non-Catholic schools did not have public recognition.[5] Grim-faced Calvinist resentment festered in Transylvania, and there were some nationalist plots, which were savagely put down.

But there was another side to all of this. In many ways the history of modern Hungary begins with Alexander Bach. The laws passed after the revolution of 1848 were indeed liberal, promising emancipation, education, equality before the law. But there were imprecise areas: who would pay for the emancipation of the serfs, what land would they get, what compensation would the landlords be given, what would happen with the common lands, belonging to no one? These, in any modernisation of agriculture, were very important matters. Old widows depended on the commons – the grazing of their one cow – for survival. Cows could be kept over the winter by turnips, but if the fields were not enclosed, there was nothing to stop them from eating turnips that had not ripened. If the commons were taken over by a private landowner and enclosed by hedges or fences to keep cows and goats away, then turnips ripened and fed the cattle in winter. This worked in Britain, with her parliament of landowners, but not in France, where, with the practice of *vaine pâture*, the old women won, and the cows were scrawny. On common land peasants would cut down trees for fuel, and deforestation then happened; common undrained marshes also supported wildlife that peasants could trap or shoot, whereas modern agriculture had no use for them. Most peasants, with a short and unpredictable life-span, necessarily thought short-term, and it was only when a class of richer ones had emerged that serf emancipation and enclosure could go ahead. In eastern Prussia serf emancipation (in stages between 1808 and 1848) meant that prosperous peasants compensated estate owners with money or land, and compensated themselves by taking over common land. Much of Hungary was still sparsely populated, and the problem of inadequately sized holdings was not, in 1850, too severe, but there were other problems. Poor peasants might drink and fall into debt, losing their lands to more prudent people; and what compensation would the serf owners get, and how much land would they keep? Who would pay taxes? The nobles – 5 per cent of the population – were exempt, and even made a fuss when asked to pay a toll for crossing the Chain Bridge. The Church also did not pay. Bach changed all that and added new taxes, collecting 23 million guilders in 1850, 55 million in 1857 and 75 million in 1864, partly from tolls and partly from inheritance taxes or monopolies (including salt). This enabled him to settle the peasant question, which a noble-dominated national assembly might have had some difficulty in doing. Commissioners in the countryside quite often favoured peasant claims, and some two-fifths of the arable land was transferred to them, but often as 'dwarf-holdings' (700,000 souls), while many (300,000) were landless. The big estates retained 25 per cent of the arable, and the landlords were given 50 guilders in compensation for the free labour of a cotter. This was paid in the form of state bonds, which the smaller serf owners – 80 per cent of the 150,000 serf-owning families – usually sold off at a one-third discount. The former serfs were supposed to pay this back to the state, in instalments reaching to 1916 in Transylvania. Serf emancipation was a minefield, but at least in the case of the Habsburg Empire a more serious effort was made at fairness than elsewhere.

The Bach administration also laid down over 2,000 kilometres of railway, an important beginning, and this connected the central plain, the Alföld, with Vienna and Trieste; there was also a route to Fiume, on the Adriatic, but trains had to cross the Danube by rail-ferry. One main concern here was the encouragement of agricultural exports, and these were given a fillip by a piece of straightforward liberal legislation: the abolition of the Austro-Hungarian customs border, which had been instituted by Maria Theresa so as to collect at least some tax from Hungary, even if this was on her exports. That barrier now went, and exports to Austria greatly grew; so did imports from Austria, largely of manufactured goods. Bach also did much for practical schooling, as distinct from the universities with their proliferating law degrees. In 1856 and 1857 a polytechnic for engineers, an agricultural high school and a commercial academy got going, though initially they taught in German.

A problem afflicting Hungary had been the absence of credit, bemoaned by Széchenyi. This was partly caused by prohibition of certain land sales, under a system of entail or 'mortmain', literally 'dead hand'. Unsellable, it could also not attract credit. This protected, for instance, monastic property, and one reason for so many central Europeans to take an interest in English history (Lewis Namier and Geoffrey Elton in the lead) was no doubt that Henry VIII dissolved the monasteries, which had a third of the land, which some way down the line was subject to agricultural improvements, including turnips. Now, with Bach, credit institutions started up, notably the Rothschilds' *Creditanstalt*, and the economy started to take off at last. The Esterházy family was close to bankruptcy in 1860, and was saved because under the new system it could have access to foreign credit (though the political acuteness of an Esterházy who backed the right political horse had something to do with it, for his inheritance tax was reduced by 250,000 guilders). With its eighteen estates in western Hungary (and two over the Austrian border) it bounced back, as grain shipments could be organised along the Danube to the new Austrian markets.[6] One final achievement of the absolutist government was in education. Count Leo Thun-Hohenstein allowed initial education in the mother tongue, though in middle school only in German, and schools spread. It was all done fast, in what was still a backward country, and there were parallels with the similar process in Russia, under Alexander II, with the significant difference that in Russia peasants only owned land through a commune, whereas in Hungary at least the principle of private property prevailed.

There was little overt rebellion against the Austrians, but much could be achieved through passive resistance. The Bach Hussars and the Austrian army officers were isolated in the countryside, and were mainly ignored in the towns; people pretended to co-operate and then found endless reasons for delaying delivery. The educated classes pretended not to understand German, or spoke it exaggeratedly badly, so that interpreters were constantly in demand. Recruits turned up late; taxes were paid at the last possible moment; and aside from a small circle of high aristocrats, no one would negotiate with the occupation authorities. At the time Irish nationalists took inspiration from these things, because they saw no sense in active resistance and reckoned that they could modify British rule in subtler ways; one of them, Arthur Griffith, wrote a book about Hungary. The country did have a national leader, or at least one in waiting. Ferenc Deák, a lawyer through and through, who had not had a prominent part in 1848 and had escaped punishment or exile, at first retired to his estate, the management of which bored him, and then took up quarters in two modest rooms in the Queen of England Hotel in Pest. Everybody came to consult him, as his knowledge of law, his discretion and his probity were irreproachable. He knew how to wait, knowing that the Bach system could not go on. The waiting went on through the 1850s.

There were three great weaknesses in the absolutist system. In the first place came the legacy of hatred that came from 1848 and the absurd petty oppression that followed, a hatred that went from relatives of Batthyány's, including members of the Károlyi family, who regarded Franz Joseph as a murderer, to simple Protestants, especially Calvinists, against whom discrimination still went on. Then there was the simple fact that, whatever the progress achieved, it was being carried through by foreigners, and moreover by Czechs, with a rasping accent and a silly uniform, who belittled anything Hungarian and were very nasty when it came to the application of tiresome rules. The tobacco monopoly was a much-resented imposition. And then there was money. Tyranny is expensive, and the Austrian treasury could not stand the strain. Foreigners lent to it on harsher terms than applied to Morocco, and though taxes had gone up, they were not enough to sustain the large army that Franz Joseph required for a foreign policy aimed at the domination of Italy and Germany. It took a quarter of the budget in normal times, but half of it in 1849, 1854 and 1859–60, when the army was mobilised. This meant taking on debt, at an interest rate that was high for the times (over 5 per cent), and the interest burden came to a further fifth of the budget.[7] There was paper money, supposedly based on silver, and although within Austria it was supposed to be interchangeable with silver, in practice it was worth 20 per cent less, especially abroad. The government could only pay its way with paper money, and cheated its own people, although it needed their confidence if the debt was to be contained. The Bach system, seemingly rational, was not going to last even if, domestically, it was able to keep the peace.

And it was in foreign affairs that the crisis started. It was not for frivolous reasons that the Austrian Foreign Minister was called 'Minister of the Sublime House', because the Habsburg Monarchy was in essence a machine for the conduct of foreign affairs. Its position as a Great Power – *Grossmachtstellung* – was all-important. Imperial ambassadors ranked together with the Pope's nuncios in precedence at the head of the diplomatic corps, and the army was essential. The high nobility made it their career often enough: both Schwarzenberg and Széchenyi had distinguished themselves as junior officers fighting Napoleon. The army was, of course, multinational, with South Slav infantrymen, Hungarian hussars and German gunners, but (not unlike the British-Indian army) it held together remarkably well, and the officers, whatever their origin, had an *esprit de corps* that does much to explain the Monarchy's survival in 1848. Radetzky was a tactical genius, the sort of leader of whom soldiers told anecdotes (he could still, at eighty, ride a horse and father a child) and a chivalrous man who made things easy for the defeated Italians: no Haynau, he. (And he warned Vienna to keep a tight leash on Haynau, seconded to Hungary from Italy.) When he died, in 1858, Johann Strauss's *Radetzky March* was played *largo* and in a minor key; it suited, as events were to prove, the final moments of the old army. Foreign affairs went badly wrong: isolation and defeat. The Schwarzenberg–Bach system fell apart: united Italy emerged in 1859–61, Prussian-united Germany in 1866–71; and in 1867 Franz Joseph had to swallow Hungarian unification as well, with a form of independence.

Metternich's iron rule had been to keep good relations with the Russian Tsar, in the name of conservatism. Nicholas I had saved Austria in 1849 from the Hungarians. He did so again in 1850, this time against German liberal nationalists. They had offered the headship of non-Austrian Germany to the King of Prussia, and the Russian ambassador, a Baron Meyendorff, countersigned the document at which Prussia (at the 'humiliation of Olmütz') once more accepted Austrian leadership in German affairs, restoring the old Confederation over which Austria presided. Schwarzenberg remarked that 'Austria's ingratitude will astonish the world', and if he had been in charge he might have managed a difficult situation with proper cunning. However, he died suddenly in 1852, and his successors were not of the same calibre; Franz Joseph too was still very young and inexperienced. The association with Russia came to an abrupt end because of an event of a nature that Metternich had dreaded: the Crimean War of 1853–6. Russia attacked Turkey; the British and French (with an Italian contingent) came to her aid.

The Crimean War was about nothing, but it was also about everything. The ostensible cause was a quarrel between Russian monks and French monks as to who should run what in the Holy Places of Palestine, then part of the Turkish Empire. In this highly religious age (with churches going up on every street corner in England) the cause made for great indignation, but it was a cover for much else. The villain of the piece was the new Emperor of the French, who passed himself off as Napoleon III. (He was a nephew of the great man, whose prematurely dead son counted as Napoleon II.) France was still the most powerful continental country, and peculiar circumstances threw up a Bonapartist régime determined to restore old glories after a generation of uninspiring peace. That changed with the revolution of 1848, which created a Second Republic. The Republicans were weak and given to sentimental waffle. They lost control of their revolution, and a presidential election threw up a candidate who obviously did not bode well for Republicans. This was Louis-Napoleon Bonaparte, who was elected President in December 1848. He had the name, and he promised all things to all men. Three years later, quarrelling with his parliament, he staged a military coup, called a referendum and became Emperor of the French; the basis of his support was the army, the priests, most peasants, property dealers and a horrible claque of journalists. Marx wrote his finest piece about this, with the famous opening line that history is first tragedy, and then repeats itself as farce. Louis-Napoleon, the one-time journalist (like Mussolini), thought in headlines and got endorsement by referendum, not elections, the priests telling the peasants what to do. He would not make his uncle's mistakes, the two greatest of which had been to take on Great Britain and to fail to patronise European national movements. Meanwhile there would be revenge on Russia for the great catastrophe of 1812, his uncle's most spectacular defeat. Liberal opinion in Britain agreed with this: it was violently hostile to Russia because of 1849, both Garibaldi and Kossuth being given a tumultuous welcome (and Haynau, on an absurdly timed visit, nearly lynched). The British also wanted to keep Russian warships away from the eastern Mediterranean, the windpipe of their Indian empire, and so meant to protect Turkey. War resulted, and the Russians attacked Turkey on the lower Danube (it spread later to the Crimea, which the Allies invaded). Western technology was much superior, and the Russians lost; Louis-Napoleon got not only headlines but victories of sorts – Alma, Sebastopol – which he could use for a bridge and a boulevard in the new Paris that his property-dealer allies were designing; he also got a sticky cake, Malakoff, and a way of serving sole, with lobster sauce: sole Walewska.

The best-known history of Germany (by Thomas Nipperdey) begins with the sentence 'In the beginning was Napoleon'. Echoing Nipperdey, for central Europe we might say, 'In the beginning was Napoleon the Third'. Flashy and inconsequential as he was, he remade the region without meaning to. When the Crimean War broke out, what was Austria to do? If, out of conservative solidarity, she took Russia's side, she might find herself fighting a war with France, with British support, in Italy. At the time the Austrians had plans for German unification, with an enormous free trade area, and if she could annex or control the mouths of the Danube

– Széchenyi's dream for Hungarian commerce – she would do well. Their Minister, Count Buol-Schauenstein, therefore served an ultimatum to the Russians, to evacuate these lands, the territory of today's Rumania but then known as the Danube Principalities. They were under a sort of Russian-Turkish condominium, and Russian troops there could have their supply lines cut by an Austrian attack from Transylvania. The Austrians mobilised (it strained their budget), and the Russians did withdraw, concentrating their forces in the Crimea. This broke the Tsar's heart. Nicholas I had kept a portrait of Franz Joseph by his bedside, and in his grief provoked his own death: he took a guards' parade at Gatchina Palace in midwinter, in 1855, without a head covering, when he already had a bad cold, and died. In the ensuing peace Austria did not get the Principalities, which Napoleon III protected, in the name of Latin solidarity, and in 1859 they were put together as a new country, Rumania.

The Russians licked their wounds, and a new Tsar, Alexander II, promised to restore his finances and to carry out immense reforms. He was not going to support Austria ever again, left European affairs to a more trustworthy ally, Prussia, and made an agreement with, of all people, Napoleon III, in 1856, even before peace was signed. This left Napoleon III free to make his next headline, in Italy, where his uncle had made his reputation in the first place. His plan was to evict the Austrians altogether, to set up a new, French-dominated kingdom of northern Italy under the ruler of Piedmont and Sardinia, whose daughter would then be married to a Bonaparte cousin; that cousin was groomed to be king of central Italy. The chief statesman in Turin, the Savoyard capital, was Count Cavour, the sort of liberal whom the British especially supported, and he had gained credibility by joining the Crimean coalition. Cavour arranged a military alliance with France at a secret meeting in 1858, agreeing to let France have Nice and Savoy as a reward. Then it was a question of provoking the Austrians, and Cavour knew how to do that. They had no idea of any of this. They had chosen a middle-class ambassador for Paris as a deliberate snub to Louis-Napoleon, the upstart Emperor, rather than the sort of grandee who could intimidate officials – a competent Esterházy was available – and that ambassador assured the Ballhaus, the Ministry of Foreign Affairs, that nothing was afoot. On receiving Cavour's provocations (as to Piedmont's rights in Modena), Buol-Schauenstein, self-righteous and crass, was duly provoked, blustered that Piedmont had no business to be challenging legitimate authority in this way and eventually declared war in April, expecting support from the Powers. But by attacking he triggered the Piedmontese-French alliance, and the (badly led) Austrian army was twice defeated, at Magenta and Solferino. This gave Napoleon III another boulevard and another bridge. It also led straight to the defeat of France by Prussia in 1870.

Napoleon soon saw what he had done, and tried to limit the damage. After Solferino the Austrians gave up Lombardy but were allowed to retain Venice. However, Cavour went far beyond what the French had expected: local revolts in Florence and elsewhere were stage-managed to let him take over central Italy as well in 1860, a process uncomfortably rounded off in 1861, when the new Kingdom took over the south and Sicily. The Pope was now confined to Rome, and Louis-Napoleon sent a force to protect him, at the behest of his own Catholic following, which was aghast. This caused tension, inevitably, with the new Italy, but in any event there would be trouble. If matters in Germany came to a head, the Austrians would face a two-front war, as the new Italy would fight to take Venice and would ally with Prussia: approaches to this effect were made almost at once. And matters in Germany did come to a head, as Bismarck became Prussian Prime Minister in 1862 and started provoking Austria much as Cavour had done. If he thought about headlines, it would be those five years hence, not tomorrow's. He maintained very good relations with Russia especially.

The other essential was to stop an Austro-French alliance. Here Bismarck needed mistakes on the other side, and he duly got them. Louis-Napoleon's headline obsession led him into posing as another

Simón Bolívar, liberator of South America, and a French expedition accordingly sailed to Mexico to set up a French-dominated 'empire', taking advantage of the American Civil War, which prevented the United States from objecting too forcefully. It became bogged down in Mexican politics, and the French puppet ruler, the most unfortunate of the Habsburg Archdukes, was shot. (Mussolini was called Benito after the leader of the anticlerical revolutionaries, Benito Juárez, who did the shooting.) In all of this, Austria was isolated, and in 1866 she had to face a two-front war, cleverly provoked by Bismarck over a question in Schleswig-Holstein that made the causes of the Crimean War look rational. The Italians pinned down a third of the Austrian army, and the other two-thirds were defeated at the battle of Sadowa (Königgrätz) on the Dresden–Prague road. Peace followed. Prussia took over some territories in north and central Germany, but Bismarck carefully avoided humiliating the Habsburgs. They, he knew, dealt with problems that might be fatal (as indeed in 1945 they proved to be) for Prussia. But the Habsburgs had to rethink. They had lost Italy and Germany. Their only way forward would be in south-eastern Europe, and Bismarck himself suggested that they should move their centre of gravity to Budapest. The question of pacifying Hungary therefore came up.

It had already come up after the battle of Solferino, in 1859. Austrian finances were badly strained, and the military expenses in Hungary were considerable. But if money were needed, it would have to come from banks and businesses, which would not lend to an Austria where matters were decided by incompetent and greedy Court intriguers. Here the Austrian-German liberals – they called themselves *Deutschliberale* – came in. They were closely identified with capital, with the stock exchange, and there was a Jewish dimension to this. There always had been Jews exempted from the usual taxes and residential restrictions because of their usefulness: an Oppenheim founded the Austrian Nationalbank in 1816, and by 1820, 135 families were exempt from Jewish disabilities, of whom nine were enobled, including the Rothschilds and the owners of the

Arnstein-Eskeles bank (two-thirds of the exempt Jews converted). In the 1850s, as railways and industry spread, many more Jews made money, and there were, of course, many more Christian professional men than before. In general, they greatly resented the powers given to the Church by the Concordat of 1855. Many Jews regarded their own religion as absurd but Catholicism as even more so, yet they had to pay a church tax and so opted for Lutheranism (as did the Wittgenstein family, although the philosopher himself eventually became a Catholic). Such people would only part with money if they could somehow control its use, and so the *Deutschliberalen* emerged. A parliament, representing them, there would have to be. Alexander Bach was dismissed just after Solferino, and his successor was a Polish nobleman, Count Agenor Gołuchowski, who had been governor of Galicia. In 1860, as Italy was uniting, the parliamentary question in the Austrian Empire came up, and this included Hungary.

However, who would do the voting, and what would their powers be? Of course, a real parliament, representing every element in the Empire, would just reproduce in heightened form the problems of each and every part of it: an oratorical civil war. It would be like establishing a parliament for the Equator (as, in Austria, was to happen when the deputies blew cavalry horns, spoke for hours in Russian and threw inkpots at each other). The Austrian liberals had money and a coherent programme, but it did not involve recognition of nationalities. In their view these were just a nuisance – languages that were bogus-romantic, and that no one with an education would want to use. German was the language of progress, and from Marx to Gladstone progressives wanted these obsolete jargons out of the way. There must be Germanic centralisation.

However, there were Czechs and Slovenes who did not take this view, and they got support from the great Bohemian aristocracy, which had resented the interference of the Bach bureaucrats. They wanted decentralisation and recognition of provincial rights. Franz Joseph wriggled on this hook. He listened to the conservatives, who well understood what problems might emerge from a central parliament for the whole Empire. Hungarian aristocrats who had favoured access at Court – Count Szécsen, in particular – argued that Hungary should be reconstituted together with her Diet, and other noblemen said, not at all stupidly, that in a multinational state it was best to settle everything at local level. In Czech and German Budweis (the American beer originated there) at this time, for instance, the town council was run by a chairman who knew everyone, who knew that so-and-so had something to say but did not speak German well enough, and so let him speak in Czech, of which others present had some knowledge. Why substitute formal rules, argued over by pestilential lawyers, who would just make everybody hate everybody? These conservatives suggested local assemblies, which would appoint men to a central Council of State, which would then, in its wisdom, draw up such laws as were needed. Of course it was decentralisation, run by local landowners, notables of various sorts and the Church. This was all argued over in an advisory Council, known as the Reichsrat (as distinct from Reichstag, the usual word for 'parliament').

On 20 October 1860 a decree went out to the effect that the Reichsrat would become an all-imperial parliament; windows in Vienna had candles in celebration. This was the October Diploma, and it was billed as an irrevocable law ('Diploma' was a feudal term for royal recognition of rights). Then the householders woke up to the small print: it would not be a real parliament, just absolutism putting on a false nose so as to extract a few coppers from the public, as the classic French historian Louis Eisenmann put it. Provincial Diets were to be reconstituted on lines favourable to the nobility and the Church, and these would send delegates to the Reichsrat, which even then did not have many powers. Money talked, and kept its hand in its pockets. Weeks later the Diploma was radically amended, with the February Patent (another feudal word, for 'decree') of 1861. There would, after all, be an Austrian constitution, written by the Minister of the Interior, Anton von

Schmerling, and there would be a central parliament, elected by men with money in the entire empire, including, of course, Hungary. Elections were held, press restrictions were lifted, and the *Deutschliberalen* duly supplied a government, under the formidably arrogant Schmerling, a man from an old military family who understood finance and law and felt comfortable in Jewish company. His electoral arrangements gave his supporters an artificial majority in the Lower House, and they confidently set about technical laws that were, they thought, quite beyond the comprehension of obscurantist Catholics and obsolescent aristocrats. Count Gołuchowski happily resigned. All of this was really done with Germany in mind, where Franz Joseph had to appeal to Protestant and liberal opinion; and meanwhile a key point was that the *Deutschliberalen* particularly disliked the Czechs and despised Slavs in general, as unprogressive. They were not keen on Hungarians either, but there they ran into people with a political sense.

There were 345 seats, 85 of them supposed to be Hungarian. But the Hungarians were absent: only a few Transylvanian Saxons eventually came, and even the South Slavs mainly stayed away, out of resentment at Bach's treatment of them. Deák advised abstention, since the Emperor was not recognising what his own predecessor had done in 1848. Hungary wanted separate recognition. The local assembly prescribed by the October Diploma met in 1861, eventually in a building next to the museum that Franz Joseph had had specially built. (It was too small and is now the Italian Institute.) It did so at a time when the absolutist institutions were being weakened – Bach had gone, to a long, dignified, told-you-so retirement – and there was a relatively free press. Many of the men present had been members of the 1848 body, and looked back to that. Why should Hungary give up her rights and send delegates to an assembly in Vienna? Members protested. Oratory, now seeming quaint, was discharged. The only debate about this was whether the objections should be cast as a petition, implying subjection to the Emperor's will, or as a resolution, implying continuity with the legally established parliament of 1848. Two parties emerged, and they shaped Hungary's relations with the Habsburg Empire until 1918. The resolution men had a natural majority, because, after ten years of humiliation, many Hungarians just hated the Habsburgs – particularly the Protestants, and especially the Calvinists. But common sense prevailed in other quarters. Count Gyula Andrássy had fought with the army that had invaded Austria, and had then represented Hungary in Constantinople. He had been hanged in effigy in 1849, and exiled to Paris and London before his mother, a Countess Szapáry by origin, and very rich, had managed to arrange an amnesty. He got the assembly to agree on a petition, a sign that a deal could be done. However, meanwhile, the Hungarians were not represented in Schmerling's Council; Franz Joseph dissolved the Budapest assembly and waited on events in Germany. Absolutism returned, but was without much conviction. Schmerling's Imperial Council, known as the 'narrower imperial council' because the Hungarians were not present, passed its laws on insurance, banking and so on at liberal behest, and the Czechs suffered some persecution. This caused bad blood with the Bohemian aristocracy, which was also aggressively clerical and had privileged access to Court.

Schmerling faced intrigues, but in any case his strategy to make Franz Joseph German Emperor failed, when Bismarck got the King of Prussia to refuse to attend a ceremony in Frankfurt in 1863 that would have started the process, and Schmerling was finally dismissed when it was plain in 1865 that his Reichsrat had failed. Rather wearily, a moderately decentralising Bohemian nobleman, Count Belcredi, took the succession and said that the Hungarians would have to be included in the deal.

Already in 1863 a Hungarian conservative, György Apponyi, had suggested terms. To him and other conservatives, union with Austria gave Hungary protection, provided that she could run internal affairs, and at Christmas 1865 Ferenc Deák, sitting in his job-lot-furnished bachelor quarters in the Queen of England hotel, heard a knock on the door. It was a Baron Augusz, chief confidant of the military governor Archduke Albrecht, and a hated man, who had almost been lynched in 1848 on the Chain Bridge. He had come to ask for terms. Deák offered them: Franz Joseph could take charge of war and foreign affairs, with finance to cover both. Everything else would be subject to a form of Hungarian independence, including, of course, a separate parliament. There would have to be some joint body to oversee foreign and military affairs. Fifty or so delegates from the two parliaments would deliberate on these matters, alternately in Budapest and Vienna. Ministers would address it. A vote would be taken, but it would have to be in silence, given the explosive nature of the language question.

Franz Joseph did not like this, as he regarded foreign and miitary matters as his business, and the Austrian liberals did not like it either. They looked on Hungary as an aristocratic racket, its chief quality ingratitude, but they thought that the Czechs, patronised by stuffy clerical grandees, were even worse. If they could get a quorate parliament just for the non-Hungarian lands, it would be dominated by *Deutschliberal* centralisers. A Styrian bureaucrat, Max von Kaiserfeld, had his own Slav menace in view, the Slovenes, and he brought a faction of the liberals round to the idea of a pact with the Hungarians, who would have a parliament of their own.[8] In all of this, it is hardly surprising that Franz Joseph and his officials did not concentrate particularly well on essentials. They were quite outwitted by Bismarck, and fell into another hopeless war, this time for Germany. The battle of Sadowa in 1866 decided things, and Franz Joseph was ready to remodel his empire. He wanted revenge against Prussia, and that must mean a settlement of the Hungarian question; it must also mean co-operation with the German liberal nationalists. If Hungary were excluded from the Vienna Parliament, these nationalists would dominate it. And if the Hungarians could be persuaded to finance a renewal of the army – universal liability to conscription was set up in 1868 – so much the better. On their side, the Hungarians were ably led by Andrássy and Deák, and these could always point to the wilder nationalists, with their origins in the Protestant gentry, who hated the Habsburgs and had fought for a resolution, not a petition, in 1861. In 1866 negotiations went ahead for a new settlement, which became law in 1867 and is generally known as the Compromise (*Ausgleich*).

The Hungarian constitution was restored, with its parliament, together with the reforming laws of 1848. But the Hungarians accepted some common arrangements. Foreign policy was to remain in the Emperor's hands, and so were military matters: the War Ministry in Vienna was called *Reichskriegsministerium*, implying the continued existence of a united Austrian *Reich*, 'Empire'. The two parliaments would decide every year how many recruits could be taken into the army for their three-year service training, and how much money the army should have. The finances of common institutions were to be managed by a Finance Minister, and these three common ministers sometimes met, together with the Prime Ministers of Austria and Hungary, as a sort of cabinet, to discuss imperial matters; there was a common bank, responsible for note issue. There was no common parliament, but delegations from Vienna and Budapest were to meet regularly, to hear what the common ministers had to say. Hungary, the poorer of the two, would pay roughly a third of common expenses.

The Empire was now renamed Austria-Hungary, although this came about, with symbolic significance, for reasons to do with foreign affairs, because in trade treaties the term 'Austro-Hungarian monarchy' had to be used. The 'Austria' meant all the Habsburg lands, including Hungary, and imperial officials were called imperial-royal – *kaiserlich-königlich* – implying equality of the kingdoms, Bohemia and Croatia especially. After a while, in 1889, the Hungarians insisted on recognition of their own special status, and *kaiserlich-königlich* had to have an *und* ('and') inserted. That same year the mayor of Budapest decreed that only Hungarian inscriptions should be carved on gravestones. In 1915 the non-Hungarian 'kingdoms and lands represented in the Imperial Council' – such was the name of the country – were called Austria.

Kossuth, in exile, wrote an open letter to Deák, his old associate. This was a sham independence, he said. Without an army Hungary would be caught up in the affairs of Germany. This was true, but if the new Habsburg Monarchy could be made to work, it would protect Hungary. This was the question that now dominated Hungarian politics. Hungary was now the fourth European country, after Rumania, Italy and Germany, to get a form of unification between 1859 and January 1871. It was the end of the French hegemony, and the new countries were, by implication, part of a German system. In the two generations that followed, Hungary flourished. Where the Compromise went wrong was in Austria. She had been saddled with a centralising parliament with a rigged German majority, and all local grievances – the language for this or that village school, the name of this or that railway station – could be raised there. Bureaucratic rules were drawn up in such detail that they occupied three thick volumes. Only lawyers could handle such things, and there were 7,000 judges in the Austrian Empire, as against 162 in late Victorian England. But Hungary survived with a workable parliament, and a programme of national modernisation.

# CHAPTER 3

# Dualism, 1867–1914

O n 8 June 1867 Franz Joseph was crowned King of Hungary, in Buda, which was now once more the royal capital, as it had been in the Middle Ages. The Mátyás cathedral, which had once been a mosque, its old decoration whitewashed over, was restored, and Franz Liszt composed a Mass; the great aristocracy were present, in ornate national costume, and the master of ceremonies was Count Andrássy, trusted both by the Court and by the Hungarian politicians. He had the task, with the Cardinal Archbishop, of jointly placing the crown on Franz Joseph's head, and the culminating moment came when the King, wearing the Crown of St Stephen, rode a horse to the coronation mound, which was put together with soil from all parts of the land, waved a sword to all four points of the compass and swore the oath to the constitution, and to defend the country from all comers. He kept his word too: to the very end, the Lands of the Crown of St Stephen were preserved in their integrity. The Hungarians had won their cause, and few people blamed their king personally for the vindictive reprisals that had followed 1849, when he was only nineteen; and Empress Elisabeth, who had learned the language, made herself popular.

In a sense, this was the first decolonisation of modern times

– pageantry, flags wobbling up and down poles, anthems sung by little girls in national costume, tears running down whiskery cheeks, followed by considerable enrichment of the nationalists. At the time it was not thought likely to last. It was the outcome of a bargain between three parties with different interests. The Court wanted revenge against Prussia and looked for alliance with the south German states; a former Prime Minister of Saxony, Friedrich Ferdinand von Beust, who detested Bismarck, was now in charge of foreign affairs. He had pushed for the Compromise, because his programme needed taxes and recruits, and he wanted the Hungarian problem out of the way. The German liberals, thanks to the electoral system, could now dominate a purely Austrian parliament that would not include Hungarian deputies. They were now free to realise their progamme, to ignore the Bohemian grandees with their claptrap about Bohemian state rights, to put the Czech nationalists back in their box and to cut back the powers of the Church. They meant to create a progressive state, as their like were doing elsewhere, together with the centralising bureaucracy, schools, inheritance taxes, laws, law degrees and lawyers that so irked the Bohemian aristocrats. The Hungarians, on their side, also wanted wide autonomy so that they could remake the nation in their own way, without reference to Austrian centralisers, who, apart from anything else, were always tempted to encourage the non-Magyar peoples of Hungary to demand rights. With these thoughts in mind, and bringing his own bottled water from Vienna, Franz Joseph came to Budapest. Laws were passed from 1867 to 1869 in both parliaments to sanctify the new arrangements.

Hungary at the time had a population of some 13 million, mostly either illiterate or literate in a language other than Hungarian. There was a country to make, and there was a formula at hand as to how this should be done: it was Progress, and such optimism dominated thinking in the 1860s, a triumph for classical liberalism. The British example was well to the fore, and an Italian Prime Minister, Agostino Depretis, dyed his beard white to acquire Gladstonian authority. The rule of law, through parliament, was part of this. So too was sound money, eventually based on gold and issued by an independent bank. Mass education was important, and the schools of that era were built on Greek and Roman lines. Town planning and public hygiene were involved, and doctors were properly consulted. The institution of the limited company was important for commercial matters, to encourage competition, and free trade at the international level belonged in the context. There was also the matter of military reform. Classical liberalism was more easily established in the framework of a nation-state, in a decade that started with national unification in Italy, saw another form of it in the American Civil War and ended with Bismarck's ceremony at Versailles setting up the German Empire. All of this involved armies, and the example was Prussian for, instead of taking recruits for twenty-five years, a system of conscription had been introduced, giving peasant boys three or more years' training, after which they went into a reserve that could be called up in wartime. This had the great advantage of making them feel part of the nation and even, in many cases, learn the national language. Austria-Hungary introduced conscription in 1868, Russia in 1874. The Habsburg Empire still counted as a Great Power, with a large army, and the Powers generally co-operated to keep the peace.

The Hungarians took their place in the Habsburg machinery: Gyula Andrássy became Minister for Foreign Affairs in 1871, and Hungarians had more than their due share of embassies and common ministerial appointments. In 1867 there was considerable euphoria in Budapest, and a cabinet dominated by magnates took office. At this time many of the great aristocrats took their national role very seriously and did their homework, in this following a British example, where the House of Lords produced considerable experts in economics or prison reform. So it was in Hungary, where a Count Lónyay turned out to be an excellent Finance Minister. The English journalist Henry Wickham Steed, who wrote a classic on the Habsburg Monarchy, had reservations about Hungary, but he noticed the rise in intelligence that occurred as the steamer moved from Vienna, with its smug aristocracy, to Budapest.

Andrássy was the first Prime Minister, and among his first tasks was to make a new capital. The Chain Bridge had linked Buda and Pest, and these two, with Óbuda, were conjoined in 1873 as Budapest, which had a powerful mayor, strongly supported by commercial interests. Much of Pest was a greenfield site, with some marshy ground that needed to be drained. The obvious immediate rival was Vienna, where the enormous Ringstrasse had gone up in the 1860s, but Paris had undergone radical reshaping at Louis-Napoleon's behest (and much to the profit of his financial supporters), and the sewers built by his chief prefect, Baron Haussmann, were famous. London was the most successful city at this time, in terms of urban transport, and although private property there was too powerful for the radical reshaping that Paris experienced, somehow an admirable body, the Metropolitan Board of Works, got rid of cholera thirty years before Hamburg, and fifty before St Petersburg. It also laid down the Underground, by far the best system of the 1860s (and still incontestably so today). Budapest also got a metro, the first on the Continent, for the city was well planned by men who thought ahead. The Budapest Board of Works, composed of serious-minded magnates – a Baron Podmaniczky (a hero of 1848), a Széchenyi, a Szapáry – worked hard, and developed a very good plan, which has guaranteed canalisation and hygiene to this day. The city's situation, with the hills of Buda on one side and the plain of Pest on the other, and with the Danube running straight through, was magnificent, and the roads were laid out in a sensible way: two concentric boulevard rings, with two arterial boulevards (Andrássy, although it was then called Ray in English, or *sugár*, and Rákóczi) cutting across them. The intersection of the great boulevard (Teréz) and Andrássy avenue was an eight-sided square, the Oktogon, with fashionable cafés, and beyond it the avenue was studded with enormous villas, now occupied often enough by embassies. A very good opera house went up in 1884, and there were endless theatres, as the city's cultural life showed much vigour, the Hungarians having considerable acting talent. (Nagymező utca, crossing Andrássy boulevard near the opera, was Budapest's Shaftesbury Avenue.) In the early period the architecture tended to be heavily imitative of Austrian, but after 1890 a distinct Hungarian note was struck, and not just Budapest but several provincial places, including Marosvásárhely (now in Rumania), have astonishingly successful Secessionist-era buildings.[1] By 1900 Budapest was heading to become a million-strong city, and in that generation much of it was a building site. Mayors of Budapest – Rottenbiller, Podmaniczky, Gerlóczy – deserve their street names.[2] As a showcase for the re-established country, Budapest was a dramatic triumph.

The new Hungary was self-consciously liberal, and adopted various arrangements accordingly. Now that there was a proper Hungarian finance ministry, and now that laws and courts guaranteed investment (until this time you could not legally get a debt back from a nobleman), Austrian capital flowed in. The Vienna stock exchange brokers and banks did very well out of initial property development, but the particular engine of growth was the railway. Eventually, this was to make fortunes for estate owners. If they had a station near their lands, they could load agricultural produce, mainly grain, and sell it to the Austrian market, which was captured for them. Early industrialisation meant food processing, particularly flour (and distillation); true industrialisation, with textiles and then machinery, came later. Austrian Germans and Czechs made up a good quarter of the skilled artisans and railwaymen, and the overwhelming majority of Hungarians were peasants, 5 million of them (in 1900) with no land, 7 million more with some land, but a third of these with less than the seven acres needed for subsistence.

The new Hungary was therefore dominated by estate owners, magnates of the Esterházy–Károlyi class in the Upper House or gentry with middling-sized estates, who occupied most parliamentary seats. This was a gentlemen's parliament, with clubs of the

English type where men could meet informally (the grandest being the Nemzeti, or National, near the Astoria Hotel, though it did not survive 1945). The parliament did not even have house rules of any strictness, which was to cause immense problems a generation later, as gentlemen's agreements were broken and the opposition deliberately obstructed legislation with endless speeches or pointless roll-calls. In the first years, under Andrássy and his successor, enlightened laws did pass, in particular József Eötvös's of 1868 concerning the non-Magyars, which gave considerable rights to them as regards schools and law courts, a reward for the way in which they had accepted the Compromise. Eötvös also did much for education, as did his successor, Ágoston Trefort, whose name marks the street in Pest, again not far from the old parliament, where they put up the model school (i.e., teacher training, equivalent to the *École normale supérieure* which distinguished a Paris that also went in for state-led modernisation). An attempt was made to curb the autonomy of the counties: now that Austrian interference was not to be expected, that autonomy, so often associated with pig-headed provincialism, would just be a nuisance for governments. Two political groupings stood out – the 1848-ers, who greatly distrusted the Austrians and their magnate collaborators, and the 1867-ers, who again and again offered the common-sense argument that a small and poor country like Hungary badly needed shelter in a great Habsburg Monarchy. This was old-fashioned politics, not much affected by a middle class, let alone a working class. The government found it easy enough to co-operate with the contemporary Austrian one, which was in the hands of liberals headed by a Prince Auersperg, who had broken with the clerical-conservative traditions of his class, and the institutions of the Compromise worked well enough.

Still, there was much money to be made out of politics. Deputies were paid 6,400 Crowns per year, with expenses, at a time when, with 10,000 Crowns, people counted as 'rich'.[3] Besides, there was much money to be made out of railways, which required parliamentary sanction, and if an estate owner could have a station built on his land, he would be able to transport bulk goods, especially grain, cheaply and profitably. In 1869 an honest minister, Ernő Hollán, revealed that he had been offered 40,000 Crowns in a Brussels bank by railway promoters, and Ferenc Deák always refused to sit on railway committees. A good part of the gentry was therefore tempted to join in government, and in 1875 a substantial part of the 1848 Party joined up with the 1867-ers. A new party emerged, generally called 'Liberal' in English because its real name, 'Free-Thinking' (*Szabadelvü*, a direct rendering of the German *Freisinn*, which is still represented in the Swiss parliament), was not easy to translate. The background to this was a resounding economic crash in 1873, known as the *Krach* in central Europe, which ruined many and brought many bankruptcies: it occurred in a world more closely connected by telegram and steamship (and railway) than ever before, and events in another hemisphere could fatally affect the Vienna stock exchange, which was new and vulnerable. It is the world of Anthony Trollope's *The Way We Live Now*, whose central villain is a fraudulent railway promoter, or Zola's *L'Argent*, where the chief figure ruins an old aristocratic mother and daughter with fantastic schemes for exploiting the Levant. It put an end to the optimism of the later 1860s and called into question the verities of the classical liberal world.

By the end of the decade the classical liberals were out of power everywhere, with different pretexts – in France over the President's powers, in Germany over free trade, in Britain (1874) over drink, in Italy over railway nationalisation (Kossuth's elder son became director of the state company). Hungary followed the same pattern, though at some remove, since she lacked the counters for the liberal, let alone the democratic, party game. Still, the gentry-and-magnate parliament did produce a political shift, and in 1875 the Compromise statesmen were replaced by Kálmán Tisza, who had led the resolution side in 1861, and now became long-term Prime Minister. The party's name implied hostility to Catholicism and thence to the reigning Habsburg ethos. Its backbone was Protestant, and

Calvinist at that – energetic, organised, charmless, speechifying. It blamed the Habsburgs for encouraging non-Magyars, especially the Rumanians of Transylvania, where they formed a majority of the population, and Eötvös's nationality law was increasingly disregarded, but it also quite successfully pursued the modernisation (or 'nation-building') programme, and by the time of Tisza's fall, in 1890, the country was gaining self-confidence. This was a tremendous period for the great aristocracy.

The era is oddly known in British writing as 'the Great Depression'. The phrase is misleading, in that a far worse Depression followed in the early 1930s, with 25 per cent unemployment in Germany. But it is anyway misleading, because these were years, the first in history, of growing mass prosperity, even of the first 'globalisation'. There was indeed a depression, but it was in the first place a fall in savings income, which affected the idle middle and upper classes. There was also a sharp fall in food prices, which affected small landowners and the farmers generally. The reason for this was simple enough: the transport of American or Argentine grain, and of Australian and New Zealand sheep and lamb, to European markets. In the 1880s the steam turbine and refrigeration made such transport cheaper and effective. Hungary also produced grain at lower cost than elsewhere, and joined the export market. Big estates profited from economies of scale and also, of course, from the captured Austrian market, but small ones could not easily attract credit, and, as elsewhere – this is the Russia of Chekhov's *The Cherry Orchard* – the gentry went under.

The great estates grew at the expense of the gentry, and one obvious problem in dualist Hungary was the enormous gap between these enormous landholdings and the peasant village. In 1853, when the emancipation of 1848 was confirmed by the Austrians, the great estates profited as the lesser ones, without free labour, collapsed. The big landowners had done well out of grain in the Napoleonic Wars, and then did well out wool: and 'sheepes eateth men', as the English had known in Tudor times. In Prussia the common lands, on which poor peasants depended for grazing, were enclosed, often enough to the benefit of the better-off peasants. In Hungary they went to the big estates. Then, after 1875, these diversified. A quarter of Hungary's arable land was owned by some six hundred families. Princess Esterházy had almost 800,000 acres (500,000 *hold*, or what could be ploughed in a day, the equivalent in English being the furlong). Great palaces went up – such as Keszthely, the Festetics one on Lake Balaton, or Fóth, one of the many Károlyi palaces, near Budapest – and there were compact but imposing manor houses and castles in today's Slovakia, where the Andrássy family flourished. (Homonna, on the Ukrainian border, is especially worth seeing.) Some of these aristocrats, again especially the Andrássys, had a very good eye for paintings, and patronised Hungarian painters as well. There is a 'Palace Quarter' in Budapest's VIII district: Festetics, Károlyi, Wenckheim, Esterházy, Zichy, Csekonics near to the (then) Parliament building and the Museum, almost all of them put up in the later nineteenth century. Fashionable architects, who could knock out Scotch baronial or Renaissance or – as with the extraordinary Anker Köz (built by Ignác Alpár for an insurance company) on Deák Square – Egypto-Masonic, made fortunes, and Miklós Ybl was kept especially busy. In the new Habsburg Empire, *fidei commissa* were set up to protect the great estates, and about 4 million acres were thus affected in Hungary by 1867. Church lands were also involved. Great estates might work well, as little worlds under a patriarch, and they have had an undeservedly bad press. A labourer with a tied cottage could well be better off in such a community than scratching a living from a field or two with no access to tools or credit. There was not much protest in the countryside, except in certain specific areas that were notoriously poor, such as Békés, on the Transylvanian border.

But if Ybl's clients flourished, the lesser gentry did not. There had been an over-production of people with noble titles – or rather, a claim to noble status through military service – in Hungary, as in Spain or, most notoriously, Poland. The gentry, with their right to vote, began to move to the towns. They sold up small landholdings that could only be made profitable with a prodigious effort, if at all, and the great estates benefited. Once in Budapest, they could, through connections, find a job in the public administration, and the flats that were built for them had aristocratic pretensions – caryatids, balconies, vast interconnected rooms, some much smaller ones for the platoon of servants. Andrew Janos, the historian of the phenomenon, notes that, where there had been 170 gentry families in Sáros county in the eighteenth century, there were only 34 by 1895; the number of small-gentry families, 30,000 in 1800, fell to 7,000 by 1895, when the population was much greater. (Such families had from 250 to 1,300 acres, but there was a sizeable element called 'felt-shoe nobility' who were part of the phenomenon.) They had been badly affected by the abolition of serfdom in 1848, when they lost their labour force, such as it was, and were then hit by tax increases (and new tithes to the Church) under Bach's absolutist rule. Many found jobs in the state administration. The Austrians had employed 16,000 civil servants, but that figure doubled by 1875 and under Kálmán Tisza reached 60,000 by 1890 and then went up to 120,000 by 1910 as the state's role in communications, education and even welfare grew. Two-thirds of the employees of the Ministry of the Interior were of gentry origin, and so were half of the parliamentary deputies, made up equally of civil servants and lawyers. In the provinces their share was two-thirds. Of course, far from all of the small gentry did find such employment. Others became lawyers or journalists or just collected rents. They would not take up trade or industry, leaving it to Armenians or Germans – Buda was still largely German. They had, as Janos said, many admirable qualities: the administration was not corrupt, and the state followed the rule of law. But Hungarian feudalism had carried on in a modernised form.

Under Kálmán Tisza politics was stable. The 1848-er agitation was under control, give or take a student riot or two, and relations with Austria were reasonable: the financial arrangements of the

Compromise were renewed. It helped that in Vienna there was also a long-term stable arrangement in the parliament, though there it came about through a conservative-clerical régime, based on anti-liberal and Slav votes: that of Count Taaffe (who entered history with his remark that, beyond the attainment on all sides of supportable dissatisfaction, he had no political ambition). Tisza dominated the parliament with his 'Mamelouks', a word taken from the name for the slave soldiers of the Islamic world: his followers – 176 out of 329 deputies – were generally county officials of one sort or the other, and he was clever in offering patriotism and profit. In any case, he soon found that it was easy enough in Hungarian circumstances more or less to dictate the outcome of an election, though there was never anything quite as blatant as in Sicily, where the results of an election were announced before polling had taken place. The problem was how to prevent puppets from developing a will of their own, and Tisza was good at that. The electoral law restricted the vote to men of property, as happened in most other countries (the great exception was France), and there were not many voters; more to the point, voting was open, and the Lord-Lieutenant in many places could keep an eye on things and make trouble for opposition voters. There were independent constituencies, but they were in the pocket of a magnate who could nominate himself if necessary. Oddly enough, the percentage of men entitled to vote went down, not up. Originally, with property qualifications (and complications of other sorts, some of them picturesque), 14 per cent had been the rule. But in 1873 a new law restricted the suffrage, and as the gentry declined, they lost their right to vote. The share of electors declined to 6 per cent around 1900. Besides, the constituency boundaries and the fixing of deputy numbers in each discriminated against the opposition, with the odd result that purely Magyar areas had less representational weight than the mixed-nationality areas, where a very small electorate reigned. The Transylvanian Saxons were over-weighted, such that in Brassó 839 men elected one deputy, as against 4,370 in Pest, and in Naszód four

electors chose two deputies (although this happened because qualified Rumanians abstained). It is not too much to claim that (in the
title of András Gerő's book) this was rule by 'an overwhelming
minority'. He points out that the governments from 1867 really
relied on German and other nationality votes, given that these
voters regarded 1867 as the lesser evil. There was much to-do about
this from critics such as the Scotsman R. W. Seton-Watson, whose
famous *Racial Problems in Hungary* (1908) did much to lessen Hungary's until then positive image in the west. But even in Great
Britain the Scots and Irish had many more seats than their numbers
warranted, and in England the agricultural weight was far more
than by proportion it should have been. Democracy is seldom
perfect, which is perhaps one reason for its working at all.

Still, in Tisza's time change was occurring, a middle class was
emerging, and a real public opinion arose. As printing techniques
improved, and advertising provided lavish revenue, newspapers and
journals proliferated (journalistic skulduggery was a Budapest speciality): by 1890, when Tisza fell, political life was due for a
considerable change, and the last real (as distinct from surreal)
magnate government, under a Szapáry, came up, not for long, in
1891. After 1890 capitalism struck Hungary with great force, and in
the forefront were Jews. They arrived in both senses in Hungary.
One phenomenon of these years was their presence in great strength,
and by 1910 they accounted for nearly a quarter of the population of
Budapest. Jews were even responsible for much of the building.
Andrássy út and the streets to its south (named after talented painters such as Gyula Benczúr) have enormous late nineteenth-century
villas, which required armies of servants, and often enough these
were occupied by Jewish families – Chorin, Kornfeld, Weiss, Perlmutter – who waxed almighty on the development of the Hungarian
economy. Some were also established on the Buda side, where the
Rózsadomb or Svábhegy districts had their own often ingeniously
designed villas, with vast gardens. Then there were the overcrowded,
narrow, tall-buildinged streets of the Jewish quarter that started

with the great synagogue and was marked by Király utca and Dohány utca between the ring boulevards. That area subsequently became the ghetto in 1944. This was the quarter where the young Arthur Koestler grew up, in an overheated flat with cats, antimacassars, endless objects, stuffy furniture and a mother whose bosom heaved up and down with incipient outrage and hypochondria.

The period counts as a Jewish golden age. The Jews very rapidly became associated with Hungarian national loyalty, took up the language and contributed considerably to cultural life. Béla Bartók was not initially at all popular; his use of Hungarian folk music went down badly with classical traditionalists, and it was only with the patronage of a dozen Jewish ladies (and of Miklós Bánffy, then director of the opera house) that he established himself.[4] Arminius Vámbéry and Ignác Goldziher led the way with oriental studies, and Miksa Falk was a characteristic figure of the era, universally interested and editor of the newspaper *Pester Lloyd.* There was much more intermarriage than elsewhere, and of course also conversion. This caused some speculation that the Hungarian Jews were, racially, close to the Hungarians, and Koestler wrote a book about this. He argued that the Khazars, a Turkish people who had run an empire in the Caspian area in the ninth century, were at the origin of the Hungarian Jews, and not, as everyone had supposed, the Jews from the Rhineland (whose newly acquired surnames indicated as much – Kissinger from Bad Kissingen, Wertheimer from Wertheim etc., and there are real places called Bacharach and Katzenellenbogen). Jews were in fact called 'Hazar' in 'Sub-Carpathia', then northeastern Hungary, and the Khazars had converted to Judaism rather than to Islam or Christianity, not liking the attitude to alcohol of the one or that to sex of the other. Koestler himself, after a Zionist moment, distanced himself, and wrote the Khazar book in that spirit. It is not widely endorsed, and may even just count as a period piece of Hungarian-Jewish assimilationism. Zionists, such as David Cesarani in his grudging biography, have never forgiven him.

Of course it helped that Jews, like Budapest Germans, accepted

'Magyarisation' much more easily than, say, Rumanians. In the 1860s there was a powerful society to promote this, and Hungarian was used in the synagogues and Jewish schools, in place of German, let alone Yiddish, which enlightened Jews considered an embarrassing folk memory. Jews had associated with Hungarian nationalism in 1848. One of their finest, Arminius Vámbéry, grew up as the son of a rabbi in a place called Dunaszerdahely (meaning 'Wednesday market on the Danube'). His father died of cholera when Arminius was a baby, and he had to help out with finances by working, at the age of twelve, as a tutor. He went to a Catholic school where, at the age of fifteen, his Latin and his memory were such that he acted as the priest's helper at morning Mass. He had no university education, but as tutor to well-off families he learned many languages in his spare time, got to know Baron Eötvös and, with a little money, set out for Constantinople in 1867, changing his name (from Bamberger). He picked up Persian and Arabic, impressed influential Turks and undertook a confidential mission to Persia. There he bethought himself to find out where the Magyars had come from, and investigated central Asia. A local Emir agreed that the languages did not have much in common: but perhaps the music? The court orchestra was brought in, sounding like defective vacuum cleaners. The Emir asked Vámbéry for a rendition of his native music and got excerpts from *Don Giovanni*. The great man soon returned to Budapest (he gave up Judaism) as professor and eventually, after collaborating with the British, was Queen Victoria's guest at Windsor Castle. Edward VII gave him a very grand Order. Publishing in Hungarian was soon almost a Jewish preserve, and the Jewish influence on cultural life was prodigious. Gustav Mahler, for instance, agreed to learn Hungarian, and in 1888, at twenty-eight, was appointed artistic director in the new Opera, built four years earlier. He staged two parts of Wagner's *Ring* (in Hungarian), and conducted his own First Symphony. Then his patron was replaced by Count Géza Zichy, a one-armed pianist of nationalist disposition, and two singers challenged him to a duel for not putting on any Hungarian operas, so he left. The great Hungarian conductors – Solti, Ormandy (*né* Jenő Blau), Reiner, Szell – have been good Mahlerians, and Ivan Fischer has set up a Mahler Society.[5]

You could also argue that in this period Hungary experienced economic modernisation through Jews, or even that they constituted the middle class. Here there is an oddity, to do with Protestantism. This is the period when Max Weber wrote his famous book identifying *The Protestant Ethic and the Spirit of Capitalism* (1903). It has been denounced ever since, a sign that Weber was on to something. In 1903 he was: Catholic countries were poorer than Protestant ones. The oddity in Hungary was that Protestants were not particularly identified with capitalism: Jews were (though they quite often converted and married 'out'). The list of successes goes on and on. In the 1860s, both in Austria and Hungary, Jewish banks and businesses made the running. In Hungary there was a fairly standard process by which a rabbi's son would take up trade, and flourish, from one branch of it to another. Thus the Schossbergers. At first it is grain trade, as middlemen for the great estate owners as they shifted their grain to Pest, from where it went up the Danube on barges to the Austrian market and sometimes beyond. The Schossbergers and others became established on the northern edge of Pest, where the barges were loaded and where now the Parliament district sits. Then they diversified – tobacco, agriculture: they acquired an Esterházy estate in 1873 and had the inevitable Ybl (who also did the splendid Opera) knock them out a turreted castle. Then came a bank. Members of the family became bored by Judaism, converted to Catholicism and married out (a descendant was Georges de Hevesy, who was awarded the Nobel Prize for Chemistry but, in disgust at Hungarian anti-Semitism, took Swedish citizenship). The Schossbergers were given a baronial title by Franz Joseph,[6] but this occurred in 350 other cases, and conversion was not necessary (though it was desirable) and the Schossberger story could be replicated many times over, whether with railways, banks, flour-milling or insurance – Kornfeld, Chorin, Manfred Weiss, Madarassy-Beck, Freudiger, Mauthner, Hatvani-Deutsch (whose picture collection was of European significance). Their monuments are all around in Budapest. Another monument remains: Pick's winter salami.[7] Márk Pick (1843–1892) was yet another rabbi's son, from Szeged, yet another grain merchant, who set up a small factory producing paprika and spirits. He went to Italy and learned about salami. In 1883 he brought Italian workmen to Szeged, and since he knew about meat-processing, he set up with the new employees, who dried the Hungarian young pork (*mangalica*), then smoked it with beechwood, adding paprika. It is called winter salami because it could not be made in hot weather without rotting. The family business survived the Nazis because an Austrian Christian relative took over.[8] There are many such tales, and Hungarian inventions (not generally Jewish but financed from there), from the light bulb and the soda fountain to the biro (the name means 'judge') and the Rubik Cube, add their bit to the industrial revolution. And of course it all came to a head when Hungarian physicists came up with the nuclear bomb. The names of the Nobel prize-winners Karman, Neumann, Szilard, Teller and Wigner resound in the context of the Manhattan Project.[9] They were products of the hothouse Budapest schools – the outstanding ones were the Fasori Lutheran, the Minta (= 'model', or 'normal'), near the Museum, and the Piarista, near the Elisabeth Bridge; there was a Calvinist one for girls, the Lorántffy, now Baár-Madas, in Buda – where the teachers, as John Lukács avers, knew more and presented it more inspiringly than today's university professors. The logical connections are not easy to make, though there is a brave American attempt (by William McCagg) to relate things. But that old Hungary treated the Jews decently of course mattered. There were indeed anti-Semites, but they were muddled, and Hungarians at this time were, if anything, fascinated by Jews and made a great deal of them. Around 1910 many deputies and government ministers (Szterényi né Stern for trade, Teleszky né Theikles for finance,

Hazai for war) were of Jewish origin. By 1914 one of the best-informed foreign observers of the Monarchy could write that 'the Jewish problem is one of the great problems of the world'.[10] He was impressed by Werner Sombart's account of the Jews' involvement with capitalism, as if the Talmud were the ledger of Heaven, although it has not really stood up to examination.

There was a shadow side, of course. In the first place, armies of Jews were not included in this charmed circle; nor were a great many Christians. There were also young Jews living not on Andrássy Avenue or on the Rozsadomb in Buda but in the Dohány utca district of Pest – hot, noisy, overcrowded – who were either alienated by the suffocating conformism of their fathers or, if not involved, resentful of the system and its workings. They were to drift into socialism or, much more rarely, Zionism. A counterpart was anti-Semitism, and efforts at political anti-Semitism began in the 1880s but fizzled out. More serious was an attempt to establish a Catholic Social party in the 1890s, at a time when Pope Leo XIII inveighed, in *Rerum Novarum*, against capitalism in a language that was almost Marxist. By implication it was anti-Semitic. Liberal Italy had taken over Rome and bundled the Pope into the Vatican, where he fulminated: as Indro Montanelli said, 'He spoke like a persecutor to claim that he was persecuted'.[11] In 1898 the Italian army bombarded a monastery in Milan, on the grounds that the monks were hiding anarchists. There was an anti-Semitic edge to the Catholic People's Party that was founded (by a Zichy) in Hungary, although it mainly flourished in western and Slovak areas. There was of course anti-Semitism, but in a sense it was even shared by the early Zionists (also a Budapest product), who wondered why Jews were not like other people and thought that a nation of strapping peasants would do the trick. A great majority of Hungarian Jews had no real notion of what they were talking about.

Although the Jewish contribution to modern Hungary is considerable, and overwhelmingly positive, there have been darker sides to this too. The best-known of these lies in the career of one Ignac Trebitsch-Lincoln: a fraud of genius. His father was a poor merchant, and at sixteen Trebitsch-Lincoln was found to have forged laundry tickets so as to steal the goods and sell them on to the rag trade. He escaped, encountered the Anglican mission to the Jews in Trieste and became a curate in Kent. Then he was taken up by the Quaker Rowntree chocolate-making family, whose influence was strong in the Liberal Party, and he became an MP. After that he was an oil man in Rumania, and in 1914 offered his services to the Germans as a spy. After the First World War he took up contacts with aristocratic Hungarian counter-revolutionaries and with their help took up still more in 1920 with German military reactionaries. When they launched a farcical coup called the Kapp Putsch, Trebitsch-Lincoln was their foreign press spokesman. He remade himself as a Buddhist monk organising spiritualist journeys through Mongolia for mothers of sons killed in the war, and then became a spy against the Japanese in Shanghai.

There are parallels to this more recently in Robert Maxwell, whose entire career was built on fraud. In Britain he passed himself off as a Czech, because by 1940 the Czechs counted as a let-down people, and they were known as competent architects or engineers or pilots, not as glamorous as the Poles but more solid. But his first language was Hungarian. His surname was Hoch, meaning 'high' in German, and the Hungarian for 'high' is *magas*: hence, no doubt, 'Maxwell'. He came from Sub-Carpathia, where the peasants spoke dialects of Ukrainian, itself then a dialect of Russian. They were very poor, and the diet was so bad that young men's voices did not break until they were twenty, and so they could not be conscripted. Smuggling was part of the culture, as all regimes unable to tax incomes taxed tobacco instead, and there were monopolies to undercut in this thickly forested region. Jews there spoke Hungarian once they had moved out of Yiddish, and were Hassidic, following the spirit rather than the letter; they drank on Friday nights, on the (defensible) grounds that it brought them closer to

God. They acted as agents for the landowners and ran the inns. Unscrupulous ones would let the peasants drink on credit – a very powerful hooch, at that – and then foreclose. These poor illiterates, wrestling to understand Hungarian legalese, would have no defence. The Jews of these parts had come straight from Galicia, not from the Moravia that nurtured Freud and Mahler, and they gave an edge to anti-Semitism; an Irishman, Edward Egan, tried to counter this around 1900, with encouragement from a good minister of agriculture, by setting up co-operatives and lecturing the peasants as to the error of their ways as no doubt he would have been doing in Ireland. He was in the end frustrated and mysteriously killed. Maxwell, born in 1920 and hence formally a Czechoslovak citizen, was a formidable linguist and was useful to British Intelligence. He used that position to do deals with the Soviet representatives in post-war Berlin, acquiring the rights of German scientific periodicals, which he exploited as a publisher. Then he became a Labour Member of Parliament and led a charmed life, his assistant being a former British Ambassador in the United States, Peter Jay; he bought a left-wing newspaper (and a football team). In 1989–90, as Communism fell apart, his deals with Moscow were revealed, and he died, probably by suicide, having tried to salvage his concerns by stealing his employees' pension fund. He is buried on the Mount of Olives, a sort of posthumous fraud.[12]

By 1890 Greater Hungary had been successfully on the map for a quarter of a century, and, as in the new Germany, a younger generation was emerging that was full of nationalist enthusiasm. Elsewhere in Europe politics took on a modern shape. In Hungary old tunes were still being played. The 'political nation' had run affairs since 1867. This grouping, of magnates, gentry, lawyers, bureaucrats and journalists struck attitudes and jockeyed for office. Gladstonian speeches were delivered; aristocrats manoeuvred against each other; newspapers sold their opinions, as George Orwell remarked of France, like so many pounds of cheese across the counter; in the background Emperor Franz Joseph could manipulate the politicians. In Hungary it was easy enough to divert energies into a national cause of some sort. There had already been trouble in 1878, over the war that broke out between Russia and Turkey. The sympathies of the 1848-ers were with the Turks, and Sultan Abdul Hamid capitalised on this when he sent thirty-five codices from the library of Matthias Corvinus back to Budapest. Austrian officialdom none the less took the view that Austria should profit from the peace that followed, by occupying Turkish Bosnia-Herzegovina, and there were strong protests in the Hungarian parliament. By 1889 nationalist muscles were being flexed. As the European populations grew, the military wanted increases in the recruit contingent: i.e., the numbers of young conscripts who could be taken in each year. This affected Austria-Hungary as well, but by 1889 many Hungarians wanted to have a properly national army, not one commanded in German. Kálmán Tisza used all of his arts to have the bill passed, but it exhausted him and he resigned. The concession that he had had to make was a purely symbolic one, which resonates. Officially, Austro-Hungarian institutions were called *kaiserlich-königlich* (in short, K.K.) or 'imperial-royal', which denoted the Austrian Empire with its kingdoms, which again implied that Bohemia and Hungary were equal. Now an *und* was inserted, making it K.u.K., implying the superior status of the Hungarian kingdom. This was the moment when Andrássy's dualism began to unravel, and there was another, tragic piece of symbolism in that Crown Prince Rudolf killed himself. He had been educated by the best economists and had Hungarian tutors; there were rumours that he might become king of an independent Hungary, but he himself was a dilettante. The clerical hoops that had bound such characters in the past were weakening, and with parents like his, the poor man probably never stood a chance. Franz Joseph was stiff and protocol-obsessed; if you had an audience with him, it was held standing up. Elisabeth was narcissistic and worked constantly at herself: rope exercises in the gymnasium, dry biscuits and soda. She knew that her weak point was rotten teeth, and did not open her mouth when speaking; when she visited the sick, no one knew what she was saying. She drove the architect of the Vienna Opera to suicide by cancelling the ceremonial opening again and again. She was supposed to have had an affair with Andrássy, but this is unlikely: Franz Joseph was no doubt a Karenin figure, but Elisabeth became her own Vronsky. They married Rudolf off to a plum-duff Belgian Saxe-Coburg and used him for public relations purposes, but he probably fell into drugs, and in 1889 shot himself together with a besotted seventeen-year-old. After that, Franz Joseph became even more of an automaton with no creative interventions, just as Hungarian politics entered a period of dangerous instability.

All of this occurred in an atmosphere of heady nationalism. Hungary had put herself well and truly on the European map in a generation, and Budapest was a European capital to be visited. Money oozed from the grand villas at the top of the radial avenue leading from the city centre to the City Park. A non-European language that had been spoken only by peasants and back-of-beyond clergymen who could not even agree on spelling, and which had been hastily cobbled together with invented words two generations earlier, was now generating serious literature, worth translating, and outstanding poetry. The music, particularly pianists and string quartets, spoke (and speaks) for itself. The time had come for a piece of grand national showing off, and roughly a thousand years had passed since the Magyars had taken over the Carpathian plain. A Millennium Exhibition was planned, just as the ultra-nationalist Bánffy government was under way. (The Prime Minister's wife had been a school teacher, and the great aristocracy indicated to him that they would not turn up if she did: she went on a journey.) The historians could not decide, within a twenty-year period, quite when the settlement had happened, and there were other grand European exhibitions that might compete. In the end 1896 was chosen, and a display was made – the statuary at the top of the radial avenue (it was called 'Heroes' Square' only in 1932), the Franz

Joseph Bridge (now *Szabadság* or 'Freedom'), the twin museums on the Square and the first continental underground from there to central Pest. A war-horse nationalist historian, Kálmán Thaly, planned events, and it was decided that seven great monuments to the conquest would go up, most of them in areas where non-Magyars predominated – Slovak, Serb, German, Rumanian, Ruthene – to show who was boss.[13] The ceremonies went on for six months, with schoolchildren gawping and nationalist songs being composed. Thaly produced some songs from the Rákóczi period, no doubt to rapture. After he died, it was discovered, in 1913, that he had passed off some of his own poetry – it was unpublishable – in the songs.

All over Europe this kind of nationalism was proliferating. It had a positive side in education, but it poisoned public life in Austria. Czechs and Germans fought in the Bohemian Diet over the language of schooling or administration, and transferred their quarrel to the Vienna parliament, making it unworkable, and demonstrating that Gołuchowski and the conservative makers of the October Diploma in 1860 had been, for all their blunders, correct. Attempts to deal with such problems through central law led to a proliferation of detailed prescriptions that enriched lawyers and increased hatreds. In 1897 a great row broke out in Austria when the Prime Minister, a Count Badeni, decreed that Czech and German should have equal status in the Bohemian bureaucracy – meaning, in effect, that Germans would have to learn Czech. Howls of rage followed, and when, in 1900, a Czech group hired a Danube steamer for a celebration, they were stoned as they passed through the Wachau, above Vienna. It was characteristic of the whole quarrel that Czechs, rather than Germans, took the low pay of administrative jobs and anyway, informally, conducted their business in Czech. But living in fantasy was common enough in that nationalist era.

In Hungary a nationalist spirit more and more took over government and opposition alike. 'Magyarisation', as it came to be called, went ahead, particularly in Bánffy's time, when villages had their names arbitrarily changed and school programmes were tightened up. By now, thanks to the Magyarisation of the Jews, Hungarian-speakers formed a small majority of the population. As Budapest, especially, grew, the German bourgeoisie, with Hungarian nannies, could and did switch character; the same happened lower down the social scale, as Slovaks (especially) poured in. (Tóth is a name meaning 'Slovak', as Horváth is 'Croat' and Németh 'German'.) Religion, of course, mattered, and here the great blockage was with the Rumanians of Transylvania. They were Orthodox, though half of them were attached to a Church called 'Uniate', which followed Orthodox ways (priestly marriage especially mattered) but, as part of a compromise with the Habsburgs, accepted the Pope as head. Enlightened aristocrats tried to win over the Uniates (there is a church in Hermannstadt, now Sibiu in Rumania, which in 1982 still had a plaque recording the generosity of the Dessewffy family) in the hope of dividing their loyalty from Orthodox Rumania; and there were indeed a great many Uniates who preferred the Habsburg Monarchy to the Balkan state beyond the Transylvanian Alps. But these Uniates were not to be won for a Hungarian Transylvania, and resentments grew. In 1892 ultra-respectable Rumanian citizens petitioned Franz Joseph for recognition of their rights and were imprisoned (although they were released in 1895 by amnesty). This was the point at which British opinion began to have doubts about liberal Hungary, which became the subject of a despairing book by a later Hungarian foreign minister, Géza Jeszenszky (*Az elveszett prestizs*, 1986), and the Hungarian image worsened when the young Robert Seton-Watson, who came to central Europe as an admirer of Hungary, found out about the shadow side and wrote about it in *Racial Problems in Hungary*. But the 1848-ers also became ambitious after Tisza's fall, and took up various causes.

The first, in the early 1890s, was religious. In Hungary the Church had not given up its universalist claims, and was a great deal more understanding of minority or underdog peoples than the classical liberals. The Slovaks (like Basques or Bretons in France) were generally fervently Catholic, and supplied more than their due share of the Hungarian priesthood (including two cardinal archbishops) and there were Catholic-Orthodox Rumanians as well. In civil affairs the Church was able not just to prohibit divorce but also to impose strict rules about mixed marriages. These had to be performed by a priest, and the children had to be brought up as Catholics. The Calvinist element was very strong in the Liberal Party, and there were also many mixed marriages because, particularly in Transylvania, there was a long tradition of toleration and also much purely political choice of religion. After a long wrangle Franz Joseph gave way, and in a sense this marked the real breakthrough of governmental liberalism, in that Church and state were separated (as was to happen in France ten years later). One consequence was that, in reaction, a Catholic Party emerged, led by Count Ferdinand Zichy, but it never really flourished outside parts of the west and the Slovak north. Another was that you could obtain a divorce in Hungary but not in Austria (and in 1915 the Chief of the General Staff, Franz Conrad von Hötzendorf, was able to marry his long-standing mistress when she took Hungarian citizenship).

Once the religious question had been semi-settled, nationalist fire turned towards the financial arrangements of the Compromise. Here was more fantasy. The original sums due to the three common ministers had been substantial enough, and the Hungarian 30 per cent was fair, given the relative poverty of Hungary. But she became richer, and a greater share would have made sense. Nationalists complained, and some of them anyway had a notion of building up Hungarian industry in a classic protectionist way, with tariff walls against Austrian competition. To some extent this was already happening, through railway policy. The system was centred on Budapest, with its two grand stations, Western and Eastern, and the chief minister, Gábor Baross (whose statue stands at the Eastern Station), ruthlessly built up Budapest's hub position, as his equivalents did in

Paris. It was quicker to go from Zagreb in Hungarian Croatia to Maribor (Marburg) in Austrian Styria (now Slovenia), a distance of forty miles, via Budapest and Vienna than by the alternative, a narrow-gauge mountain railway. Nineteen Hungarian railway lines ended in buffers on the Austrian border. In the same way the port of Fiume (Rijeka), which the Hungarians in 1868 had by surreptitious methods made dependent on themselves and not, as the Croats wanted, on Zagreb, was artificially built up as a rival to Trieste. The common bank was another apple of discord: without its control of the note issue, based on gold, would credit for up-and-coming Hungarian enterprises not be more generous? The party of 1848 began to make headway as Hungarian industrialists grew hungry. None of this had anything much to do with the common budget, but in the 1890s it was held up. In any case it was dwarfed, as it had not been in 1867, by the budgets of the two states, which reflected a prodigious growth of the overall economy, and the sums voted by the two parliaments reflected their preoccupations with internal affairs. Especially in Austria, the nationalities were bought off, with duplicated jobs in the public services, and common matters came off badly. Foreign affairs did not cost much (ambassadors were generally rich aristocrats who paid out of their own pockets), and the Finance Minister had little to do beyond counting the small change (he was given the job of running Bosnia). It was the common army that came off badly, and this struck at the whole purpose of the Compromise: to maintain Austria as a Great Power. The common war minister found that his needs came some way behind local domestic ones, and he ended up with an army eight times larger than the British one, but with a budget no greater: even the military bands, Austria's pride, were in part suppressed.

Around 1900 Hungarian triumphalism was such that several well-known commentators thought that a Hungary of 30 million souls could dominate the Balkans as in the time of the late medieval king János Hunyádi, who held off the Turks. Before 1914, in that era of nationalist euphoria, as Hungarians contemplated their superb capital, the historic recovery of the Lands of the Crown of St Stephen, from their Adriatic port of Fiume almost to the Black Sea, and the cultural effusion that had put them once again well and truly on the European intellectual map, the delusions piled up. Of course, such delusions were common in Europe at the time. Lord Curzon, for instance, as Viceroy of India in 1904, thought that the British 'should rule as if for ever'. They were out forty-three years later. In Budapest the chief editor of a main newspaper, Jenő Rákosi, said in 1902 that soon there would be 30 million Hungarians dominating south-eastern Europe as in medieval days of yore. The chief thinker of the governing party, Gusztáv Beksics, thought the number too high but the effect the same. A best-selling book, *Greater Hungary* (by Pál Hoitsy, otherwise a decent astronomer), dispensed the reader from reading any more than the title, and there were serious suggestions that the Habsburg Monarchy should be renamed 'Hungary-Austria'.[14] In Transylvania the Hungarians had certainly achieved much, and the chief town of the Székel district, Marosvásárhely, is a turn-of-the-century architectural masterpiece. But the Hungarian Transylvanian Cultural Association was offensively triumphalist. Historians wrestled as to whether the Rumanians, with their Latin words, descended from old Rome or were just shepherds who had wandered in, with a dog-Latin vocabulary for rudimentary matters, during the thirteenth century, when the Mongols had temporarily smashed Hungarian power. Hungarians danced their nationalist round dance and hurt the feelings of the local Rumanian majority without reducing its size.[15]

In the common army these things were kept under severe control. The officer corps was firmly imperial, its loyalties regimental. There were famous military educational institutions which took recruits from all backgrounds. Franz Joseph considered himself to be the father – by now, the grandfather – of his peoples, and he spoke nineteen languages. A multinational army had, of course, to be commanded in universally comprehensible ways, and the language of command – 'Attention' etc. – was German; so was the 'language of service', a hundred or so words such as 'trigger'. This was obviously sensible, and it worked quite well. Then there was the regimental language, which professional officers were expected to learn. (Franz Conrad von Hötzendorf, the later Chief of the General Staff, spoke seven of them, and there was an old tradition, going back to the Military Frontier, that favoured Serb and Croat.) Odd ways round were found, as in 1914, when a Slovak regiment was commanded in English, which the officers knew from school, the men having acquired it from returned emigrants. Hungarian nationalists wanted to extend the use of their language in the army and raised a great fuss about it. Now there were demands for Hungarian to be used alongside German for military purposes in Hungary, along with red-white-green insignia. Such causes kept the opposition together, and student demonstrations took place about them. Military bills were held up, and the opposition had a weapon to hand: parliamentary obstruction. In the 1860s, when the Vienna and Budapest parliaments began to operate, the assumption was that gentlemen would behave as such. There were no real rules for procedure. The Irish at Westminster, and worthies in Congress, discovered that they could stall proceedings with very long speeches or demands for a roll-call and the like, and the Hungarians hit upon the same device. Parliaments in Vienna became unworkable because of this, and if Austria became a home for Fascism, this discrediting of parliament has something to do with it. More and more there were disputes about language in mixed localities. The German liberals of the 1860s now paid the price for setting up a central Reichsrat where everything was discussed, including such matters (in 1895) as the language of instruction in a small-town Styrian grammar school, instead of leaving matters under October Diploma localisation. Germans, Italians and Poles said that proper schooling in Czech, Slovene or Ukrainian (Ruthene) was not possible, at any rate not for them: the professor of law at the Prague German University blew a cavalry trumpet to interrupt a Ruthene deputy speaking for eleven hours in Russian, in pursuit of some point or other. Young Hitler, looking upon all this, made certain conclusions about parliamentary democracy.

Hungary after 1900 moved in the same anarchic direction, as obstruction wrecked proceedings. The opposition had this on its side, that elections under Kálmán Tisza had become government-controlled, so that a natural majority of the electorate was under-represented. Parliamentary obstruction then went ahead, and the moderate obstructers would have somehow to be placated. The financial question was put on ice, but concessions were then demanded over the military question, and this was too much for Franz Joseph, who defied the Hungarians with an army order in 1903, to the effect that oaths had been sworn and that the army would respect every nationality. More rows, more obstruction, and the appointment of a strong man as Prime Minister, István Tisza, the son of Kálmán. He was to be the last dominant figure of Habsburg Hungary, a formidably well-educated man who had studied law at Heidelberg (his German was very elegant) and an astute bank director. He was also a nationalist (he regarded the 'idea of a Rumanian university' as 'a contradiction in terms', having inherited the Calvinist contempt for these non-Elect shepherds) but took the longer-term view, that Hungary needed a strong Empire. He tried, through wheezes, to obstruct the obstructors. There were more rows, and even when the brand-new Parliament, the national monument, was opened, they did not stop. Enraged deputies smashed the elaborate carving; duels (a weird survival) were fought, even by Tisza himself and a leading opposition figure, Count Mihály Károlyi.

It mattered, of course, in all of this that minds were not concentrated by larger dangers: the modern mass parties existed only in embryo. Peasants in great estates, especially in the wine country of the west, were generally quiet, looked after by a beneficent and paternalistic landowner. In the poorer, spirit-drinking centre there were disorders in the 1880s and 1890s, in which the gendarmerie were sometimes involved, but emigration – in all, 1.25 million between 1869 and 1910 – was a safety valve, and the remittances (by 1902, 100 million Crowns, rising to 250 million in 1910) helped. Some half a million also migrated to Budapest, a city, by 1914, of a million inhabitants. There was also not much of a working-class movement outside Budapest, where a socialist intelligentsia counted for more than trade unions. Migrant peasant labour arrived, as elsewhere, but many were Slovak, and peasants were not usually inclined to part with even a pitiful sum for trade unionists, whom anyway they mistrusted. No doubt many of the migrant labourers employed in construction in Budapest moved back to rural areas for the harvest. The socialist party set up in 1890 remained embryonic.

'The political nation' had a last field day, and played old tunes with enthusiasm. It no doubt helped their cause that no war was in sight: Austria-Hungary had struck an agreement with Russia in 1903 over the southern Balkans, and in 1904 Russia, anyway defeated in war with Japan, was on the verge of revolution. The opposition could ignore reality and was itself a strange creation. At this time Hungarian politics was still very much a matter for great aristocrats, middling gentry (now usually transmogrified into urban officials or lawyers) and some middle-class modernisers, often of Jewish origin, with an echo chamber of vociferous journalists and some industrialists or bankers in the background. Transylvanian Protestants generally liked the sound of their own voices, and took the nationalist and independence-minded side. The governing party was not more than very loosely kept together, and defections were liable to happen, particularly if one or other of the great aristocrats wanted to make trouble. A leading figure here was Count Albert Apponyi, who set up his own party, although, having been educated at the upper-class Jesuit school Kalksburg, he sat uneasily together with a Transylvanian Protestant such as Gábor Ugron. But over the army question the opposition coalition held together and was joined by senior government bloc men over other issues. Tisza then called an election, did not tell the Lord-Lieutenants what to do and so deliberately lost it. He flung responsibility at the opposition.

In 1905 the opposition coalition was therefore in a position to govern, and had an audience with Franz Joseph. It lasted five minutes. A military government of sorts was then appointed, as an interim measure, to keep the show on the road: an old General, Géza Fejérváry, who ran things without parliamentary sanction. A sort of ghost of 1848 then appeared, as the political nation went on strike, with taxes uncollected and Lord-Lieutenants boycotted and (in Debrecen) roughed up. Franz Joseph still had a trump card to play. The Hungarian voting system was notoriously weak, and the country had progressed so far that the kind of mass party that now figured in European affairs had a shadowy presence. There were socialists, with demonstrations promising doom to the rich. There were Catholics, who promised doom to the Protestant and Jewish rich. In Hungary there were also national minorities: Rumanians especially, but also Serbs, Slovaks and Ruthenes. National movements had developed, uneasily kept at bay by police or other administrative action. If the government introduced universal suffrage – votes for all (men) – then the parliament would altogether change. The Austrians had been driven mad by Hungarian obstinacy, and their Prime Minister, Baron Gautsch, expressed exasperation at the 'arrogant oligarchs, small noblemen, clergymen, lawyers who make up the Hungarian parliament and make it unworkable'. The German experience showed that the socialists formed *eine ganz traitable Partei*, he said, in Viennese idiom: i.e., one you could deal with. In the summer of 1905, as Russia exploded in revolution, the Minister of the Interior, József Kristóffy, proposed the decreeing of universal suffrage in Hungary.

The backdrop to this was the character of the heir to the throne, Archduke Franz Ferdinand. He was Franz Joseph's nephew, and Franz Joseph was already seventy-five. Franz Ferdinand was devoutly Catholic and detested Hungarian Protestants; travelling by train through Hungary, he pulled down the window blinds. He saw Hungary's pretensions as ruinous to the Monarchy, especially the army. He occupied Prince Eugene's grand Belvedere Palace, and there had his own Court; his military cabinet (*Militärkanzlei*) followed developments in Hungary quite closely, with press cuttings. He regularly held meetings with Slovak or Rumanian and particularly Croat figures, discussing what was to be done in Hungary when his old uncle died. If he came to the throne, would he make a return to absolutism, this time with the threat that masses of hitherto silent voters would swamp the Hungarian political nation? There would be a parliament containing a large majority of Reds, Blacks (Catholics) and nationalities: the end of Hungary, in other words. Some men among the nationalist opposition were also prepared for an extension of the suffrage, but not many. In the view of the political nation Hungarians had done a remarkable job, one not to be stopped by fancy Austrians and gullible peasants. The threat of universal suffrage was enough, and in April 1906 the opposition buckled, with a formula that barely saved its face. It accepted Franz Joseph's conditions. The political histrionics came to an end. Hungary would pay somewhat more of joint expenses, reflecting the increase in her prosperity. Recruits came to the colours, learning the few dozen German words of the language of command. Large questions as to the functioning of the common bank, or the possibility of protection for Hungarian industry from Austrian competition, were shelved. The new Prime Minister, Sándor Wekerle, was an old hand, practised in financial questions, and a Protestant to reassure the large Protestant component (he was also the first non-noble Prime Minister). But the government could at least indulge in triumphalism and nationalist gestures. The enormous Stock Exchange off the Parliament Square in Budapest – the largest in Europe – opened for business, and the remains of Rákóczi were brought back from Turkey and reburied in the Kassa cathedral (they are still there, in St Elisabeth's Cathedral in what is now the Slovak town of Kosice, but under lock and key). Albert Apponyi as Minister of Education opened the splendid Music Academy, but he also applied harsher laws as regards compulsory Hungarian in nationality areas, chipped away at the salaries of teachers in private

Rumanian schools and even instituted linguistic inspection of kindergartens. He decreed that even the Croatian railways should use Hungarian. (This in its way was fair enough, given that railway accidents occurred all too frequently, and a common language for such purposes made sense, as with English in today's air traffic control, although German would then have made more sense.) Universal male suffrage was, of course, shelved, although it was introduced in Austria. Elections there returned parties representing the masses – socialists and Christian Socialists. For a time the nationalists were cowed, but they soon recovered. Austrian Catholics divided along national lines; so did the trade unions. By 1909 the usual futile pretext came up, over a clerical matter, and Austrian politics went back to its dismal old pattern: by 1913 the Bohemian Diet was closed down in chaos, and in 1914 the same happened with the Vienna parliament. Hungary avoided this. There the coalition also fell apart (over the National Bank, but it was divided by much else), and Tisza made a return to politics, renaming his old party (it became the Party of Work) and eventually, over a military bill, overcoming obstruction by using main force. But this stability came at a cost. When the Austrian nationalities declared independence in 1918, it was more or less bloodless, a matter of a few telephone calls. In Hungary there was Communism and civil war.

Tisza overcame the 1848-ers' obstruction of a military bill because, by 1912, the European situation had become doom-laden. War was in the air, as Germany practised naval rivalry with Great Britain and military rivalry on land with France and Russia. In 1911 the Italians started the final crisis when they attacked Turkey, and late in 1912 a Balkan alliance, sponsored by Russia, defeated the Turks in a few weeks. This victory especially profited Serbia, which doubled in size, and Serb nationalists now looked to liberate these lands now occupied by Austria. This opened up the area in which Hungarian nationalists had been least creative: Croatia. It was over the South Slav question that the deadly trouble came about. Archduke Franz Ferdinand had the right instincts about this. Croatia and its shadow kingdom, Slavonia, were historically part of the Lands of the Crown of St Stephen, but there were Croats in Austrian (ex-Venetian) Dalmatia as well. A South Slav movement aimed to join Croats and Serbs, since they had a more or less common language, but many Croats, as Catholic Habsburg loyalists, saw in Greater Croatia an answer to the South Slav question. There was also a Croat and Catholic minority in yet another South Slav area, Bosnia-Herzegovina. It had been a province of the Ottoman Empire, taken four centuries earlier, and there was a very substantial Moslem element as well, including the landowners. About half of the population was Serb and Orthodox.

In 1878, at the Congress of Berlin, two European Powers made a considerable mistake as regards the Ottoman Empire. The British took Cyprus, which gave them headaches two generations later. The Austrians took over Bosnia. At the time the Hungarians protested, partly out of solidarity with the Turks, but at the time Vienna simply saw the advantages: more security on the Dalmatian border, more protection for the projected Austrian railway to Salonica, with its commercial opening. The common Finance Minister given the job of governing Bosnia was a Protestant, Count Kállay, who in his youth had written an enthusiastic history of Serbia, as had the great German historian Leopold von Ranke (*Serbien und die Turkei*, 1879). (The Serbians had the desirable qualities of not being, like the Croats, Catholic, and also of being against the Turks, whom the Gladstonian Protestants of the era regarded as embodiments of major vices.) However, Bosnia was an object of Serb nationalism, and to discourage this, Kállay's own book was banned. The place then developed along colonial lines, with some picturesque buildings in Sarajevo, the capital, being built and a school system instituted. The railways had a narrower gauge than those of southern Hungary, because the Hungarians wanted to make the export of Bosnian pork more expensive, and it had to be unloaded at Bosnisch-Brod and trans-shipped to a different train. There was another Croat grievance of a commercial nature. Fiume in north-western

Croatia, as an old Venetian and still largely Italian-speaking town, was their outlet to the Adriatic, the hope for Hungarian exports. In 1868, when they made their own sub-Compromise with the Croats, the Hungarians had smuggled in a clause that made Fiume a Hungarian port (which anyway Maria Theresa had decreed).

One demand of the rising Croat nationalists was for a union of Croats in a Triune Kingdom: Croatia-Slavonia, comprising Croatia with Slavonia (to the east) and Dalmatia. The Hungarians formally accepted this ambition, but in practice did nothing, and to control Croatia they had a tool at hand. About a quarter of the population were Serb and Orthodox, and Hungarian governors favoured them: they made up the police, for instance. In Zagreb there was much resentment, as Croats, Catholic and European, regarded the Serbs as heretical, rough and crypto-Turkish. In Dalmatia, where sea ports and an international tradition dictated different ways, and where in any case there was common hostility to the Italians, Serbs and Croats came to an agreement that they were 'South Slavs' – i.e., Yugoslavs, rather than Serbs and Croats – and in 1905 they produced the Fiume Resolution as to future co-operation. The Zagreb parliament soon became Yugoslav in sympathy, though there were still Croat nationalists who resented everybody and looked to the Habsburgs for semi-independence and a Triune Kingdom.

This became complicated again because of Bosnia-Herzegovina. There the population was made up of 10 per cent Catholic Croats, 50 per cent Orthodox Serbs and the rest Moslems, a legacy from the Ottoman Empire, though speaking Serbo-Croat. In the 1870s, anxious to restore their Great Power role, the Austrians looked to the Balkans and the ports of the Ottoman Empire, with railway projects. These involved Bosnia, and anyway Habsburg rule over the South Slavs also implied expansion into Bosnia. In 1878 Austria-Hungary had occupied the land, which became its colony, with a military governor. Serb nationalists regarded it as Serbian, and wanted union with Serbia; Croats thought of a Greater Croatia or a Yugoslavia with its capital at Zagreb, and Franz Ferdinand was obviously inclined to agree. The Bosnian Moslems still looked to Ottoman Turkey but were otherwise content enough with the status quo. In 1908 Franz Joseph formally annexed the place, a defiance of Serb nationalism. One great question mark over this period concerns Hungary. Why did Budapest obstinately block the creation of a Habsburg Yugoslavia? This went on right to the end of the Monarchy in 1918. Even Hitler's later commander in Croatia, Edmund von Glaise-Horstenau, who largely wrote the Austrian official history of the First World War, said that Yugoslavia was the only good creation of the post-war treaties.[16] Croats and Serbs had enough in common for it to work and Bosnia was a case in point, in both cases. A Yugoslavia, its capital at Zagreb, was one possible answer. However, the Hungarians did not want a co-partner, and Tisza was still refusing this in September 1918, near the very end. In Sarajevo a South Slav delegation asked for unification and he blew up: 'impertinent … Do they think Hungary will collapse? We might but before that we will still be strong enough to smash her enemies.'[17] (Here he was quite wrong. At the very end of the Monarchy, when most Croats were adhering to Yugoslavia, the extreme Catholic loyalists managed to get the Hungarian government to agree to a Triune Kingdom. Did anyone really notice?) Franz Ferdinand never had a chance to put his plans into action and was shot by a Serb in 1914, when he visited the Bosnian capital.

On 28 June 1914, to display grandeur to the citizenry, he paid a visit to Sarajevo. His relations with its Governor, Oskar Potiorek, were frosty. Potiorek, of Slovene origin, was a neurasthenic homosexual who had been given the job as consolation for not being Chief of the General Staff (Franz Ferdinand preferred Conrad von Hötzendorf). He disliked social events, and loathed his own chief of staff, a Colonel Böltz, with whom he communicated with scribbled pieces of paper, in nearly unreadable Gothic script, pushed under the door. Penny-pinching reigned. Security for the Archduke's visit was handed over to a firm of Budapest private detectives. Seven young Serb conspirators picked up training and weapons in

Belgrade, and one of them brought it off. Another of those few men who saw what disasters would come from a great war was, curiously enough, Archduke Franz Ferdinand himself, and it is a considerable might-have-been in history: if he had been wounded rather than killed at Sarajevo in 1914, he would certainly have refused to go to war. But killed he was, in an extraordinary chapter of accidents.[18] The assassin, Gavrilo Princip, thought that the plot had failed, and Franz Ferdinand's driver, by mistake, turned into the street where Princip happened to be. He was too young to be executed, and was imprisoned in the fortress of Theresienstadt, where he died before the war ended. The prison psychiatrist asked him if he had any regrets. He answered, 'If I had not done it, the Germans would have found another excuse.' And there the wretched creature was right. Great wars in the modern era start off with ridiculously dispropor-tionate causes, and so it was in 1914. The tensions were released by a trigger. Vienna could see no other answer to the South Slav problem than a demonstration of might against Balkan monkeys.

But Serbia was protected by Russia, and only Germany could help in that case. On 5 July the Germans said: move. They did so because they saw this as the last moment at which they could deal with Russia, and the diary of the German Chancellor's secretary spells it out: if war now, we will win; if later, not. The Austrians were told to provoke a war. The Austrian Crown Council deliberated, and Tisza, alone, spoke against: the Rumanians would come in, and anyway the Empire did not need any more Slavs, such as would accrue if Serbia were smashed. But in the end he gave way. He knew that Greater Hungary had come about because of Bismarck, and that one of the main boulevards in Budapest (now Bajcsy-Zsilinszky) was named after Kaiser Wilhelm I, and he voted for war. He told the Belgian Minister, '*Mon cher, l'Allemagne est invin-cible.*' War followed against Serbia on 28 July, and there were paroxysms of enthusiasm in Budapest. Even Count Apponyi said in Parliament, 'At last' ('*végre*'). The Russians did protect Serbia, and Germany went to war, provoking trouble with Russia's ally France, and then giving the British no choice by invading Belgium, which the British had guaranteed. In the last three days of July a freak storm hit the microclimate of hilly Buda and flat Pest. It blew and blew, carrying off roofs, smashing the plate-glass windows of the cafés on the embankment and the Oktogon, as the recruits marched towards the mobilisation trains. Two men saw through this. Endre Ady, a poet of provincial Calvinist origin in Transylvania, whom students can quote by heart, guessed where it would end. More statesmanlike, Archduke Franz Ferdinand's main adviser, Count Czernin, said two things. Minority problems are a bore, and the only difference in Austria is that we have a particularly multifarious collection. The main thing is to avoid a war. In his memoirs he also said: 'we were bound to die, we were at liberty to choose the manner of our death and we chose the most terrible.'[19]

# CHAPTER 4

# War and Revolution

The Chief of the General Staff, Franz Conrad von Hötzendorf, had been arguing for some time that war was coming, and that Austria's only way out was to attack first before all her neighbours united against her. His prime target was Italy, when she attacked Turkey in 1911, and then he argued for war against Serbia, after the Turkish collapse in 1912. At that time Russia was not ready for war, but Archduke Franz Ferdinand and the Germans rejected Conrad's line (and he was briefly out of office). Now, in 1914, with Italy and Serbia both victorious, Conrad himself described war as a *Vabanquespiel* – a risk-ridden gamble. But the Austrians had been enraged by the provocations of Serbia, a country that they regarded as barbarous, and now the Germans, instead of arguing against war, encouraged it. What was really at stake was a German Europe, a challenge to France and Russia. Within weeks of the outbreak of war, the German Chancellor roughed out his war aims, and they amounted to a Europe controlled from Berlin – France 'weakened for all time', and Russia thrown back to the frontiers of 'pre-Petrine Muscovy' (that phrase is from a later memorandum), meaning that she would lose the Baltic states, Poland, the Ukraine and the Caucasus. Quite soon a book appeared in Germany, *Mitteleuropa* (1915), by Friedrich Naumann, arguing in effect for a united Europe, run from Berlin, and in that scheme of things Greater Hungary would have her place. Kossuth, back in 1867, had written an open letter to Deák warning that, without control of her foreign policy and without her own army, Hungary would be dragged into Austro-German adventures. He was proved right, fifty years later. But at the time Hungary's involvement with Germany seemed overwhelmingly positive, the more so as Kossuth's alternative, a Balkan federation, lacked attractiveness. Germany had become the most successful country in Europe. The heavy industry of the Ruhr, the inventiveness of her chemists, the ingenuity of her engineers, generally overtook Great Britain and challenged even the USA. Her educational system was acknowledged throughout the world as superb. German universities attracted Hungarians in great numbers, including István Tisza, who had studied law at Heidelberg. (Three members of the British Cabinet that went to war in 1914 had also studied in Germany, and the Secretary of State for War, Lord Haldane, even translated Schopenhauer.) Hungary firmly belonged in the Germanic world, whatever Kossuth might say, and in 1878 Gyula Andrássy set up an Austro-German alliance. In 1914 the German cause was very popular: very few Hungarians opposed the war. Miklós Bánffy ends his Transylvanian novel trilogy – the comparison with *War and Peace* is not far-fetched – in 1914, with his cast of characters pulling on hussar uniform and galloping off to what they think will be a glorious time.

There was a belief, which now seems incomprehensible, that the war would be short. The generals, of course, knew that with millions of men and thousands of guns, and with endless supplies of food and clothing, it could go on for a long time. But the economists and bankers ruled this out. If trade were interrupted for more than six months, there would be mass unemployment and bread riots; and in any case credit, based on the gold standard, was not limitless. Few people foresaw that paper money would fuel the war effort, and when the Hungarian Finance Minister was asked how long the

Empire could fight, he said, for three weeks.[1] The emphasis every-
where was therefore on immediate attack – France in Alsace,
Germany in Belgium, Russia in East Prussia and Austrian Poland.
Conrad von Hötzendorf also planned offensives, but this was com-
plicated. There had been an exchange of letters between him and his
German opposite number, Helmuth von Moltke, since 1909, when
the Bosnian crisis had first put a war with Russia on the table.
Moltke hinted that Germany would send most of her forces against
France, and the idea was that the Austro-Hungarian army would
keep the Russians busy in the meantime, in southern Poland
(Galicia). Another illusion was that cavalry could sweep over the
plains of Russian Poland, where the Hungarians especially would
be useful, and the Austrians even nominated a governor of Warsaw
just as the war broke out. Of course, they would also have to contend
with Serbia, and that would mean keeping a small part of the army
in the Balkans for the time being.

One initial problem was foreseeable, and Conrad raised it in the
correspondence with Moltke. If Austria went to war with Serbia,
she would of course send a large part of the army south, to the
Balkan front. But if Russia intervened, Austria would need most of
these forces in the north-east, in Galicia. What would happen if the
Russians delayed intervention until these forces were committed to
the south? The Germans do not seem to have worried about this:
after all, if Austria-Hungary took a proper part in the great battles
with France and Russia, Serbia could easily just be sorted out later.
But Conrad did have a serious problem. The fact was that the Austrians were just trying to do too much and, in a spirit of imperial
vainglory, would not admit it. Their army, with forty-eight infantry
divisions, would have to take on the Serbians' fourteen and the Russians' fifty. Conrad found what appeared to be a way round. The
army was divided into three groups. Group A, half of it, would go
to Galicia in any event. A 'Minimal Balkan Group', somewhat less
than a quarter, would face Serbia. Group B, the rest, four army corps
in strength, two Hungarian and two Bohemian, would go south if

Russia stayed out, north if she did not. All very well, no doubt, but when the time came, a quarter of an army already not large enough for its purposes did not take part in the fighting for a whole month.

The fact was that the Austrians did not want to fight Russia and found excuses. Berlin had told them to provoke a war with Serbia, but they delayed presentation of their ultimatum for a month, and when the Serbians rejected it, took another three days before declaring war (28 July). Then, when the Russians did mobilise (31 July), they did declare general mobilisation but delayed the start of it for a week. Not only that: on 28 July Conrad ordered the army corps of Group B to proceed to the Serbian theatre, for that was a war the Austrians indeed wanted to fight. This was done for the alleged reason that the Russian response was not clear, that the diplomats had let him down. But the Russians' response, general mobilisation, in fact happened quite quickly, and in any case the War Minister, Alexander von Krobatin, said that no one had ever had illusions otherwise. When the Germans heard that their ally was proposing to fight a European war by sending half its army to a very secondary Balkan front, they hit the roof – the military attaché, Chief of the General Staff, the Kaiser himself. Conrad asked his railway chief whether the trains of Group B could be stopped and sent to Galicia instead. The railway chief, Johann Straub, was aghast. Telegrams would have to be sent out for the trains to be stopped, some of them on one-track lines where turning them round would be difficult, and maybe coal and water (and food for the men) would have to be brought up, whereas the lines were needed for other trains proceeding elsewhere. Maybe the man overdid it: but if he got anything wrong, the consequences could be catastrophic. In the lead-up to the battle of the Somme in 1916, for instance, there was an eighteen-mile log-jam of British army trains outside Abbeville station. He told Conrad that the trains should just go on as planned, wait at their destinations and get to Galicia after the general mobilisation was over. As things turned out, these army corps did reach the Serbian border and sat in tents while the Minimal Balkan Group, too small for the job, was humiliatingly defeated by the Serbs.[2] Then they trundled across Hungary and reached eastern Galicia just in time to take part in an enormous defeat.[3]

In Galicia there were three Austro-Hungarian armies, and their mission was to deflect the Russians from Germany. But when the war broke out, as Conrad was ordering Group B to go south, he also took a fateful decision as regards Galicia. The troops there had been intended for the frontier. But they were now ordered in effect to avoid a battle, and to disembark from their trains very far from the border, in fact in the northern foothills of the Carpathians. Now they were supposed to march forward, in the scorching August heat. The campaign began with another display of illusion. Austro-Hungarian cavalry, splendidly arrayed, made a magnificent sight. Ten divisions cantered over the border. They ran out of fodder, and the military saddle, designed to present cavalrymen at their best, rubbed the skin off the backs of requisitioned horses. The cavalry soon returned, the men leading their horses on foot. In any case, even obsolete Russian rifles could stop a horse a mile off, and the only cavalry engagement occurred (at Jaroslawice) when two cavalry divisions decided just to re-enact the Napoleonic Wars with a lance-and-sabre engagement. (It ended inconclusively.) The two armies of left and centre gave a good account of themselves at the end of August, but that on the right was prodded into attacking vastly superior forces and retreated in panic, abandoning the chief city of Galicia, then known as Lemberg (now Lviv), on 3 September. The other two armies, thus threatened from the side, also fell back, after a failed attempt at counter-attack, and just at that moment (8 September) Group B arrived, also exhausted from weeks of train-journeying. A retreat then got under way, taking the army back, through a constant downpour, to Kraków and the Carpathians. The Russians were not in any condition to pursue energetically, and a line was reformed. It was then revealed that the entire operation had been unnecessary, because the Germans in East Prussia gave not only a good account of themselves but a spectacular one.

They took advantage of the slowness and poor co-ordination of the two Russian armies invading East Prussia, and at the battle of Tannenberg captured 100,000 men, including four corps commanders, from one of the armies. The other was soon driven out of East Prussia altogether. The old professional Habsburg army was almost destroyed in these first weeks of the war, and lost some 500,000 men. But conscripts flowed in, and there was still enough devotion to the imperial cause to keep the army going. This was particularly true in Hungary, where nationalism was so strong, and there was no trouble among non-Magyar recruits, especially Croats. There were even Serbs as well who followed the old military-frontier traditions of dynastic loyalty. However, Austria-Hungary was being pulled into a German vortex.

At first the Germans had not quite known how to handle the Austrian emergency. The moving spirit behind German strategy in the east, Erich Ludendorff, Chief of Staff of the Eighth Army, which had won the battle of Tannenberg in 1914, was at first overawed by Habsburg grandeur. Austrian headquarters were at a small palace in Teschen, in Silesia, which was owned by the nominal commander-in-chief, the very rich Archduke Friedrich (he charged rent), whose wife, Isabella de Croÿ, was from a very old Burgundian family. Liaison officers with imposing names to-ed and fro-ed. Ludendorff, a Pomeranian farmer's son, who went there after the initial disaster, was at first on his best behaviour. To start with he could offer only limited support, and his own chief, Erich von Falkenhayn (Moltke's nerves had collapsed), resented having to part with troops for the eastern front when the western one was so obviously more important. But the very existence of Austria-Hungary, by the spring of 1915, was in question. Another disaster had come about in the Carpathians. There was a fortress, Przemyśl, with a garrison of 120,000 men that had been cut off in the Galician retreat. Conrad tried to relieve the place, with three winter offensives in the Carpathian snows that ended in frostbitten calamity: a Czech regiment collapsed. The Russians then entered north-eastern Hungary and threatened a cavalry sweep onto the great plain. A Hungarian general, Sándor Szurmay, fought them off and a German force, *Beskidenkorps*, swung into action on Easter Sunday.[4] In this period the Serbian army had also defeated all Austro-Hungarian attacks, and late in April the British and French landed on the Gallipoli peninsula, threatening an end to Ottoman Turkey, allied with Germany.

Conrad's pre-war fears were coming true, for there was worse to come. In Italy the disasters were noted, and nationalists (who now included Mussolini, the editor of a socialist newspaper) said that the time had come to intervene: how could Austria-Hungary survive? They wanted not just to round off the unification of Italy but to establish a sort of Mediterranean empire: they would take the sub-Alpine Tyrol, Trieste and much of Dalmatia as well as part of Asiatic Turkey, which the Allies were offering. On 23 May the Italians mobilised, supposing that the Habsburg Empire would just collapse. This did not happen, for the Italians had not taken account of the fearful terrain they would have to cross – impassable mountains, or granite soil where trenches could not be dug, while caves offered safety for the defenders – but still Austria-Hungary was hopelessly over-stretched, and Falkenhayn had to rescue his ally. A German army went east, this time to considerable effect. The Russians were almost driven out of Austrian Poland, and then lost most of Russian Poland as well. More good fortune came the Central Powers' way in the autumn, when Serbia collapsed, and the British gave up at Gallipoli.

Of course, it would have made sense at this point if Austria-Hungary had offered to get out of the war. The western Powers had no interest in destroying the Habsburg Monarchy – quite the opposite, for its destruction could only profit Russia or Germany. One prominent figure in Austria did somehow guess how it would all end. This was Professor Tomáš Masarýk, the leader of a small Czech progressive party, who got himself to London on a wintry evening in 1915 and tried to persuade the British that Czech independence might be a winning cause. Beyond politeness, he got nowhere.

Hungary did not even produce a Masarýk. The only prominent figure who might have reacted in this way was Count Mihály Károlyi, who had even been in France when the war broke out and used his connections to avoid internment. Otherwise, Hungary was solidly behind the war and, with control of food supplies, was able to assert herself more and more. A new crest was designed for the Empire in 1915, giving more prominence to Hungarian insignia; the non-Hungarian half of the Empire (not including Bosnia) was finally officially called Austria. Tisza was able to insist on medal factories being set up in Hungary because Hungarians were being awarded most of the output. But state money was being showered on arms factories in Hungary in any event, and there were scandals to do with profiteering.

Meanwhile Austro-Hungarian confidence revived, and so did resentment at German domination. The two allies started wrangling about the future of Poland, and Conrad in September 1915 launched an independent invasion of the Russian Ukraine, announced as the 'Black-Yellow Offensive'. It did not flourish, but he went on, without telling the Germans, to plan a more serious attack on the Italian front, when the snows had cleared. Equally, without telling the Austrians, Falkenhayn planned a great attack on France. Here is a might-have-been of the war: if the German army had joined in with Conrad in 1916, as it was to do in 1917, Italy might well have been knocked out. But there was no question of that at the time. The Germans had no quarrel with Italy, had not even declared war, and by this stage mistrust between them and their ally was considerable. The wrangle over Poland – 'the Austro-Polish solution' – went on and on, and since tact is not a German virtue, German criticism of Austrian inefficiency was wounding. Falkenhayn planned a knock-out blow on France, and in February began the huge artillery bombardment at Verdun. Somewhat later, in May, Conrad launched a well-planned assault on the Italian front, on the Asiago plateau, north-west of Venice. Victory there would have brought Austro-Hungarian troops onto the plain of Lombardy and cut off the Italian army fighting to the east, on the River Isonzo. Both offensives in the end failed. In the Austro-Hungarian case, the failure was fatal, because the best troops had been withdawn from the Russian front to support the attack, and the forces left there were weak and badly led. Retribution followed on 4 June, when a very well-executed Russian offensive, generally called after its designer, Brusilov, led to the collapse of the Austrian front in Galicia. Here the Germans had what they had feared, what had even driven them to provoke war in 1914: a Russia that was at last mobilising her enormous potential.

She had overcome a severe armaments crisis, and at last produced an intelligent general. Brusilov had studied the war, and attacked, in an original style. He achieved surprise, for a start, because he avoided the days-long bombardment that told the enemy where an attack would come and where to place reserves for a counter-attack. He also attacked in different places, which further confused the reserves. Brusilov used shock-troops tactics, the troops emerging from huge bunkers that had been carefully concealed and racing forward to catch the defenders before they knew what was happening; and the Austrians had made the mistake of concentrating their defences in the vulnerable front areas. In the brick-dry Ukrainian plain the bombardments raised clouds of dust, which blinded the defenders. An entire Austro-Hungarian army disintegrated, and a message went back to Vienna, 'Fourth Army has in effect been taken prisoner'. Another army was very badly mauled. German troops again came to the rescue, and the Germans performed miracles with the few railways at their disposal. However, this time there was a proviso that the high command in the east should pass to Ludendorff; a month later he also took charge of the western front from Falkenhayn. Now the Austrian and German armies were inextricably intertwined, and German troops were deliberately used as 'corset staves' (the tactless phrase of a prominent German general, Max Hoffmann) to prop up Austro-Hungarian units, even at regimental level, because, although Czech and

Ruthene troops might not be frightened of Austrian sergeants, Prussian ones had a terrifying effect. There were so many German troops intermingled now with Austro-Hungarian ones that separating the two was impossible. Prince Leopold of Bavaria took overall command of the eastern front. There was a separate Austro-Hungarian army group, under the heir to the throne, but even then the Chief of its General Staff was a German, Hans von Seeckt. The Habsburgs might well anticipate the words of Count Ciano, Mussolini's foreign minister: 'If England wins, we lose. If Germany wins, we are lost.' With apt symbolism Franz Joseph died on 21 November 1916.

Franz Joseph's successor, his great-nephew Karl, was well-meaning but utterly inexperienced and not very bright. Of course he could see what was coming, and his Foreign Minister, Count Czernin, was an intelligent, sophisticated man. Karl tried desperately to parade himself as a People's Emperor. He brought in some social welfare provisions, and recalled the Reichsrat; he tried, in particular, to bring about peace. He used his brother-in-law Prince Sixtus of Bourbon-Parma, who served in the Belgian army, as an intermediary with the French; he did not inform his German allies. The British and French of course showed interest, but they had to consult the Italians. Negotiations broke down on a simple question: would Austria concede anything to Italy? But the Italian war was popular, and had gone relatively well. Karl refused to concede anything but said that he could recognise 'the just' French claims to Alsace-Lorraine, so that a bargain could be done. He was silly enough to put the phrase 'just claims' in writing, and silly enough not to tell his Foreign Minister. When, later, Czernin denied that the phrase had been used, Karl looked foolish as well as, in German eyes, treacherous. But as the Reichsrat sessions soon showed, the peoples of the Empire were now in effect divided: could they live with a Europe arranged by Ludendorff's Germany? Germans and Hungarians went on with the war, seeing no alternative. Croats and Slovenes might fight it, out of fear of Italy. The others were now alienated. The Poles had kept good relations with the Central Powers but by 1917 recognised that they would do better if they dealt with the western allies. The Czechs had at first been loyal to Austria – where else to go? – but Professor Masarýk in exile was gaining influence, and in Russia the Czech prisoners of war had formed a legion to fight the Germans. There were Croat Yugoslavs as well, though fewer, and a deal was done on Corfu with the Serbian government in exile.

Matters were different in Hungary. Her 'political nation' had remained solidly in control of affairs. Karl had at first seemed to be a threat, the more so as Franz Ferdinand's advisers, especially Czernin, were close to the new Emperor. Would he push for universal suffrage in Hungary, and maybe some rights for the nationalities? To offset this threat Tisza decided that he must be made to swear the famous oath to the constitution, which would mean a coronation. As soon as Franz Joseph was dead, he appeared in Vienna to urge this cause. At the time Hungary seemed to be the chief motor of the war effort, and Austria depended on her for food deliveries. Karl gave way, and on 30 December 1916 a scene of preposterous unsuitability was staged in the Castle district of Buda. Miklós Bánffy, with his experience at the Opera, was put in charge of the Cathedral's lighting and décor (his memoirs, *The Phoenix Land*, are eloquent as to the difficulties of obtaining the right swathing materials in wartime), and the painter Gyula Benczúr also had a hand; seamstresses worked overtime. The entire aristocracy appeared in traditional dress, and the ceremony went ahead, as Tisza and the Primate placed the Crown of St Stephen on the royal head. The text of the oath had been forgotten, and the Cardinal was discreetly told to drone on for an extra half-hour while a Prince Lobkowitz raced off to retrieve it, after which the King read it, at the foot of the Plague monument in Trinity Square, mounted his horse and galloped to a mound, containing soil from all parts of the land, and on it waved the sword of St Stephen to all corners to indicate he would never give up anything.

Karl would have been very uncomfortable if he had broken his word (although he had no trouble in doing so later on, when he left Switzerland in an effort to regain his Hungarian lands without telling the Swiss, which he had promised to do). The most he could now achieve was a change of personnel: Tisza was dismissed, and an Esterházy was appointed, whose first act was to burn the enormous amounts of paper generated by attempts at rationing. Quite soon he was replaced by an old Calvinist war-horse, and Tisza returned to the influential wings (from a spell as Colonel on the Italian front). This combination of arsenic and old lace went on almost to the end. There is a good question involved. Why did no Hungarian go into exile, as Professor Masaryk did, to represent the Czech cause in the west? It never seems to have occurred to any Hungarian that a proto-government in exile would be a good step, and in any case after the Russian Revolution there was even a strong possibility that the Central Powers would win the war. Despite the penury at home, 1917 saw no great disasters. There were strikes and mutinies, but in the circumstances surprisingly few. Wars generate their own illusions and momentum, and common sense now had no part to play.

Even at the turn of 1916–17 the Central Powers could still hope to win the war. Their submarines, sinking ships that supplied Great Britain, might, if properly used (i.e., without humanity), bring starvation. This did not happen: instead, the United States entered the war. But at the same time Russia in effect dropped out, as a huge army mutiny got under way and the Tsar abdicated. This culminated in the Bolshevik Revolution in November 1917, and the Bolsheviks asked for an armistice. The eastern front had ceased, and Germany could concentrate on the western front. Ludendorff meant to mount a great offensive in 1918 that would break France before the Americans could arrive. Meanwhile, he had eastern Europe at his mercy. In the headquarters town of the German army in the east, Brest-Litovsk, negotiations with the Bolsheviks began. They were concluded in the early hours of 3 March 1918. The Treaty of

Brest-Litovsk laid down the lineaments of German domination, and Hungary had her part to play. There is a ghostly similarity to the Europe of today.

Early in 1918 President Woodrow Wilson of the United States set out Fourteen Points as his war aims. They included freedom of this and that, but they also addressed the self-determination of nations. The Allies were already speaking more than vaguely of Czech independence, of a southern Slav kingdom; not long before, the British had declared support for a 'Jewish National Home' in Palestine, and went on to promote an Iraq, with the French (mainly) promoting a Syria – all of it at the expense of Ottoman Turkey. At Brest-Litovsk the Germans developed a parallel logic. The Baltic states, including Finland (which was to have a German monarch, from the House of Hesse), would receive independence of one sort or another. So would Poland, though with smaller borders. The Caucasus states, especially Georgia, were favoured. The greatest new state was the Ukraine, with a population of 40 million and a good part of Russia's mineral resources, and although Ukrainian nationalism was weak or non-existent in the east (the Germans even at Brest-Litovsk could not determine its eastern border), it was strong enough in the west, where the Austrians had encouraged it. (Alexander Solzhenitsyn said that the worst mistake of Tsarist foreign policy had been to give East Galicia back to Austria in 1814: Napoleon had given it to Alexander I in 1809.[5]) Berlin perhaps missed a trick, in that it might have taken a lead as regards the Jewish National Home, where a ferocious row developed as to whether modern German, rather than antique Hebrew, should be the language of education. At any rate, here were new states to replace old empires. Most of them contained large dissident minorities, and almost all were ramshackle, subject even to civil wars. The German system was not significantly different in principle. The Allies topped their system with a proposed League of Nations that would adjudicate minority rights. The Germans topped theirs with a plan for a great free trade bloc, from Narvik to Baghdad – in effect, a scheme for European union dominated by Berlin. In May 1918 a conference was held in Budapest to inaugurate this. It broke down fairly quickly with wrangles about the common agricultural policy, in which the Hungarians obstinately fought for concessions. All would depend on the Germans' winning the war in the west, and Ludendorff staged five great offensives, from March to July. Austria-Hungary also gambled, in Italy.

These efforts failed in dramatic circumstances, and Allied counter-offensives got under way. It became clear that the Central Powers were losing, and the central European peoples responded accordingly. The migrant communities in the United States became enthusiastic for national liberation. Millions had emigrated from Austria-Hungary, and, as ever with diasporas, when they crossed the Atlantic to reach America they changed planet rather than continent, forgetting the complications and accommodations back home and swallowing a hard-luck version of the national past. The Hungarians were not well organised, were divided along religious lines and anyway were not desperately enthusiastic for the Habsburg Monarchy. However, the Czechs could easily be mobilised, and when old Masaryk went to Pittsburgh, he started by saying how pleased he was to find himself in the largest Czech city in the world. He appealed for financial support and got it, saying that Czechs and Slovaks should unite, in a new independent state to be called Czechoslovakia: possibly hyphenated, possibly not. The languages were rather similar, though not the same, and there were considerable differences otherwise: Bohemia was industrialised, with a large middle and working class, whereas Slovakia was heavily peasant, and moreover religious. (Masarýk's Slovak supporters came mainly from the Lutheran minority.) Bratislava, the present capital, was then, as Pressburg or Pozsony, a German-Hungarian town with a large Jewish element. The new state would contain a very large German minority, at odds with the Czechs for a good generation, a smaller Hungarian one and Ruthenes as well. In other words, another sort of Hungary. In June 1918 the French recognised it.

Masarýk had two great advantages, apart from American-Czech money: he was a very dignified professor (of philosophy) with an east-coast American wife of Unitarian background, capable of addressing the American President, Woodrow Wilson, in the same austere idiom (which Lloyd George could also use, not very appropriately); and he had an army.

This came about because there were, in the Russian prisoner-of-war camps, some 2 million Austro-Hungarian soldiers. There were many potential volunteers for a Polish legion, a Czech legion, even a Yugoslav one. But the Czechs were the most active, and 50,000 men volunteered. With the Russian Revolution in full swing, they found themselves running the trans-Siberian railway, and a fight began with the Bolsheviks. This endeared them to the British and French. By June 1918, in any case, they had given up on a Habsburg Monarchy that had obviously been captured by Germany, and so the Allies recognised a Czech government in exile; the same was obviously possible for a new kingdom of Serbs, Croats and Slovenes – Yugoslavia. A reconstituted Poland and a Rumania enlarged by Transylvania were already agreed. Hungary in these circumstances would lose two-thirds of her territory. There is a question in this. The Czechs ended up counting as allies of the western Powers, the Hungarians not, although until relatively late in the day Czech troops fought well enough on the Italian front, and a great many Czechs fully understood that a future for them outside the Habsburg Monarchy was not altogether safe. Why, then, did Professor Masarýk go into exile in 1915 to talk to the British, but not Count Károlyi? Again this is a question that anticipates a far worse situation in the Second World War. Károlyi led parliamentary opposition to Tisza and had the right instincts, but he was self-indulgent, and in the end had caste pride. (He says in his memoirs, of uncomfortable exile in London, that a member of the middle classes might have felt let down by fate if he had had to lug heavy coal-bags up flights of stairs; but a Károlyi was a Károlyi, of a lineage so old as to pre-date Habsburg titles.) The Czechs timed things right, and the Hungarians did not time them at all. Yet the vital matter in central Europe was the relationship between Vienna, Prague and Budapest: Yugoslavia or Poland could be lost, but it would not be the end of the world. But there were few constructive suggestions. Hungarian nationalism was very much caught up in the war, presented – especially as far as the Russians were concerned – as a historic matter. A few voices were raised against the war and the German alliance, but they were drowned out by patriotic clamour: Greater Hungary would go down with Germany.

Ludendorff's offensives broke the German army, which lost a million men and after 18 July was in constant retreat. Allies dropped out – first Bulgaria, then Turkey – and that was a sign for Austria-Hungary too to give up. An armistice on the Italian front was signed on 3 November. Then Germany herself exploded. Mutinies in the navy, and strikes in the armaments factories, produced chaos in Berlin, and the Kaiser was forced to abdicate. An armistice in the west was arranged for 11 November. Under its terms Germany had to repudiate Brest-Litovsk and withdraw from the whole area. The Habsburg Empire was already disintegrating. Emperor Karl could not truly compete with President Wilson when it came to offering the self-determination of peoples, and the determination to run to the help of the victor, as the French say, was overwhelming. However, Karl tried, and on 16 October issued a 'Manifesto to my loyal peoples' inviting them to set up national councils which would meet to discuss a confederal future. Notables everywhere had been discussing what would happen when the end came, and such national councils were indeed set up, the Prague and Vienna ones containing representatives of substantial trade unions who, alone, could keep vital services running. The appeal for confederation was ignored. It was too late: this was to be independence, an independence that, for the Austrian Germans, was expected to mean union with Germany. In Prague the declaration came on 28 October, in Zagreb the next day. The day after that, the Austrian Germans set up the institutions of a new state as well. It would not have room for a Habsburg, and on 11 November Karl was prevailed upon to 'withdraw from the conduct of affairs': he did not abdicate and withdrew to a castle, Eckartsau, east of Vienna, where he was guarded by loyal-to-the-end officers until, in March, he went to Switzerland. There was no fighting of seriousness. In Prague there was a telephone call to the Governor, General Zanantoni, who was briefly interned and then let go, and the nearest Vienna came to reaction was a Mass at St Stephen's, where many were in tears.

There were indeed, however, exiles. In Russia there were about half a million Hungarian prisoners of war. When the Russian Revolution broke out, they too could look forward to liberation, and a great many took lessons from Bolshevik propaganda. If you were kicking your heels in some camp in Kazakhstan or Tomsk in Siberia, fearing typhus, with time on your hands, there was room for resentment, and there would not be much respect for an Austro-Hungarian establishment that had launched the war and then run it so badly. Bolshevik propaganda appealed to international working-class solidarity, and many prisoners of war were affected by it. There was Tito, a captured Croat sergeant. Then there was Ernst Reuter, later Mayor of Berlin at the time of the Stalin blockade in 1948, who was even in the Red Army and became a Communist member of the Reichstag before imprisonment by Hitler and refuge in Turkey (as professor of town planning in Ankara). Of the Hungarians, four enter history (perhaps we should say five, given that Tito was technically a Hungarian). The least-known, Endre Radvanszky (who later was in charge of Bolshevik propaganda in Tashkent), was the brother-in-law of Zinoviev, a moving spirit of the Communist International, or Comintern, which was supposed to organise revolution abroad. There was Imre Nagy, the central figure of 1956, and Béla Kun, a journalist from Kolozsvár in Transylvania. And then there was Mátyás Rákosi, the Stalinist monster of post-war Hungary. In 1918 these men returned to Austria-Hungary, with hatred and contempt for the establishment that had produced this war and their own misfortunes. Bread,

Peace and Land had won Lenin his revolution, and these slogans applied in Hungary as well.

War at the front ended in chaos. Of the 9 million men mobilised, over a million had been killed and over 2 million captured (800,000 of them Hungarian). A further 3.6 million had been wounded, and the cities were full of cripples living on a pittance. For want of labour, agriculture had suffered, and the government had mismanaged matters by imposing fixed prices and requisitioning, which simply created a huge black market or caused farmers to slaughter animals that could not be sold at a profit, which meant less manure. With the black market, peasant houses filled with pianos and Persian rugs as townspeople came to the villages, rather than, as before, the other way round. Everybody hated everybody, and there was a notable rise in anti-Semitism, as the Jews were alleged to be adept at black-marketeering, and synagogues in the centre-east of Hungary were raided by the police.[6] The Hassids were supposed to be particularly adept, and their synagogue in Máramarossziget – Maxwell country – was raided in September 1918. Inflation, since the government experts just printed notes, shot up, and real incomes dropped by half – by and large, impoverishing the middle classes more than others.[7] When 300,000 Hungarian former prisoners of war returned in 1918, having seen what the Bolsheviks could do, here was material for a Red Revolution. When Austria-Hungary asked for an armistice in Italy, and got a humiliating one at the Villa Giusti outside Padua on 3 November, the soldiers began to go home.

In Budapest, after brief resistance and a few casualties, great demonstrations caused the government to change. Tisza had already admitted on 24 October that the war was lost, and his detested rival, Mihály Károlyi, came to the fore, as the obvious opposition candidate. On 25 October a National Council was set up of Károlyi's followers, radical liberals and Social Democrats, and when a crowd supporting it moved on the Vár, there was shooting, with three dead and seventy wounded. Tempers, of course, rose. The King/Emperor prevaricated, appointed a Count Hadik as Prime Minister, and found that rebels had occupied stations and telephone exchanges, milling round the Astoria Hotel, itself close to the aristocrats' National Club. At that the Palatine Archduke József appointed Károlyi as Prime Minister on 31 October. The new War Minister decreed that Hungarian troops should just get home, as did the other nationalities, and the army in Italy broke up. The atmosphere in Budapest for a time was euphoric, and this was known as the Aster Revolution: just before All Saints' Day the custom was to wear a button-hole, and the soldiers used that as a revolutionary symbol. The Astoria Hotel was the new centre, and from there on 31 October some soldiers, inspired by journalists, drove to the house of István Tisza, beyond the City Park, where they decoyed the security guards and, in front of his wife and a niece, shot him. Károlyi proclaimed land reform and distributed his own land to peasants. (It was not, strictly speaking, his to give away, as it was heavily mortgaged.) By now a great epidemic of Spanish influenza, a virulent form, was striking, and everything was breaking down: a republic seemed to be the only answer to revolution, and a deputation of high aristocrats – an Esterházy, a Wlassics, a Dessewffy, a Széchényi – went to ask the Emperor to abdicate. He did, or at least renounced participation in public affairs, on 13 November.

Károlyi had the immediate problem of an Allied invasion. In the very last days of the war Rumania had again entered it, and her army was advancing into Transylvania. There it was met by local Rumanians who intended to unite the country with their fellows in Moldavia and Wallachia. In the southern provinces there was similar disaffection among the Serbs, and the Croats had already set up their national council, aiming to create a new South Slav state under the Serbian king. The first problem was to establish armistice lines, and here Károlyi was helpless, because he had allowed the army to disintegrate. This was not a mistake that the Turks made; they had functioning troops in Trans-Caucasia and on that basis became the only defeated Power to survive and defy the Allies. Their leader, Mustafa Kemal Atatürk, then acquired a certain cult status in Hungary. As things were, Károlyi went to see the French commander in Belgrade, Louis Franchet d'Esperey, and announced himself as head of the Workers' and Soldiers' Council, getting the famous answer, 'You've fallen that low, have you?' The only force offering resistance was a Székely Division, of brigade strength, and it got no encouragement from Budapest because it was seen as counter-revolutionary. There was only one Hungarian success, at Balassagyarmat, and even that occurred despite contrary orders from the Károlyi government.

In March 1919 a French colonel, Vyx, handed in a note requiring Allied occupation of more still, and the much-shrunken boundaries of the Hungary to come were in view. Károlyi's nerve snapped. He had hoped that long overdue reforms that might be called bourgeois-democratic would stabilise the situation, and even that his nationalities commissar, Oszkár Jászi, an old Edwardian progressive, would be able, through federalisation, to retain the loyalty of the non-Hungarian peoples. The Slovaks, in particular, might be won over. But the Czech National Council had troops, and enough Slovak sympathisers to establish Czechoslovak rule in the north. Jászi got nowhere. In Budapest there were sufficient socialists and there was a Communist element, not as yet very coherent; unionisation had not progressed very far, and former soldiers made the running. The Communist leader, Béla Kun, was a former insurance clerk from Transylvania and had learned his Communism at source, in Russia: he had been taken prisoner in 1916 and interned at Tomsk; he went to Petrograd just as the Bolsheviks took power and became associate president of the Red prisoners-of-war organisation, as such taking part in the suppression of the Left Socialist Revolutionaries in June 1918.[8] He was a good orator, and a competent political organiser; he could make common cause with some of the Social Democrats. The Károlyi government did arrest him, as a trouble-maker, but was careful to keep him in play, perhaps as a threat that might be used against the western Powers. His cell was comfortable, and he could continue to edit his newspaper.

The threat failed, and the French, with Rumanian allies, ordered the Hungarians to withdraw from even more territory. Károlyi had become discredited, and in any case the situation was desperate. There was now real hunger, as only half of the transport requirements for flour could be met, and potatoes rotted, while the paper money degenerated; there was also a crippling housing shortage.[9] Now Kun was let out, and Károlyi resigned. What followed, from March until July, was a Hungarian variant of the Bolshevik Revolution called the 'Republic of Councils', a clumsy translation of 'Soviet' but one that will do. As with Soviet Russia, irate soldiers were a dominant force, and many of the leaders were Jewish, which caused much trouble later on. There were twelve commissars for this and that, nearly all of them young Jews, and of thirty-six chief figures, twenty-eight were Jews – allegedly of first- or second-generation Galician origins, as a later and very enlightened Minister of Education, Count Kuno Klebelsberg, said, stressing that the properly Hungarian ones had been entirely loyal, unlike the Galicians.[10] Nationalisation affected all firms, of any size. Rations went to the workers; others starved. Of all absurdities, land reform was reversed. It was in any case a complicated question, perhaps even insoluble, since great estates were often not just efficient but also looked after the workforce better than if the peasants had to struggle on their own. The Communists preferred to keep large estates, and therefore took land back from the peasants who had benefited from Károlyi's land reform, and of course the countryside mainly went over to counter-revolution.

There were positive aspects just the same. Efforts were made to bring culture to the masses (this was particularly successful with paintings, the expropriated ones being exhibited with great success in the Andrássy Palace), and some of Hungary's great names collaborated – Bartók and Kodály, for instance, in music and even the considerable historian Gyula Szekfű, although he later turned conservative. A rival, popular, Academy of Sciences came into existence, challenging the calcified established one, and was named after the national poet Mihály Vörösmárty. The great poet Endre Ady, who had foreseen the calamities, was its president. (He could not manage his opening address, as a life of considerable dissolution caught up with him, an admirer of Baudelaire and Rimbaud, at the age of forty-one.) The Marxist philosopher György Lukács was commissar for culture and suppressed religious teaching in schools; the later Cardinal Mindszenty, who had a starring part in 1949, had already been interned under Kun for his stubborn resistance. Illegitimate children (a fifth of births in Budapest) were legitimised, a factor probably of some importance in the making of János Kádár later on, as he was born the son of an ill-used young servant girl in Fiume in 1912 and grew up in desperate poverty while his mother chased after the father's family, in vain. The workers' regime also strongly discouraged alcohol, and the pubs in Old Buda were used to house people: 100,000 proletarians were shifted into the houses and flats of the middle classes, the class war being fought over shared bathrooms and kitchens. There was, however, an aspect of sinister farce to the new government, as there was, generally, to Hungarian Communism. Béla Kun looked somewhat like a bit-part actor in *Casablanca* – a film made by a Hungarian director, who turned Mihály Kertész into Michael Curtiz (it means 'gardener'). The Hungarian Soviet ran a terror machine: the 'Lenin Boys', many of them former sailors, whose uniform was a dinner-plate hat and leather jacket. They specialised in house searches for food or textiles, and their headquarters were in the Batthyány Palace on the Teréz körút. There were some extra-judicial killings, while hostages, including ministers, rich Jews and a Habsburg Archduke were put into the Gyűjtőfogház, a grim remand prison (on the way to today's airport) that now bears a plaque. The overall head of the machinery of repression was one Tibor Szamuely, who went around the countryside with an armoured train, in the manner of Trotsky, and if there was trouble, it was put down in two or three hours in short order.

Kun had great problems with the Allies. In April General Smuts steamed to the Eastern Station in Budapest and stayed for twenty-four hours; Harold Nicolson, who had known Budapest from before the war (and was anti-Hungarian), observed the city: the Communists laid on scenes for him, such as a gathering of middle-class figures in the Hungaria restaurant (now the New York Palace), supposedly taking tea undisturbed. He was not deceived. (The Reds' own headquarters were in the Hungaria hotel on the Danube embankment, ruined in the later siege and demolished: the site is now occupied by a Marriott.) The Allies authorised the Rumanians and Czechoslovaks to move forward, whereupon Kun organised a Red Army of his own, which did retake towns in Slovakia, including Kassa, but his forces were overwhelmed and in late July he had to do more or less as Károlyi had done: resign in failure. There was a final meeting of the government at Gödöllő on 1 August, just ahead of a Rumanian occupation, and then Kun took the train to Vienna with his colleagues. Once there, he went by taxi to the Hungarian legation in the Bankgasse, leaving a folder of names of people left behind to organise an underground network. They were picked up by the police and, Communists being Communists, there is a supposition that Kun had done this deliberately so as to dispose of rivals more courageous than himself: two of the chief 'Lenin Boys', László Szamuely and Ottó Korvin, were picked up and killed shortly afterwards.[11] Kun and the others went on to Moscow, where he became a commissar in the Crimea, had 50,000 people massacred when the Russian Whites collapsed, and, as agent of the Comintern, attended the Baku Conference of the Toilers of the East in September 1920, which was intended to raise revolution against the British Empire. He was then used particularly but not successfully in Germany in 1921 and 1923; Stalin eventually had him shot.

Central Hungary, and even Győr in the west, were occupied by the Rumanians, who looted comprehensively and were only stopped when they threatened the precious exhibits of the National Museum, by a Colonel Bandholtz in the American section of the Allied mission in Budapest (earning him a statue). Once a proper government was organised in Budapest, the Rumanians left, but forming a government took time – a socialist briefly took over, then a liberal conservative, and even briefly an Archduke. But a counter-revolutionary organisation was already in being, partly through British support, and White officers gathered in the Britannia Hotel on the Teréz körút. The right had gathered strength, as prosperous farmers of the west linked arms with ferocious officers, the formula that gave Germany the Freikorps that defeated the Communists, and in time this developed into properly organised counter-revolution, with groups such as the Ébredő Magyarok ('Awakening Hungarians') led by a staff officer, Gyula Gömbös, together with a new party, the Nemzeti Egyesülés Pártja ('National Party of Unity'), organised by aristocrats, the most astute of whom was Count István Bethlen, in Vienna. In Germany, even by the end of 1918, a Communist revolution had been stopped, and a parliamentary republic was soon to be proclaimed in Weimar. The key to this was that the Social Democrats were in charge, and used the Freikorps on their own terms. In Hungary the reactionaries made the running, and in Szeged the Habsburg navy's last commander, Admiral Horthy, had a force under arms, built up partly from a contribution of 150,000 Crowns gathered by the town's Jewish businesses. He now entered Budapest on a white horse, on 16 November 1919.

# CHAPTER 5

# Admiral Horthy

Admiral Horthy was self-consciously a gentleman of the old school, an Anglophile of the double-breasted blazer, governess-accent class; and he had a sense of honour that touched at times on the absurd. (He drafted a letter challenging President Masaryk to a duel, with a query as to whether this elderly professor would choose sabres.) He was born in 1868, into a Calvinist family of middling gentry (though with Catholic connections). He was ambitious, courtly, an excellent sportsman, not very bright but a considerable linguist, and he looked the part as head of state. His weakness was that of a man who knows he is not brilliant: he was very stubborn, uncomfortable with imaginative schemes and new ideas. His nation was his world, his class its natural ruler. He was good at running a team, having been a (very brave) commander of the Austro-Hungarian navy. He rode into central Budapest, occupied rooms at the Hotel Gellért and received a deputation of the city notables. He spoke severely of 'this sinful city', and thereby sharpened a contest, already brewing, between the country, supposedly healthy and unselfconsciously natural, and the big city, always looking abroad, depraved and, of course, with a large Jewish presence. In most countries this contest exists, but in Hungary it could take on a vicious quality. Writers of the two schools were often very hostile to each other.

Hungary's three-month experience with the Republic of Councils had some resemblance to France's in 1871. After defeat, Paris also experienced a commune, with red flags well to the fore. The Communards had shot an archbishop, and when the conservative forces restored order, they put 147 Communards against a wall – the Mur des Fédérés – and shot them all. They also planned to put up the Sacré Coeur in expiation on the highest point in the city – Montmartre – where it could be seen from all around, but particularly from the working-class areas where the Commune had flourished. It is not the best monument in the city. The Eiffel Tower is much more convincing, as a testimony to the engineer, and if France recovered rapidly from the disaster of 1870–71, this had much more to do with progressive republicans than vengeful conservatives. In Hungary, progressive republicans were lacking. On the other hand, the conservatives' desire for vengeance was intelligently contained, and a recovery did indeed take place under their leadership. By early 1920 the Allies themselves wanted a proper government in Budapest with which they could make formal peace. They dealt with Horthy and his team.

It had been easy enough for the team to convene in Vienna, where they had friends and relatives, and although some of them waved swords in romantic style, and conspired with crackpots of the German right, the most intelligent of them, Count István Bethlen, had serious plans for the future. He knew that he would depend on British good will – the French had been making the running, in full support of their Rumanian and Czech allies – and made his contacts. His group financed its doings with a daring raid on the Commune's representation in Vienna, in the Bankgasse. There was another centre of counter-revolution, in Szeged, in the south, close to the Entente lines, and there army officers gathered, with Admiral Horthy at their head, protected in effect by the French army. Another highly intelligent and realistic Transylvanian nobleman,

Count Pál Teleki, offered wisdom, along with a Pallavicini and an Andrássy, and Admiral Horthy offered an old-fashioned decent and honest presence. They reined in the wild men, and they struggled towards recognition of Christian Democracy as a way for the future. They were essentially monarchists, but understood that this was not a moment to re-introduce the Habsburgs. Wild men did make the running for a while, with 'the White terror', a backlash from the red one. Because the Commune had been led often enough by Jews, there was an anti-Semitic side to this. Seven thousand people were interned, and possibly 1,000 killed.[1] However, now a proper Hungarian government could be sorted out and peace arranged.

At the end of the First World War Wilsonian ideas were triumphant: free elections, self-determination and, to ensure international standards, a League of Nations. Hungary had an election in January 1920, with something not far from universal male suffrage, and secret voting. It threw up a conservative majority, Christian and agrarian; the Social Democrats abstained because of victimisation against them by the counter-revolutionaries, including the 'Awakening Hungarians' (Ébredő magyarok egyesülete) movement and the police. The older parties did not figure. The majority of their adherents would no doubt have preferred a monarchy. However, the Allies made it clear that they would not recognise a Habsburg restoration, because they had already achieved 'the liberation of peoples bound hitherto to servitude' (an absurd line). On 1 March Horthy took over as Regent – i.e., stand-in for an absent monarch – with wide powers. He faced an immediate problem, in that poor Karl, who was not very bright, expected him to remember his oath, and he turned up twice to reclaim the throne in 1921: once by car from Switzerland and then in October by plane, a daring thing to do. It was a characteristic Karl performance. His train stopped at every station, Mass was said, huzza-ing peasants were rounded up and after a week Karl turned up in Budapest, his thoughts dominated by the question of which medal to give Horthy for enabling the restoration. Horthy's advisers were just then negotiating to keep part of the country's west (the Burgenland) from annexation by Austria, and the country had only a few thousand soldiers. Czechoslovakia and Yugoslavia complained, and Horthy had to explain that the moment was utterly wrong; there was even a brief shoot-out, and Karl was interned in Tihany monastery, on Lake Balaton, before a British warship took him via the Black Sea to Madeira. The Empress Zita's jewels were stolen. A banker then gave him a hilltop house gratis, but it was very damp, and Karl died in 1922, aged thirty-five and penniless, of a lung infection.

Foreign recognition followed. An initial government (under Károly Huszár) now had to deal with the Entente and the Americans as regards a final peace treaty, and the parties concerned gathered at the Trianon Palace in Versailles. The Hungarians arrived with maps and experts, including the now venerable Count Albert Apponyi. They were isolated, forbidden to have contact even with an envoy in London (who secretly passed information about his Presbyterian contacts from a park bench in the Bois de Boulogne). In a vintage crop of stupid treaties that of the Trianon, signed on 4 June 1920, was the worst. The argument for self-determination was ultra-modern, but the boundaries that were fixed generally could only be justified in historical terms. Hungary came off worst of all the defeated Central Powers. Yugoslavia and Czechoslovakia, new states, took much, and might even have been awarded a 'Slav corridor' through western Hungary (there were Croat villages in the Burgenland) between Bratislava and Zagreb. Rumania took all of Transylvania, and some properly Hungarian territory as well. Hungary's population fell from 20 million to 8 million as she lost two-thirds of her territory. Three million Hungarian-speakers were taken over by the successor states, and there was only one plebiscite – in western Hungary, where Austria was allowed to take over the Burgenland, but not all of it. At the time people seem to have assumed that, the larger a country, the stronger it would be. Rumania was allowed to take over purely Hungarian areas on the border, particularly the towns of Nagyvárad and Szatmárnémeti. This was

done partly because after a year and a half of wrangling, the negotiators were very tired and could not be bothered listening to any
more central European grievances: they would be sorted out at the
League of Nations. Trianon was immoral, in that it broke President
Wilson's own rules as regards national states: here were unworkable
countries, with grand aspirations and explosive minorities. The
handling of Germany was absurdly clumsy. She was told to install
a parliamentary republic, which was then hobbled by impossible-
looking demands. A French general called it an armistice of twenty
years – which was right, almost to the day. Germans were handed
an enormous bill, called 'reparations'. These were meant to compen-
sate the French and Belgians, and to burden the Germans with such
a bill that they would not recover for two generations. All Germans
blamed their economic troubles on these, and when the time came
in 1932, nearly two-fifths of them voted for Hitler and almost
another fifth for the Communists. But the reparations were really
paid for by American investment, and if the German economy went
downhill there were other reasons. Hungary was also absurdly
handled. The government (and Count Apponyi, whose wisdom had
been waved aside) refused to sign the treaty, but the Rumanian
army threatened to stay, and an unknown politician had to sign
instead, on 4 June 1920. The nation went into deep mourning:
Trianon from then on was to be a national obsession. Budapest was
filled with Transylvanian refugees, and the slogan of non-
recognition, 'No, No, Never' (*nem nem soha*), reverberated.

The backdrop to the 1920s was financial confusion, and eventual
recovery – much as happened, on a much larger scale, in Germany.
The Monarchy's end was for Hungary an economic disaster. The
common currency and captured markets went. Industries that had
been stimulated by the war – metallurgy and textiles – would go
bankrupt, and besides, the raw materials they used were now often
enough over some border or other: timber in Rumania, iron ore in
Czechoslovakia. And while she retained her railway factories, she
now had only two-fifths of the railway length. There was a milling

capacity for 65 million tons of flour, but now she produced only 28 million. By 1921 industrial production within the new borders was half what it had been. C. A. Macartney wrote an influential book showing what a calamity Trianon had been for 'Hungary and her Successors': idiotic interruption of railways and river transport, and pointless disruption of essential trade. A third of the workforce was unemployed, and the essential thing was to get agriculture back to work.[2]

Count Pál Teleki took over as Prime Minister. He was an enormously dignified and versatile figure, but his judgement let him down. He mishandled the return of Karl (many of the grand aristocracy did not forgive him), and he lent his name to a piece of anti-Semitic legislation that was both offensive and counterproductive. Most Jews, then and later, were entirely loyal and even enthusiastic Hungarians, but the Jewish preponderance in the Councils regime had been marked, and there was a reaction. As Mária Schmidt remarks, part of the political nation regarded the alliance with Jews as broken, because they had not observed the unwritten rule, not to be directly involved in politics. Teleki brought in a *numerus clausus* (1920), which affected Jewish numbers in universities: the bill did not even mention Jews, and merely stated that ethnic-minority students should be admitted in proportion to their share of the overall population, which was set at 12 per cent for Jews, later reduced as proposed by the Dean of the Faculty of Theology in Budapest to 6 per cent. Later generations might describe this as affirmative action, since Jews had until then made up a third of some university student bodies.

However, there was more to this. In the first place there were almost 500,000 refugees, many of them anxious for an education but not rating as highly as Jewish candidates, especially when it came to law and medicine; and since the landowners who formed a good part of the political class had no intention of permitting land reform, the burden of social engineering could be shifted elsewhere, at the Jews' expense. Teleki himself was a distinguished academic (a geographer, who undertook surveying and mapping, even in Japan) and had excellent relations with the superb orientalists Goldziher and Vámbéry, with whom he had collaborated before 1914 on a journal called *Turan*, which made much of Hungarian-Turkish affinity. A prominent figure in all of this was Ottokár Prohászka, Bishop of Székesfehérvár (and of Slovak origin). He enters history as one of Hungary's most prominent anti-Semites, and in parliament he spoke in favour of the *numerus clausus*. But this is not straightforward at all. He had this to say: 'I honour and respect the good fortune of the Jews. They are a fortunate people. I honour and respect Jewish genius and strength, insofar as it is strength of spirit.' And he went on that some of his best friends were Jews, that he had Jewish godchildren and that he particularly admired the doctors in his bishopric. But they were not the same as ordinary Hungarians, for they had never had their own state, with aristocrats, peasants, chivalry and so forth, and they therefore concentrated on money. Arthur Koestler in his memoirs says exactly the same about his Zionist period. Jews would be reformed by having their own state, where they could learn to live as other peoples did. A few Zionists were present when Prohászka spoke, and applauded. Other Jews were, of course, appalled: assimilation was their aim, and Zionism was a fantasy. The bill went through, a small beginning of the tidal wave of legislation that was to sweep Europe from 1933 on.[3] This drove many Jews abroad, if they could afford it: Arthur Koestler to Vienna, Leo Szilard to Berlin, and Peter Bauer, subsequently the hardest-hitting development economist in Great Britain, to Cambridge, and many, many others.[4] Bauer's father had got him into an upper-class Catholic Pietist school by putting a red line through the gambling debts of the chairman of the governors, Count Sigray. Bethlen, another Transylvanian Count, and another Protestant, succeeded Teleki as Prime Minister in 1921, and occupied the post for a decade; his judgement was a great deal better. He knew that the country had a badly damaged economy, knew very well that it was not wise to offend Jews in this way and relaxed the *numerus clausus*; it was in any case widely ignored, as most academics wanted after all to have good students to teach, and many in any case resented the injustice of the whole thing. But it was a terrible portent, and alienated numbers of young Jews. Many of them moved to the left in the 1930s.

Bethlen was Prime Minister for ten years,[5] and repeated Tisza's feat of one-party rule (this time, unoriginally, with the Egység Pártja, or Party of Unity, although it was actually quite divided). The party was under the theoretical chairmanship of an old agrarian, Nagyatádi Szabó, who might have been expected to address the basic question of land reform, as vast estates co-existed alongside one-hut poverty, but the Hungarian estate owners were strong in Bethlen's circles, and reasons were found to put off the reform. Why weaken productive estates to benefit small peasant plots, which would not have access to credit or even (in a poor peasant or gypsy neighbourhood) the proper drive to make use of it? The party was soon filled with co-opted civil servants, as Tisza's had been, and its nominees filled administrative posts in the provinces, where elections could be controlled. Bethlen arranged for a new restrictive voting decree, such that not much over a quarter of the population could vote, and the secret ballot was shelved in countryside constituencies. Three-quarters of the voters therefore had to declare in public, under the watchful eyes of cock-feather-hatted gendarmes. Bethlen said that the secret vote was 'not compatible with the Hungarian people's open character'. The governing party then governed for the next two decades. True, the cities had secret voting and there the governing party won only a quarter of the votes, but Bethlen managed a deal with the socialists in December 1921, by which they were given secret voting in towns, an amnesty, a political presence and a free press; in return they accepted limits on trade union activity – no political strikes. The parliament was not in fact as manageable as Bethlen wanted. The suffrage had widened to 27 per cent (though it had been narrowed from the 40 per cent of 1917), and there was a popular opposition – Social Democrats, Democrats (radical liberals) and Octobrists, Károlyi's faithful – which was vocal and also took up obstruction. Bethlen had to re-introduce Tisza's rules against this, although he had earlier opposed them. Eventually, Horthy's old Szeged associate, Gyula Gömbös, seceded to set up the 'Race Defenders Party'. It was crypto-Fascist. Mussolini had taken power in October 1922, and the example was infectious, for he appealed to veterans who felt that their sacrifices had been for nothing, and that the country was being run by corrupt old men and was going to the dogs. Horthy bluntly supported Bethlen against this, and some 'Awakening Magyars' were put on trial for their anti-Semitic atrocities. In the 1926 elections the Race Defenders got nowhere, nor, subsequently, did similar groupings for a decade, when the political nation began to lose control. It is quite wrong to identify Horthy with Fascism.

Hungary in the 1920s was a very conservative country, but it smelled of mothballs. The old ceremonial titles were used – 'Greatness' for a university rector, 'Refulgence' for a general etc. – in their semi-Japanese complexity: there were different ways of greeting, depending on the rank that was doing the greeting. There were 745 magnates, with a third of the land; the Church had a great deal; and even the Protestant foundations held land in plenty. This was the last gasp of the old political nation. Eighteen of Bethlen's twenty-nine cabinet members were either high aristocrats or gentry, and these, with the upper middle class, dominated politics. The universities of Pozsony and Kolozsvár were shifted to Pécs and Szeged, producing law graduates who aspired to jobs in the civil service, in some ministry, with its 'paternoster' revolving lift, men stepping be-briefcased on and off it at each floor. There was much meaningless paperwork, theoretically to stop corruption but in reality following a tradition that went back to Joseph II, a believer in bureaucracy.

Hungary, like Germany, was supposed to pay reparations – a humbug word meaning crippling tribute. As with Germany, she therefore had no particular interest in keeping her own currency stable – quite the contrary; and besides, inflation would knock out the real value of debts taken on by industry for investment during the war, and by landowners for acquisitions during and after it. Inflation had reduced the value of paper crowns against gold crowns from ten to one in 1919 to 18,400 to one in 1924 – an inflation not as dramatic as the German mark's fall to 11 billion to the dollar but heading that way. One hundred Crowns fetched 11.6 Swiss francs in 1919, but this fell to 1.4 late in 1920 and then to 0.03 in 1922. Of course, this reflected overuse of the monetary printing press, but at that time most bankers claimed that this had nothing to do with them, that they were just responding to demand for credit. But chaos produced its solution. A Great Coalition government, including Social Democrats and right-wing Liberals, came in, and its financial expert, Hjalmar Schacht, knew what had to be done. The government ruled by emergency decree, and a new currency was introduced, backed by the industrialists. Credit was throttled back, the head of the Reichsbank dropped dead of a heart attack, and a foreign, mainly American, gold loan underpinned things. The price was a rise in unemployment, which the Social Democrats accepted for the sake of stability. Within months the inflation had stopped. Five years of boom, fuelled by foreign investment, followed. (The German inflation brought more dollars, through speculation, into Germany than the Marshall Plan.) A similar pattern affected Hungary. Bethlen and his Finance Minister, Tibor Kállay, handled this well, and the western powers already had a sense of guilt at what they now saw as a bad peace. Even the successor states were persuaded not to insist on reparations, and a new stable currency was introduced in 1925 – the pengő, worth some 13,000 crowns, and theoretically based on gold. In 1926 the international supervision of Hungary's army and finances came to an end. A recovery now got under way, partly owing to foreign investment and the Bank of England. Bethlen interested foreigners in a sort of privatisation, with Swedes buying the match monopoly, for instance. From 1924 to 1931 Hungary had 1,300 million pengő in long-term loans and 1,700 million in short-term, usually with an interest rate, high for the era, of 7 per cent. By 1931 she had become the most indebted nation in Europe, and the cost of servicing the debt (excluding large private liabilities, 4,300 million pengő) ran to 10 per cent of the national income. Raw materials for industry could only be bought if agricultural exports earned the money. But there too was trouble. Half of the young peasants had gone off to war, along with most of the draught animals, so that land was unused. In 1920 wheat yields were half what they had been, natural manure having fallen as live-stock shrunk by two-thirds. In 1921 the farm exports of Trianon Hungary were only two-fifths of the pre-war figure, and American grain had taken their place even in central Europe. There was a recovery, and in the 1920s agricultural goods (including live animals) were 60 per cent of all exports: in other words essential, but also a trap.

Bethlen was determined to industrialise, as Tisza had been, and that meant giving protection to home manufactures: in 1924, a 30 per cent tariff on agricultural machinery and equipment, for instance, which of course held back agriculture. Because flood control and irrigation did not go ahead, with fertiliser and machin-ery expensive, agriculture produced hardly more in 1929 than it had done in 1913, although small farmers did show enterprise, such that the number of fruit trees rose by 50 per cent in the 1920s, and the peaches of Buda or the apricots of Kecskemét were in demand. So was wine, of which the Hungarians got through a prodigious amount – 40 litres per head, whereas the French, known for not being abstemious, managed eight. Industrial output rose by 12 per cent, and per capita GDP by perhaps 40 per cent. However, a country like Hungary was well placed as far as light industry and ingenious invention were concerned. She had largely missed out on the coal-and-iron stage of industrial revoution, but, like Italy, she did well enough when it came to the electricity stage. Textiles were a success story, and there were odd flashes of genius – the helicopter owes much to Hungarian engineers, trained in the Austro-Hungarian air force (although the reputation of Oszkár Asbóth, a self-promoter, is contested), and Albert Fonó came up with the essential step towards the jet engine.[6] Imre Brody invented the wolfram electric light bulb, now exported to fifty-three countries, and the Orion Works produced X-ray equipment.

Bethlen also introduced paternalistic reforms for the benefit of the working class. This was mainly a Budapest phenomenon, and it had had its like elsewhere, in the Manchester of Engels or the Berlin of the 1880s: families in a single room with outdoor plumbing (if that) and high rates of tuberculosis and infant mortality. In 1927 and 1928 provision was made for health insurance and pensions, and ten years later for a minimum wage, holidays with pay and a forty-eight-hour week. This did not apply in the countryside, where in places there was terrible poverty. The rural share of employment was 55 per cent in 1920, and 48 per cent two decades later. Land reform was announced, but not much was done: dwarf-holdings came about in tens of thousands, not enough for survival, and most went bankrupt as they had to pay the landlords for the land. There were 300,000 substantial farmers, with fifty acres, 1.2 million dwarf-holders, 600,000 labourers tied to the estates and 1.2 million landless day labourers, only able to work for half of the year. Gyula Illyés, himself the son of a labourer, wrote about the near-starvation that was endured in the Great Plain. The day labourers received food and tiny amounts of money; they would have hens and pigs. If they did not drink, if their children benefited from education, there was a chance of escape through promotion or migration to the city. But a great many did drink and neglected their studies.

The great credo of liberalism had been education. In the inter-war period realism about Hungary's post-Trianon situation prevailed in the Ministry of Education, where two long-serving men, Count Kuno Klebelsberg and the distinguished historian Bálint Hóman, ran things. They knew that the chief task was to remake the nation, and Klebelsberg concentrated on primary schools – six years of elementary education in (by 1938) 7,000 schools, which also gave teachers proper accommodation. For peasant children, who by the age of twelve would have to work, Hóman built 'people's houses' in which literacy and reading could be encouraged for the rural poor. New grammar schools came in, with a demanding examination covering many subjects. Ten per cent of the adolescents were involved. By 1938 illiteracy had been almost abolished, a sharp contrast with the Balkans or even Poland (23 per cent). There was, of course, a nationalistic tone to the system, but it produced results, and the cultural life of the Horthy era was exceedingly interesting. Whatever the ills of the era, the intelligentsia in Hungary produced an extraordinary culture, affecting everything, writers and film-makers and composers of European stature. The main figures were divided, some cosmopolitan and urban, others striking a social-realist and countryside note; they had their problems. Ferenc Molnár, Paul Ignotus (originally Veilsberger) and Lajos Hatvany, who wrote, emigrated. So did the Korda family, much to the profit of the British cinema. Others stayed, looking left.

The later 1920s had been the eye of the hurricane, a period when you could pretend that all was heading back to 1914. In Budapest the high aristocracy could show off with grand marriages, and the capital was still putting up interesting buildings, in this case Art Deco. The recovery period ended in 1931, with the fall of Bethlen. After ten years he was tired, and made misjudgements. His life was complicated by an affair with a Countess, with whom he spent time in Venice on the Lido just as the financial crisis broke in July of that year, in the middle of negotiations with the French. Hungary was dependent on the international context, and in 1929–30 a great world economic depression started – the second half of the hurricane. The immediate problem was that American money, lent short-term ('hot'), dried up as Wall Street crashed in October 1929. American money had financed European recovery. British money had helped as well, but had been lent 'long', on the strength of money borrowed 'short'. The world had gone back to the gold standard, but not to the basics that had made it work in the later nineteenth century: i.e., free trade, including in gold, which the

Americans and the French just stored. Germany, then Great Britain and finally France clung to gold, and subjected their economies to 'austerity' to choke back demand for imports. At the same time they protected their own industries, so that other countries' exports suffered. But the banks in central Europe had been lending money on Ponzi principles, and in May 1931 some of the largest just failed; foreigners called in loans. This badly affected Germany, which could not pay debts to Great Britain. The Reichstag could not solve the problem, and when the British abandoned the gold standard in September 1931, international trade fell by two-thirds. Every country spent less on agricultural goods from abroad. Peasants did not go unemployed; they just relapsed into subsistence where possible, and starvation where not. This left Hungary extremely exposed to economic trouble. She lost two-thirds of the value of her wheat exports and half of other agricultural exports. Use of fertilisers dropped from 15 kg per hectare in 1929 to 4.2 in 1935.[7] In all, by 1933 her export income fell by 70 per cent from 1929. That in turn affected domestic demand. Industrial output fell by a quarter between 1929 and 1933, property auctions were common in the countryside, village shopkeepers went bankrupt. This was a spiralling-down nightmare, which could be halted only in two ways. The first was through international co-operation, such as had been known, at Anglo-French behest, in the days of the gold standard. The other was autarky: a self-sufficient economy, with all the tortuous long-way-round attempts to do what was done more successfully elsewhere. Public works, four- or five-year plans, state boards to buy up surplus produce at guaranteed prices marked the decade (and beyond). This went together with stringent control of foreign exchange: travellers searched at borders for Swiss francs and valuables. One ingenious Hungarian found a way round. He melted gold into long, thin bars. Once on the train, he swapped them for the iron curtain rails, and got through to Switzerland undetected. With connections, you could negotiate a way through the bureaucratic jungle, but it took an effort.

Nowadays governments co-operate, but in 1931, with wartime hatreds still alive, they did not: the French, for instance, would not use their gold because it was insurance for all the war pensioners, and they would certainly not use it to save Germany. In accounting for this seamless-web nightmare crisis, everyone fell back on a reach-me-down explanation: for Communists, whose numbers grew, the whole problem was just capitalism; for much of the right it was the excessive powers of trade unions and the growth of welfare. For another part of the continental right it was the Jews. Autarky was the answer, in Germany especially. Hungary depended on her. There were already agreements with Austria and Italy, guaranteeing a quota of agricultural exports at something above the world price, but in 1934 came an agreement with Germany which sent a quarter of Hungary's exports there. The Germans were stockpiling raw materials and agreed to send industrial goods in return. However, they were slow payers, and the raw materials and goods were late in delivery: there was not much the Hungarians could do, given the absence of other customers. By 1937 they were sending to Germany half of all fruit, vegetables, eggs and bacon, and 20 per cent of exported flour and beef cattle. By 1939 Germany had 53 per cent of Hungary's trade, and on German terms at that. However, in the short term this worked. Hungary recovered from the Depression, and by 1937 agricultural and industrial production were both above the levels of 1929. Discovery of oil and natural gas deposits helped, and helped also with artificial fertiliser. In Veszprém bauxite was discovered, which gave metallurgical industries a new edge; already in 1935 the German air force needed aluminium, produced on Csepel Island, one of the great industrial centres of Budapest. New industries – electrical, pharmaceutical – developed, and Hungarian industrial goods made a strong appearance. Unemployment dwindled. Of course, as a still chiefly agrarian economy, Hungary was a long way behind western Europe, but she had done better than her neighbours to the east and south.

A less effective conservative than Bethlen, Count Gyula

Károlyi, took over for a year, but by this stage (1932) Hungarian politics had something of an Austrian flavour: sympathies with Fascism were coming to the fore, and one Tibor Eckhardt, leader of the independent Smallholders – nationalistic and lazily anti-Semitic – did well in a by-election against a minister, and Horthy's brother-in-law at that. This was parallel to the rise of Dollfuss in Austria, rather than that of Hitler, but in 1932 Hitler was on the rise as well. Horthy now appointed Gömbös as Prime Minister. Here was the spirit of Szeged in 1919: nationalist, anti-Habsburg, anti-magnate, anti-Semitic. Horthy made Gömbös promise to leave Bethlen's supporters alone, as a majority in the lower House, to refrain from attacking Jews and to forget about land reform. Gömbös agreed, and famously spoke in parliament to renounce his anti-Semitism. One of his associates, Baross, formally signed a pact with leaders of the reformist Jewish community, but Gömbös brandished authoritarianism, extended censorship and snooping, and stuffed the civil service and the army with followers. Then he approached Mussolini for trade pacts, and visited Hitler for good measure in 1935 (it was Gömbös who invented the phrase 'the Axis' for Berlin–Rome). He broke his promise as to elections and in 1935 staged elections of violence and corruption, replacing Bethlen's men with his own; he even broke with Tibor Eckhardt, the former crypto-Fascist leader of the counter-revolution west of the Danube but now growing up and out of it. Horthy was taking alarm, and Gömbös made things easier for him by dying of a kidney disease in October 1936. He was followed by less colourful figures who were nevertheless of a similar cast of mind. Mussolini had co-operated (and the Oktogon became Mussolini Square), but by 1936, with German economic recovery, the great question came over how to handle Hitler. Germany had vastly more to offer, whether in trade or in foreign affairs.

In 1936 Horthy followed the troop of visitors to Hitler at Berchtesgaden, saying silly things, and pronounced the Führer 'a moderate and wise statesman'. In that year Hitler began his aggressive and treaty-breaking steps. The part of Germany west of the Rhine was supposed not to have troops, for the sake of French security (the French would rather have annexed it). In March 1936 Hitler sent in soldiers, and Horthy approved. Now crisis followed crisis, as Mussolini came round to Hitler's side as well. He had attempted to turn Abyssinia into an Italian colony, whereas she was formally a member of the League of Nations. The British high-mindedly took a lead in opposing this, by laying sanctions on Italy. Horthy took Mussolini's part, and so did Hitler, though with less consistency. The next crisis came over Spain, where, as the Civil War got going in July 1936, Hitler and Mussolini supported the rebels' crypto-Fascist cause. There were Nazi-inspired developments in Austria as well, where the clerical-minded rulers were compelled by economic pressure to appoint Nazis to essential ministries: war, finance, the interior. The Italians, far from opposing this, joined Hitler's Anti-Comintern Pact, the air filled with shrill denunciations of Communism. Hungary was gravitating towards 'the Axis', and Gömbös's successor, Kálmán Darányi, in vain approached the British for understanding. They also wanted agreement with Hitler, and would let him remake central Europe, provided he set about it peacefully. In November 1937 Lord Halifax visited Berlin and indicated as much. This was 'appeasement', as it came to be known. The Germans indicated that Hungary could recover her lost territories in Czechoslovakia, provided that she helped with German plans for the destruction of the country: there was a 3-million-strong German minority in Czechoslovakia, and another million Hungarians, with grievances aplenty. Austria, too, was sucked into Hitler's orbit, and he annexed her on 13 March 1938. No one seriously objected; the Hungarians were the first to congratulate him, and their legation in the Bankgasse in Vienna was closed. But it was a brutal business just the same, for the Nazis fell viciously on the Viennese Jews.

Some Hungarian feet tapped. By now there was a wave of pro-German sentiment, and there were rumours of a right-wing coup, not least because the officer corps was known to be in the main pro-German – Gömbös's doing. In the meantime, a rearmament drive was going ahead and a military programme was announced at Győr – a thousand million pengő to be spent, with 200 mainly German aeroplanes. Hungary was not supposed to have a large army but re-introduced conscription, and by 1936 the atmosphere was again one of war. To appeal to Berlin, the half-million Hungarian Germans – Swabians – were allowed collective representation, inevitably of a Nazi tendency. There were warnings: the ever sensible Bethlen warned against the adoption of Nazi ideas and pointed out that Hungary was losing her independence. It was also clear that in the trade negotiations Hungary was being degraded to a mere provider of raw materials; the Germans also refused to pay more in hard currency for the agricultural imports, although world prices had now recovered somewhat; and there was nowhere else for the Hungarians to go. The British and French had their own agricultural trade to consider. And there were Hungarian would-be imitators of Nazism. As the old political nation lost its predominance, these surfaced.

The most sinister of them was one Ferenc Szálasi. He was born into a family of very mixed origins (the name was an adaptation of an Armenian ancestor's) in Kassa (now Košice in Slovakia), in 1897, and saw action in the latter stages of the war, joining the general staff. He believed in uniforms, discipline and the inspirational power of the Nation, a Greater Hungary cleansed of Jews and Communists: 'I have been chosen by a higher Divine authority to redeem the Hungarian people.'[8] There would be a 'Hungarist' state, on Fascist lines, and its badge was the crossed arrows that supposedly represented the original Magyar conquest. The party, calling itself National Socialist, became known as the Arrow Cross, and Szálasi must have had something to hold it together for there were other such movements, none of which lasted. However, the Arrow Cross made inroads, not just among the lower middle class, where Hitler especially recruited, but also among the working class, where anti-Semitism could mean combating capitalism. Horthy contemptuously refused to give him office, and appointed as Prime Minister a banker, Béla Imrédy, a man of Swabian origin who had headed the National Bank (and according to Macartney was a considerable authority on chamber music). Imrédy was well known to the British and looked for favours from them.

Hungary grew closer to Germany in the summer of 1938. Horthy, the old sailor, was invited to Kiel, to the launch of a German battle cruiser, *Prinz Eugen*, and was asked to assist in the destruction of Czechoslovakia. Imrédy had signed a non-aggression pact with the three countries of the Little Entente, the winners of Trianon, at Bled in Slovenia. Hitler meanwhile turned up the pressure on Czechoslovakia, using the German minority for the manufacture of incidents and making warlike speeches, and he expected the Hungarian mine to explode. But it did not, and instead of marching into Czechoslovakia, Hitler had to accept an agreement with the British and French, which gave him only a part, and peacefully at that. The question was decided at the Munich conference, on 30 September, and there was encouragement for Hungary to deal with her own claims separately, and a meeting with the Slovaks concerned did occur, fruitlessly, at Komárom. It broke up after four days, and then a Hungarian offer went to Berlin for invasion, with German support, for which Hungary offered to join the Anti-Comintern Pact and leave the League of Nations. At that Hitler and Mussolini agreed to mediate, and in the Belvedere Palace in Vienna on 2 November the First Vienna Award gave Hungary part of Slovakia, including a strip north of the Danube with a largely Hungarian population, and the town of Kassa, as well as Munkács and Ungvár, which are now in Sub-Carpathian Ukraine. This was old Rákóczi territory, but Hungarian Calvinists were in a minority. Horthy rode his white horse again, and scenes of liberation followed – little girls in Sunday best throwing flowers, a march-past by the boy scouts and the fire brigade, tears running down aged cheeks, much *pálinka* downed. Shopkeepers in that part of the world were often Jewish, and if peasants wanted to have groceries on credit, there could be problems. Roughly a million people were affected, in an area of 12,000 square kilometres. Early in 1939, under a different foreign minister, István Csáky, Hungary did join the Anti-Comintern Pact and left the League. The Germans were then told that Hungary would do something about 'the Jewish problem'.

The record of Horthy's Hungary was besmirched by anti-Semitic legislation. A first law was passed at the end of 1938, limiting Jewish employment in certain areas. The framers had a difficult time in establishing who exactly was Jewish: what about the great numbers of converts, and of mixed marriages? And what of the Jews, including several generals, who had distinguished themselves in the war, or otherwise, in literature or as Olympic champions? A hundred and ten generals of the army protested against the law, and so did great figures of Hungarian cultural life (Béla Bartók, for instance: he considered Turkish citizenship). On 4 May 1939 came a Second Jewish Law to clear up the grey areas, and one of its framers was the distinguished medieval historian Bálint Hóman, who had been guest of honour (as Minister of Education) at Jewish events, who sat on the Board of the National Museum with Kornfelds and Chorins, and was a *bon vivant* with friends in the Jewish intelligentsia: what *was* he thinking? This time round, citizenship restrictions were tightened, and the quota of Jewish employment was reduced to 6 per cent (though in finance and commerce 12 per cent). Still, Jews in the media and the professions did suffer, and 300,000 lived on charity by 1942, but the law was applied patchily, and in any case doctors and lawyers (or actors) could count as self-employed and escape the restrictions. There was, for instance, a 'Christian doctors' association', which monopolised employment in state hospitals and public health, but if they had offered their services in private practice, most would not have flourished. And the rich Jews, the industrialists especially, were not affected. Horthy's bridge partners (the Chorin family) were Jews, and they kept him going in penniless exile later on. Imrédy himself looked foolish, and had to resign when journalists dug into his ancestry and found a convert great-grandmother. He fainted when Horthy told him.

Teleki took his place, and benefited (in a sense) from Hitler's next move. Six months after Munich, Czecho-Slovakia (as it had been renamed) fell apart, when Slovak Fascists, under German pressure, declared independence on 14 March 1939. The next day Hitler marched into Prague and turned the Czech lands into a Protectorate. That left Sub-Carpathia, the once Hungarian Ruthene (or Ukrainian) north-eastern corner, and here a clergyman, Mgr Vološín, declared a republic that lasted a day. Hungarian forces staged a provocation and occupied 12,000 square kilometres of thick forest, to more bellowing of anthems, more *pálinka*, more marching of boy scouts and more marching by the fire brigade and the municipal rubbish collectors. There was at least this to be said for the Hungarian case, that many of the locals did not even consider themselves Ukrainian but thought of themselves as specifically Carpatho-Ruthene, and therefore looked to Hungary, as a minority within a minority, for protection. Learned men got to work to establish a separate language. Other men, and women, in Budapest could see where all this was heading and advised proper contact with Great Britain and Washington before civilisation collapsed.

Still, the revision of the terms of Trianon brought about huge national jubilation, and even the left-wing poets (Mihály Babits, for instance, who had been involved with Béla Kun) joined in. Wild nationalism was now in vogue, and the anti-Semitic laws did not reduce it: on the contrary, since now, by implication, Jewish property could legally be stolen. The government had faced endless criticism from the left for Hungary's failure to introduce universal suffrage, and responded to it with tinkerings. The suffrage was now widened, and in the elections of May 1939 the radical right won some 15 per cent of the vote, with forty seats, becoming a substantial political party. Szálasi had been imprisoned; now he was released, taking over headquarters in the old Perlmutter Mansion on Andrássy út, which subsequently became the centre of the

Communist secret police, complete with torture chambers. (It is now a museum, the 'Terror House'.) Here was a sort of Nazi Fifth Column, to join with a further one, the list of ethnic Germans, compilation of which, again, Teleki allowed.

His horizons were now narrowing. Hitler was about to engage on his final aggressive step, which came over the matter of Poland's borders. If Hungary supported him, she would be ratting on an old alliance, Poland being a friendly associate (and the annexation of Carpatho-Ruthenia gave the two a common frontier, much celebrated). On the other hand, if Hungary stayed out, she might lose the chance of further revision of the Trianon borders; Hitler ranted to this effect on 8 August 1939, and Mussolini pressed the Hungarians to follow Nazi instructions. Again Teleki prevaricated, and a letter of his was disavowed by his own foreign minister. A decisive moment on the road to war occurred on 23 August 1939, when Hitler concluded a pact with Soviet Russia. Nazism was at deadly odds with Communism, or so it seemed, but a brief coincidence of interests occurred as regards Poland, and the two decided to partition that country and by implication to divide central and eastern Europe into zones of influence or occupation. The Second World War started on 1 September, when Germany attacked Poland, and two days later the British and French declared war. Teleki knew, as did Horthy, that sea power would in the end prevail, and that the British would win. But the immediate German pressure was overwhelming, and Hungary allowed the Wehrmacht to use railways east of Kassa at least for goods. When Poland collapsed, 150,000 Poles took refuge in Hungary, from where most went on to fight in the west. The Germans blustered again, and Werth, chief of the General Staff, threatened to resign if such courses were followed, but Hungarians defied this.

Still, Hitler seemed invincible. In June 1940 France collapsed, and though the British famously fought on, he was now master of the continent; Hungary, with misgivings, had to court his favour. He alone might offer further revision of Trianon, the most important part of which was Transylvania. Horthy wavered this way and that – reassuring the British that he would behave honourably but also sending a basket of Hungarian fruit to Hitler with a fulsome letter. Hitler was concerned that Hungary might attack Rumania, because he depended on her oil, and she was already under threat from the Soviet Union now that she had lost French protection. In June 1940, after the fall of France, the Soviet Union moved, demanding retrocession of north-eastern Rumania and offering co-operation with Hungary. Teleki and Horthy hated the Soviet Union and ignored the approach, but they did mobilise the army, and public opinion was in wild uproar at the possibility of regaining Transylvania. Hitler called Teleki and Csáky, the foreign minister, to Munich, and told them he would find an answer. Again there was arbitration, the Second Vienna Award, on 30 August 1940. Transylvania was partitioned and the Hungarian part called Northern Transylvania, although the expression was quite inaccurate. The partition was not easy, because the largest single Hungarian element was the Szekel territory in the east and south-east, abutting the Carpathians, and it could only be joined up with Trianon Hungary via territory further west that was often Rumanian. Admiral Horthy got on his horse again and rode in triumph through historic Hungarian towns – Kolozsvár, Marosvásárhely – to vast celebration. This time Hungary obtained 43,000 square kilometres and 2.5 million souls, but two-fifths of these were Rumanian, while the Rumanians in southern Transylvania retained 400,000 Hungarians. There was a bill to pay for this: adhesion to the Tripartite Pact of Germany, Italy and Japan (in September 1940, implicitly against the United States), German military transports through Hungarian territory and privileges for the Hungarian Germans' association. There would also be further measures concerning the Jews, and permission for extreme-right activities.

There remained one item on the revisionist agenda, the partly Hungarian Voivodina (where there were also Germans), which was in Yugoslavia. This was complicated. Hitler wanted a Yugoslavia that would be aligned with the Axis, and anyway had enough on his plate with the British. The Hungarians therefore cultivated good relations with Belgrade, and a treaty was signed, in December 1940, to the effect that 'there will be permanent peace and eternal friendship' between the two parties. However, Hitler was drawn into the Balkans after all because of Italian blundering. Mussolini had attempted an invasion of Greece and had badly failed: he had to be rescued. Yugoslavia had formally joined the Tripartite Pact on 25 March, but at once there was a pro-British coup, and a German invasion followed. Teleki was informed that Hungary, by joining this, could have a further revision, and a German army delegation arrived in Budapest to arrange this. Teleki had sworn to the British that he would not comply with German demands 'irreconcilable with honour', but on 1 April he himself voted for re-annexation of Voivodina. The minister in London, György Barcza, sent a telegram to the effect that if Hungary went ahead, it would mean war, and the British minister in Budapest, the vastly respected Owen O'Malley, vigorously accused Horthy himself of underhand conduct. Teleki came under terrible strain and on 3 April shot himself, having scribbled a note to Horthy: 'We have become breakers of our word [...] taken the side of scoundrels [...] the most rotten of nations.' Horthy was unmoved, and appointed the pro-German Bárdossy as Teleki's successor. Hungary joined in the invasion of Yugoslavia, which broke up. Horthy was warned that, for breaking a treaty of eternal friendship that had just been signed, he could expect no mercy from 'a victorious Britain and the United States of America'. Out of this, Hungary did get another 11,500 square kilometres with a million inhabitants, just over a third of them Hungarians. All in all, she had taken back about half of the lost territories, some 80,000 square kilometres with 5.3 million souls, of whom 40 per cent were Hungarian. But there was a considerable price to pay, for the country had now been captured by Germany.

The Arrow Cross was in parliament with (including allies) 25 per cent of the vote. It took a large number of working-class votes, in the Csepel area, where the Social Democrats advised abstention and the Communists urged a vote for the Arrow Cross (the same destructive tactics as in Berlin, where the party sought to end the Social Democrats' and Catholics' rule, at any price). It organised a miners' strike in 1940, but it also spoke for poor peasants, and had their vote in the poorest areas. In a sense, it was driving Hungarian affairs, and its anti-Semitism grew worse, no doubt because of the possibility of booty to come from more laws against Jews. A third law was passed in August 1941, this time following Nazi lines, prohibiting mixed marriage, which the Minister of Justice, László Radocsay, said 'damaged the development of the national soul'. There were also deportations of non-Hungarian Jews to camps in Galicia and the Ukraine, although these were stopped when the ministry heard of mass killings, and 14,000 Polish Jews got 'Christian papers'. There was a further atrocity early in 1942, when the Hungarians went into northern Serbia and 3,000 civilians were shot, including women and children, in Novi Sad. There was, much later, a court martial, but the five principal accused, of Swabian origin, escaped in German vehicles and were given high ranks in the SS.

In June 1941 the Germans attacked the Soviet Union, and of course Hungary was involved. She had had surprisingly good relations with Moscow during the months of the Hitler–Stalin Pact: Stalin had sent back dozens of captured standards from the war of 1849, and the Hungarians agreed to release the Communist Mátyás Rákosi from prison – as it turned out, a disastrous exchange. On 23 June the envoy, József Kristóffy, announced that Molotov was willing to recognise Hungary's territorial demands on Rumania; but Bárdossy suppressed the report, and took advantage of an unexplained episode when foreign aircraft dropped bombs on a provincial town – probably a plot by Hungarian and German staff officers – to blame Moscow and declare war. Forty thousand men crossed into Galicia to join in the invasion of the Soviet Ukraine, and Hungary helped Germany with grain and bauxite, for which she was not paid. At first the eastern war went astonishingly well, and Hungary seemed to be on the winning side; but one of the generals, Szombathelyi, and Horthy's older son, István, guessed that matters would not go so easily, as indeed they did not. By December the Germans had been held before Moscow. That same week came the Japanese attack on Pearl Harbor, and the USA thus entered the war. Quite absurdly, Bárdossy declared war on America without consulting even Horthy, let alone the whole cabinet.

It would have been sensible of Horthy to organise at least a shadow government in exile, such as the Czechs and Yugoslavs had in London or Washington. That step was urged by far-sighted men with diplomatic experience, such as Domokos Szent-Iványi and Aladár Szegedi-Maszák, who detested the Nazis, and they said that the gold reserve should go as well. The most that Horthy would do was to replace Bárdossy with a figure uncompromised by Germanomania. The aristocracy (with a few striking exceptions) detested and despised the Nazis, and the new Prime Minister, the then unknown Miklós Kállay, was yet another Count, with Protestant origins. He hated Communism, but he also disliked the Nazis and their racial policy, and the Germans were suspicious of the whole class. They also knew that Cardinal Primate Serédi and Bishop Apor, of Győr, regularly in sermons attacked the persecution of Jews (they were particularly concerned with the fate of Jewish converts). Allied prisoners on the run in Hungary were looked after. Hungary was still a peaceful island in Europe, and Kállay ran down exports of food to Germany by 25 per cent, so that his own people were reasonably well fed – there were no disasters, as in the previous war – and he also defied Hitler, in Rastenburg in April 1942, when he was told to deport Jews and have them wear the yellow star. By now fear of German occupation, with all the horrors, and of German favouritism towards Rumanians or even Czechs had become dominant, and Kállay did make some concessions – for instance, another Jewish law in March 1942, cancelling the law of 1895 that gave the Jewish religion all civil rights, and

expropriating estates larger than 150 acres. Jews were also conscripted into labour battalions, and out of 50,000 conscripted only
a few thousand survived the winter of 1942–3. On the other hand
– as ever in this story – Jews were still part of the Upper House, and
the War Minister, Vilmos Nagy, did his best to help the labour battalion Jews. And until 1944 Jewish schools and concerts went on, in
the Goldmark Hall, the Jewish theatre.

But disaster was impending. Horthy received a terrible personal
blow, at the age of seventy-four, when he was told, by Kállay, that
his elder son and designated successor had been killed in a flying
accident in the east (on 20 August 1942). Then came military collapse. The German army had taken an extraordinary gamble to seize
the oil of the Caucasus, and its long north-western flank, on the
frozen River Don, was guarded by sub-standard troops – Italian,
Rumanian, Hungarian. The main defence was conducted by a
German army, pinned down at Stalingrad on the Volga far to the
east, and on 18–19 November the Red Army broke through its
northern and southern defences, to entrap it entirely in the city. It
surrendered, half-starved, at the turn of January–February, and
90,000 men were marched off to captivity, including its commander,
a Field Marshal. At the same time the Russians broke through on
the Don. Here, at Voronezh, stood the Hungarian Second Army,
defending a hundred miles of frozen front, with inadequate weaponry, outnumbered three to one in men and by ten to one in guns,
without tanks and with half-starved horses, and between 12 and 14
January it broke – 130,000 men, out of 200,000, killed or captured,
along with 36,000 of the 40,000 men in the Jewish labour battalions. The general, Jány, exploded in contempt at the 'panic-stricken,
cowardly flight'. But these troops were bewildered peasant boys,
some of them Slovak or Rumanian, a thousand miles from home,
freezing, sometimes without boots. The Italian Eighth Army had a
similar disaster, and the Nazis were now losing the war. They were
cleared from North Africa by May 1943, with the loss of 300,000
prisoners, and the Russians retook Kharkov in July, while Hamburg

was wrecked by a firestorm; at the same time Italy was invaded and Mussolini fell. In November the Russians took Kiev.

Horthy and Kállay were now struck by these Allied successes, and a small group of ministers, with Ferenc Keresztes-Fischer at the Interior and Szombathelyi of the General Staff, discussed how Hungary might get out of the war. The atmosphere in Budapest in 1943 was surreal, and this no doubt contributed to illusions – the restaurants full, the grand hotels humming, the Jewish-owned Arizona Bar night club on Nagymező, the theatre avenue, full every night. Contacts – too many – went ahead in Stockholm, Bern and Istanbul, always with the same message, that Hungary would drop out of the war if the western Allies could save her from Soviet occupation. Of course, the Germans heard: Budapest was not a capital where secrets could be kept. In any case, even then the great likelihood was that the Red Army would reach Hungary first, and it was already close to the Rumanian border. Horthy went to see Hitler at Schloss Klessheim, near Salzburg, in April 1943, and received a rant – Hitler knew of the Istanbul and Swiss intrigues, and he also demanded action against the Jews, with their demoralising influence. Horthy was not, after the death of his son, at his best, and he was getting old (he was seventy-five). He waffled that, as an old naval man, he might suggest that German submarines should have observation balloons attached, which would deter Allied flying boats from attacking them. He also said that the Jews were essential to the economy, that Hungarians were gentlemen who left business to others, and anyway what could be done with them – 'they can't all be clubbed to death'. Hitler now cut off contact with Kállay. But by now the British were also offended. They had suggested that two Hungarian army officers should talk to Special Operations in Istanbul, and Kállay hesitated, partly because the man the British used as intermediary, György Pálóczi-Horváth, had once been a spy for Gömbös before taking up with the extreme left, and partly because the British seemed to be more interested in sabotage than in peace terms. Kállay did get heavily involved in exchanges with the British,

and Endre Bajcsy-Zsilinszky wrote a memorandum urging immediate withdrawal from the war, cancellation of the Jewish laws and
defiance if the Germans occupied Hungary. He was right, but as
ever the great fear in Horthy's circle was of a German occupation.
In any case, Churchill's attempt to intervene in the Balkans was not
supported by the Americans, who preferred the great landing in
France, in June 1944. And besides there was still a considerable pro-
German and violently anti-Communist element in Hungary;
maybe, too, the miracle-worker Hitler would come up with a wonder
weapon. In the army, pro-German officers abounded. Horthy would
not risk outright resistance.

The western Powers certainly spared Hungary the worst – no
bombing, for instance. They knew how difficult Horthy's position
was. But now, without reference to Kállay's prevarications, they
were forced to make some arrangement with Stalin as to the future
of the whole area. Churchill, Roosevelt and Stalin met at Teheran
in November 1943, and implicitly agreed that the Soviets could have
their way as regards borders. Churchill went further in Moscow the
following October, proposing that a swap would be made of zones
of influence: Greece mattered more than anything else to the
British, with their concerns east of Suez, and in exchange they
would let Rumania and Bulgaria fall into the Soviet zone. This was
a bargain that stuck. Greece might well have turned Communist at
the end of the war, but Stalin gave no help to the Greek Communists and did not even include them in the organisation that he
set up to replace the Comintern. British wishes were supposed to
be respected in Hungary, but not much could be done for her. Kállay
wriggled and wriggled, but short of a direct approach to Stalin he
could do nothing.

Hitler had already worked out plans for the occupation of a
Hungary now essential to his communications (and for oil), and in
March 1944 he invited Horthy to Klessheim. Kállay told him not to
go but he went, and on 18 March Hitler told him the occupation
would go ahead, if necessary with Rumanian and Croat help. He

was then told – a fiction – that he could not travel back by train because of Allied bombing, which had also brought down the telephone lines, and he could not communicate with Budapest. Early on 19 March the Germans moved in, tanks trundling through a Budapest where the trams were running. The situation that Horthy had managed to avoid since 1941 had arrived, and for the next ten months Budapest went through a nightmare. Edmund Veesenmayer, Nazi plenipotentiary, and the Gestapo chief, Ernst Kaltenbrunner, travelled back on Horthy's train, and when he arrived at Kelenföld station (after a twelve-hour journey, at 10 a.m. on 19 March), there was already a German guard of honour. Kállay resigned and took refuge in the Turkish Legation, and Bethlen hid in the country; others were captured. Horthy stayed on, arguing (to Kállay) that he could help if he did. The new Prime Minister, Döme Sztójay, had been Minister in Germany and was appointed when Horthy refused other German nominees, including Imrédy. Sztójay brought in other men from the extreme right – not, as yet, the Arrow Cross – and the Nazis' racial policies were put into effect. Adolf Eichmann arrived on 19 March with a detachment of thirty-two Gestapo 'specialists', and Sztójay approved an immediate plan to send 100,000 Jews for 'labour' – in fact, to Auschwitz. László Baky and László Endre, fanatical both, became senior civil servants in the Interior Ministry with special responsibility for measures against Jews: the yellow star, prohibitions on buying food in short supply, freezing of bank accounts, closure of shops. There was even some censorship of library books – no Proust, no Franz Werfel, not even *Bambi*, by a Vienna-based Hungarian Jew, Felix Saltén. By the end of April ghettoisation went ahead, starting with Kassa and going through the rest of the country, with Budapest last; and then the deportations got going, on 15 May. The ghettos were run by Jewish councils, following a now well-established pattern.

In France and Belgium Jewish notables had the sense not to volunteer, and the Germans – not more than a dozen Gestapo officers in most towns – were at a loss to find names and addresses. But elsewhere there was no shortage of men who deluded themselves that collaboration of this sort would stave off the worst.[9] By mid-July, Veesenmayer reported that 437,402 Jews had been moved from the provinces, including Transylvania and Sub-Carpathia, escorted by Hungarian gendarmes. There was little resistance, and Gerald Reitlinger, writing the first (and still a valuable) book on the Holocaust, remarked on the passivity with which the people met their fate, especially in Sub-Carpathia. The Hungarian gendarmes punctiliously obeyed their orders, and the young Edward Luttwak was told by a sympathetic German officer that he should run at once from Nagyvárad to the nearby Rumanian border: the Rumanians had given up this nonsense and anyway could be bribed. Days of travel crammed into insanitary freight waggons took them to Auschwitz at a time when the Russians had retaken Odessa and were probing the old Rumanian border. Then Eichmann turned his attention to Budapest, where since May 170,000 Jews were concentrated in 1,900 'yellow star' apartment houses, while 120,000 lived illegally in Christian households. On 25 June a curfew was imposed on the ghetto Jews, and they were unable to receive guests; and the deportations were to start on 6 July. The very rich Jews – Chorins, Weisses, Kornfelds – had stayed on, safe in their grand villas and buttressed by factories that kept the economy going. Now they too were rounded up in the cellars of the Astoria hotel, just next to the old magnates' club. They made a deal with the Germans, of a sort also made by the Wittgenstein sisters in Vienna.[10] Chorin and Kornfeld were first transferred to a work camp in Austria, then brought back to discuss the transfer of their firms. A Nazi art expert and lawyer, Kurt Becher, installed himself in the Chorin villa at 114 Andrássy út, and terms were agreed.

The Chorin, Kornfeld and Weiss families, with more than a ton of luggage, went by lorry to Vienna, then by train to Stuttgart, and then, with two planes at their disposal, thirty-two of them went to Portugal, with a stopover in Spain. The Portuguese would not let them in for thirty-six hours, because the Gestapo had forged the

Jewish inhabitants of the impoverished Angyanföld ('land of angels') district on the outskirts of Budapest in 1915. György Aczél, later the powerful deputy Minister for Culture in the Kádár-era Communist dictatorship, was born in Angyanföld. (Fortepan)

An aristocratic Hungarian wedding around the beginning of the twentieth century. (Fortepan/Magyar Bálint)

Admiral Miklós Horthy (in uniform at centre) with his family in 1936. Horthy was head of state from 1920 until forced to abdicate by the Nazis in 1944. (Agence Meurisse/Bibliothèque National Français)

Heroes' Square in Budapest in 1935. (Fortepan/Szent-Istvany Dezsö)

The Oktogon at night in 1930. This eight-sided square at the heart of Budapest lay at the intersection of two main thoroughfares and was a hub for fashionable nightlife. (Fortepan/Pesti Brúnó)

The Széchényi thermal spa in Budapest in 1930. (Fortepan)

A house in Budapest marked with a yellow star in 1944, indicating compulsory quarters for Jews. (Fortepan/Lissák Tivadar)

A German supply glider (top left) after crashing into a house during the Red Army's siege of German-held Budapest in 1944–5. (Fortepan/Album 011)

An everyday rally under Communism, with banners depicting Lenin,
the Hungarian leader Mátyás Rákosi and Stalin.
(Fortepan/Magyar Rendör)

Marchers protesting in 1956 against the 25 October massacre by Soviet
and Communist forces: some are carrying bloodstained banners.
(Fortepan/Nagy Gyula)

A May Day rally in Budapest after Communist rule was reinstated in 1956. The grandstand at the centre was previously the pedestal of a vast statue of Stalin, destroyed during the 1956 uprising. (Fortepan/Magyar Rendör)

A young Viktor Orbán, Hungary's future leader, speaking in Heroes' Square at the 16 June 1989 reburial of Imre Nagy and his comrades, executed by Kádár's Communist regime for treason in 1958. This ceremonial reinterment and Orbán's bold speech marked the end of Kádár-era Communism. (MTI/Nagy István Csaba)

Cutting through the Iron Curtain: Gyula Horn, Minister of Foreign Affairs in the last Communist government of Hungary, (at right) and his Austrian counterpart, Alois Mock, ceremonially cut through the barbed wire of the Austrian–Hungarian border on 27 June 1989. (MTI/Matusz Károly)

In 1990 József Antall (standing at centre) became the head of the first freely elected Hungarian government since 1944. Here he is speaking to his party members, with two iconic 1990-election placards in the background. (Fortepan/Szalay Zoltán)

Viktor Orbán, Prime Minister of Hungary, in 2018.
(Árvai Károly/Miniszterelnöki Kabinetiroda)

visas, but a Wodianer relative from a convert family (and married to a Thurn und Taxis), who was in the diplomatic service, helped and on they went, eventually, to Park Avenue in New York. Another plane took others to Switzerland. Becher went on to sort out the quasi-legal looting of paintings, especially from the 2,500-strong Herzog collection, with Courbet and Cranach the Elder and much else (mostly now it seems in Russia), and took time off to do another deal, with Rudolf Kasztner and his Jewish Relief Committee, allowing some 1,500 Jews to leave by special train after they had paid $1,000 each. Three hundred and eighteen did reach Switzerland; the others were held at Bergen-Belsen, where they were joined by the many Jews who had arranged foreign and neutral passports, usually South American. Meanwhile, prominent conservative anti-Nazi Hungarians whom the Germans had arrested were sent to Mauthausen – an Apponyi (György), a Szapáry (Antál) and a Sigray, along with the father of the first post-Communist Prime Minister, Antall, who had done much for Polish refugees, including Jewish ones, and even old Gusztáv Gratz (1875–1946), who had been involved in the counter-revolutionaries' doings in Vienna in 1919, and who wrote a classic on the whole period of Dualism. The former Minister of the Interior, Keresztes-Fischer, who had upheld the rule of law, was caught; many others, including Bethlen, went into hiding.

The Allies by now knew what 'the Final Solution' involved, and protests came thick and fast to Horthy, from within and without. The Pope, the nuncio in Budapest, the King of Sweden, the BBC all spoke out; Roosevelt threatened to bomb Budapest (and a British air raid had occurred on 3 April 1944). Bethlen had written to Horthy from his hiding place in the country: 'all Christian Hungary will soon be irreversibly contaminated.' The churches, though primarily concerned with the fate of converts, denounced the whole business, and the Cardinal-Archbishop said he would publicly denounce the deportations unless Horthy stopped them; in Kolozsvár and Szombathely sermons were delivered against them, and

Catholic bishops concealed Jews (although there were also here and there some stupid anti-Semitic clergymen). Horthy was very uncomfortable with what was happening, had told Baky that many of the Jews were just as good Hungarians as he and Baky were,[11] and had only stayed on to prevent worse. On 26 June a Crown Council did decide to halt the process, and the main organisers, the Minister of the Interior (Jaross) and his two secretaries of state, Endre and Baky, were dismissed. Horthy now moved loyal troops to Budapest to prevent deportations, and the last train reached Auschwitz in mid-July.

A new government was sworn in, under a general, Géza Lakatos. The Jews had a breathing space, and some left the ghetto, while neutral diplomats began giving out documents. By now the Third Reich was clearly collapsing. Paris was liberated on 24 August, and Rumania dropped out of the war in a well-managed coup (the young king managed to imprison the Fascist dictator Ion Anton-escu in his stamp collection room) on 25 August; Finland followed, both countries declaring war on Germany. The question for Hungary was now of armistice with the Russians, and though the cabinet unanimously opposed any direct approach to the Soviets, contacts with the Slovak resistance (through a Count Zichy) and with the Soviet military ensured that a delegation could go to Moscow over the lines, arriving on 1 October with a letter to Stalin from Horthy. The terms were uncompromising, as the Red Army had already taken Transylvania and was threatening Debrecen and Szeged in Trianon Hungary. On 11 October the armistice was indeed signed, and Horthy was persuaded to receive two stalwarts of the opposition, Zoltán Tildy of the Smallholders and Árpád Szakasits of the Social Democrats, to tell them what was impending. But it was all bungled: Horthy suddenly put off the armistice announcement, and no preparations had been made; the Germans knew what was going on, and sent their special operations expert, Otto Skorzeny (who had rescued Mussolini after his fall in July 1943), to Budapest. With a ruse, he kidnapped Horthy's surviving son on 15 October. The proclamation of armistice was then read out on the radio, but many officers were outraged at the news, and Veesenmayer persuaded the Hungarian commander even to countermand Horthy's order. By the evening all stations and the radio were in German or Arrow Cross hands, and at 5.30 a.m. on 16 October Veesenmayer came to the Castle to take Horthy and the others to Gestapo headquarters in the Hatvany Palace in Buda. There he abdicated, forced by threats to his son to give Szálasi authority to form a government. Their surviving son, Nicky Horthy, was kept in Mauthausen and Dachau, and Horthy himself was taken by train to Bavaria; he was not subsequently sought as a war criminal, as Stalin had noted his effort to get out of the war, and he left in 1948 for Portugal, where he died, aged ninety, in 1957.

There followed a mad episode. Szálasi preposterously insisted on a legitimate installation as Nemzetvezető (Leader of the Nation) and head of state. With full ceremonial, holy crown, guards in traditional garb and, no doubt, the growling of Soviet artillery in the background, he took the oath, and needed a quorum in Parliament to go through the performance. He had to have even opposition deputies present: a Count Pálffy, who was utterly opposed and who was in hiding, was promised safety provided he was present as a Member. The oath was duly sworn and a cabinet assembled – generally men of the right, whom the Germans trusted more than they did Szálasi. Another Count Pálffy, who unlike the rest of his family and almost all of the rest of his class had adopted a variant of Nazism, became, of all things, Minister of Agriculture and is credited with inventive schemes of horse-breeding.[12] The oddest adhesion came from a Dr Baron Gábor Kemény, who accepted the Foreign Ministry. There is an extreme mystery as to this. He was an educated man, from a Transylvanian family that had links on both sides, through Protestant connections, with the British royal family (the Queen descends from a Transylvanian family called Rhédey, which was grand enough to marry into Württemberg) and published a book in 1943 on a very thoughtful observer of the turn-of-the-century Sub-Carpathian problem, Miklós Bartha. He even had an Austrian Jewish wife, Elisabeth Fuchs. Kemény's ambition was to gain recognition from neutral states such as Spain and Sweden, and black farce in the Céline class duly followed. (In March 1945, by this time well and truly on the run, he signed a treaty in Zagreb with his Croatian counterpart concerning mutual respect for each other's minority.) Otherwise Szálasi's cabinet contained men of the 1930s' right, Imrédy and Reményi-Schneller, and again it is a mystery why they did not just use their brains. All were to be publicly executed in 1946, some hanged from lampposts in the Oktogon. On Christmas Eve the Red Army had Budapest surrounded, but Dr Baron Kemény got out just before.

But in these two months there was a paroxysm of horror in the city. As soon as the Arrow Cross were installed, the German extermination machinery rolled in. Eichmann had even been fanatical enough at this stage – 13 September – to travel to Arad and the Rumanian part of Transylvania, which the Hungarians briefly occupied, and impose the anti-Jewish laws. Seventy thousand Jews were herded into the main ghetto, which ran between the two boulevard rings, claustrophobic streets clustered near the Great Synagogue on Dohány utca, between Király utca and Rákóczi út. Its centre was Klauzál tér, and the whole area is still recognisable for what it was (not least because of the many Hebrew signs, since every year people return from Israel). There were also 'Jewish houses', marked with a yellow star, dotted around the city, and there was a smaller 'international ghetto' concentrated on the Danube embankment facing the Pest side of the Margaret Island. This contained, and was supposed to save, Jews who had foreign papers. Many thousands of Jews were hidden by Christians, and others had false papers, but the Arrow Cross were vicious.

Violent anti-Semitic propaganda issued from the radio, inciting pogroms. Thousands of Jews were marched off to Germany, allegedly to labour camps there; on the march, in winter conditions, there were many deaths. From early November 2,000 Jews were driven to march 200 kilometres to Hegyeshalom, with only a thin soup, and handed over to the Germans. When the siege began, the Arrow Cross were still murdering about fifty Jews every night, and in early January three Jewish hospitals were ransacked: 17,000 Jews were killed in this period. Just before the Red Army arrived, the militia had picked up children in the Jewish orphanages in Pest and Buda and were deterred from shooting them only because they themselves now had to flee.[13] In this period some foreign diplomats acted splendidly, abandoning their rule books. Carl Lutz, the deputy Swiss consul-general, represented the interests of fifteen states at war with Hungary, and the Swiss Legation in Stefánia út, with its Red Cross connections, supplied food and papers to thousands of Jews, using the 'glass house' on Vadász utca as a base to help people in the International ghetto, which was close by. The Swede Raoul Wallenberg made a great name for himself, hauling people from the columns marching towards Hegyeshalom on the border; the nuncio did his best, and so did an extraordinary Italian former Fascist, Giorgio Perlasca, who passed himself off as a Spaniard and issued passports from the now emptied Spanish embassy. False papers were quite easily obtained, and since the Arrow Cross were stupid and usually drunken, they could pass muster. Even Szálasi told the Germans he must respect these documents, as he wanted above all foreign recognition and anyway wanted to take Jewish property for himself. And above all, unlike the case of the Warsaw ghetto, there was audibly, in the sense of gunfire, hope. But the costs were enormous. A calculation of 1946 showed that 70,000 had survived in the ghetto and another 25,000 in protected houses, 25,000 by hiding, and another 11,000 from labour service. Fifty thousand returned from deportation. These figures were based on religion, and of course many Jews had by this time not registered as such. Figures later supplied by Tamás Stark are higher for survivors. About a third of the Budapest Jews had died or were killed, and roughly half of the Jews in Trianon Hungary.

On 27 December Budapest was encircled, although tens of

thousands of able-bodied males had left before then. Szálasi absurdly supposed that he should send all Hungarian males between fourteen and seventy to serve and leave, but many just ignored the order. Huge amounts of food and machinery were in fact taken to Germany after 15 October by river barge or 2,000 trains. The Soviet Marshal Tolbukhin (Third Ukrainian Army Group) reached Buda on Christmas Eve from the River Sava to the south, and two days later the encirclement was complete. The Arrow Cross left for Kőszeg (the Somssich villa, via a lunch with Archduke József in Alcsúth on the way, as he wanted to get his wine cellar out) and settled in Austria until the Americans arrested them. They had taken the crown. And now Budapest was encircled.

The siege was one of the great battles of the Second World War, comparable almost to Stalingrad. The German commander, Karl Pfeffer-Wildenbruch, had an impossible task: he had 100,000 troops, half of them Hungarian, but was short of food and ammunition, against a Red Army that had now become a formidable machine, mobile because of American jeeps and lorries, and with inexhaustible ammunition to be fired from sturdy weaponry. He handled his Hungarian allies very clumsily, despising them, even though the Hungarian commander, Hindy, had betrayed Horthy in order to stay loyal to the German cause. German communications ran across the Danube bridges, vulnerable to air attack, and the Luftwaffe was now almost useless – jet planes were pulled onto the air strip at Munich airport by oxen to save petrol. Gliders flew in supplies, but they were vulnerable and inaccurate. It was a hopeless battle from the start, and Hitler had only insisted on it out of a vague hope that the Allies would fall apart. As things turned out, the siege lasted until 13 February 1945. Pest itself was cleared by 18 January, but then there were artillery exchanges across the river, between the Castle, where the Germans were concentrated, and the Pest embankment, with its grand hotels. (The Ritz and the Hungaria were destroyed.) Then the encirclement of Buda tightened; there was a final battle on Széll Kálmán square as the Germans attempted a breakout, and then a forlorn surrender. This was not a moment that endeared the Hungarians' cause to Stalin: they had proved to be Hitler's last allies, and the siege had cost the Red Army 80,000 dead. The bridges and the embankment were wrecked; the Castle was a near-ruin; 40,000 civilians died, and as many German and Hungarian soldiers; gliders, attempting to supply the Germans via a racetrack and a park, had crashed into the top storeys of buildings on the boulevards; there was ruin, pestilence and hunger. A new Hungarian provisional government arrived, as soon as water and electricity had been halfway restored and the streets cleared of the dead animals and the human corpses. Its master was the Red Army Marshal, Tolbukhin.

# CHAPTER 6

# Communist Take-Over

O n 21 December 1944 a 'Hungarian Independence Front' was set up under Soviet patronage. There were echoes of Hungarian rebellions of the past: it met in Rákóczi territory, and moreover in the Calvinist College at Debrecen, where in 1849 Kossuth had dethroned the Habsburgs. Hungarian Communists arrived from Moscow and teamed up with Social Democrats, agrarian reformers and progressive figures from Horthy's Hungary – a general, and even Count Pál Teleki's son Géza. The Communists played nationalist tunes, and consorted with Calvinist clergymen who no doubt regarded the catastrophe as a judgement of Heaven on the foreign-inspired corruption that had hit the land.

By now the Communists had learned much about taking over other people's countries. It had been a slow learning curve. To start with, in the early 1920s, the Comintern, the international revolutionary movement based in Moscow, had got it wrong, and Béla Kun himself bore some of the responsibility for this. In Germany he provoked the police and the army but did not have solid support from the trade unions, and so revolution was therefore shrieking fanatics, middle-aged men in raincoats reading long words in a downpour, and thugs. The party got nowhere and in 1923 even provoked Hitler to stage a *putsch* (from the failure of which he also learned much). Communist tactics in China were a disaster, with the near-destruction of the Shanghai Party, and the greatest disaster of all occurred in Prussia in 1932, when the Party joined with the Nazis in destabilising the last decent government there, a coalition of Social Democrats, Catholics and left-wing liberals. Once the Communist leaders found themselves in concentration camps or exile, they gradually came to see that they had made a mistake. In 1934 the Comintern embarked on a new policy, that of a 'Popular Front', and made overtures to precisely the sort of people whom they had refused to support in Prussia.

The testing-ground was Spain. Here was a country quite similar to those of central-eastern Europe that the Red Army was now overrunning: many peasants, Catholics, patches of backwardness and modernity, and complications with minorities, such as Catalans and Basques. Religion divided the country, in that one half blamed it and the other half blamed the lack of it for the nation's woes. In 1936 a civil war had broken out when a progressive's nightmare blew up, as army generals, backed by the Church, and with Moroccan (Moorish) mercenaries in tow, rose against a Popular Front government, launching a war that lasted for three years and killed 500,000 (with another 500,000 going into exile). There was international involvement, in that Mussolini and Hitler supported the rebellion and the Soviet Union the government side, while the western Powers tried to avoid intervention at all. The Communists had learned from previous failures, and now joined the Popular Front. They made common cause, for progressive purposes, with the moderate socialists and the middle-class liberals, not winning many votes but securing posts of influence in the trade unions and the army. The Foreign Minister, Álvarez del Vayo, was a Soviet agent, and Moscow had a control in any event because the Republic depended on Soviet weaponry. International Brigades were formed, consisting of volunteers, and these were under Communist control.[1]

Stalin's aim was not necessarily for the Republic to win: he had learned how to play international politics, to drop revolution where required. He wanted the Civil War to go on, because it divided Germany and Italy from France and Great Britain, thus preventing the formation of an anti-Soviet coalition. At the same time, using fellow-travellers in the western intelligentsia – Arthur Koestler was for a time a case in point – he fostered a myth proposing the Soviet Union as the only true anti-Fascist power. The Comintern was portrayed as enlightened, and a huge propaganda campaign was orchestrated by Willy Münzenberg, an impresario-publisher of genius who could charm or buy great cultural figures to give the Comintern unwitting or semi-witting support. Arms arrived when the Republicans were losing, and stopped when they were winning. There was a side-effect. There were on the Republican side genuine revolutionaries, who seized land, proclaimed equality and persecuted the clergy. These formed the POUM, or Workers' Party of Marxist Unification, based in Catalonia. The POUM made itself unpopular with the Catalan middle classes, partly because it was violently anticlerical and partly because it put up notices outside its quarter of Barcelona reading, 'Catalan is not spoken here'. But the Communists had already worked out that they could use minority nationalism, and Stalin had even been the Party's main theoretician of the subject.[2]

In May–June 1937 a civil war broke out within the civil war, when the POUM were bloodily put down by the Communists because they got in the way of Stalin's foreign policy. George Orwell, who was present, wrote about it in *Homage to Catalonia*, and had good experience of the Communist influence even in Britain when he tried to publish articles on the subject. By 1938 the Communists in effect ran the Republican side but were very careful to operate from behind the scenes, not bothering much with elections and speech-making, for they understood, now, that the important things were the media, the trade unions, the army and the police. The party schools taught men and women how to deal with such things – talk soft soap to feminists and minorities, infiltrate your men into trade unions, organise platforms of sympathisers with grand cultural names, such as Thomas Mann or Romain Rolland, and control the media, especially film, the importance of which they appreciated. As Vladimir Bukovsky observes, you can watch the entire output of Hollywood and have no idea what the twentieth century was all about. It was even possible to identify Catholic priests whose social radicalism would make them useful allies. (A Mgr Plojhar in the post-war Czechoslovak government played a key part in the Communist takeover.) Some of the Comintern's brightest men and women were involved in Spain. There was Tito, soon to be boss of Yugoslavia, and from Hungary came Ernő Gerő, László Rajk and Mihály Farkas. They now flew back in Soviet aircraft in time for the Debrecen assembly, their takeover toolkit at the ready.

Gerő had been born Móric Singer in 1898, the son of a bank clerk; he went to school in a working-class district, Újpest, and then started medical school. But in 1919 he joined up with Béla Kun and worked in the youth apparatus; he escaped to the west and a Comintern life followed. Gerő was used for various clandestine missions, picking up languages along the way, was arrested and sentenced in Hungary to fifteen years, but was released after two, in 1924, after which he went to the Soviet Union and became an agent of the political-police NKVD, reporting on fellow Hungarians. Somehow he made himself trusted (as did Tito and Imre Nagy) and was used in Spain, where his ruthlessness in putting down the POUM earned him the name 'the butcher of Barcelona'. It was characteristic of his understanding of the western media that he trained one Dolores Ibárruri, a Basque Communist whom he successfully groomed to be a sort of Joan of Arc, all bosom-heaving passion. (She ended up in the Soviet Union, and her granddaughter became interpreter for the King of Spain.) Gerő had a cutting intelligence, was a formidable linguist (after his forced retirement he made a living as translator) and could play the foreign gallery.

He came back to Hungary with others who had a similar background. The chief was Mátyás Rákosi, again of an ardently repudiated and poor Jewish background (he was born Rosenfeld) and again a formidable linguist. Mátyás Rákosi came from Moscow in February 1945. He was then fifty-three, the many-siblinged son of a village shopkeeper, was a clever schoolboy in Budapest and got a scholarship to study in Hamburg, after which he worked in London for a year as a clerk. He was captured on the eastern front in 1915 and came out in 1918 a fluent Russian-speaker and convinced Communist. He fled to Vienna with Béla Kun, having had a junior post with him, and went on to Moscow. In 1925 he was arrested in Hungary as a Comintern agent, but was re-sentenced by the Gömbös government and only released in 1940 in partial exchange for the 1849 battle standards. He was very sharp, had an excellent memory and could use his charm, but at bottom he was a bullying sadist, and hideous-dwarfish besides. Another in the group was József Révai (born Lederer), the chief ideologist and wordsmith. He had worked on the Moscow Hungarian radio, and was involved with the intelligentsia, particularly György Lukács, a polymathic philosopher of Marxist disposition who carried weight in the west, particularly in France. Révai was to edit the party newspaper, and to run cultural matters generally. All of them had Russian (in Rákosi's case, Yakut) wives, and Gerő was obviously the Soviets' principal agent.

On a much lower level there was Vladimir Farkas, who wrote memoirs of much frankness.[3] He was born in poverty in northeastern Hungary (now Slovakia), to parents who fell out quickly enough: his father, Mihály (originally Löwy), abandoned his wife, who tried to kill herself and the baby by jumping into a river. Then she left, and he was brought up by his grandmother, a washerwoman who lived in a basement. His father meanwhile acted as a Communist agent in Czechoslovakia and spent four years in prison. (His mother used to bake for him there his favourite cake, called *Linzer karikak*, a plum and chocolate concoction.) Then he went to Moscow, to work in the Comintern and marry a German woman; he too was involved in Spanish doings. In 1938, when

Czechoslovakia was falling apart, he sent for his son, who crossed the Soviet border to find that the customs men even cut open his apple in case anything had been hidden in it. The Comintern people had apartments in a sinister building, the Hotel Lux, a mile or so from the Kremlin, and there the father lived with his new family. Everyone spied on everyone, and the NKVD came to arrest people in the middle of the night; it was best not to answer the common telephone and there was a check on who went in and out. Vladimir complains that his father neglected him, never taking him to museums or the cinema, as other fathers did with their sons. In 1941, when the Nazis reached the outskirts of Moscow, the father joined a flight of the Comintern families. With suitcases they got into the lift, Vladimir being last. His father pressed the button before he could get in, and then left with the bus to the station before the boy could get down the stairs. He saw it drive off. Then he went to the station and travelled for a week to Samara (Kuybishev) in the company of a hideous woman, Erzsébet Andics, who kept him going with tins of sardines. (She was later a war-horse historian.) He attended a party school – bare floorboards, pseudonyms, endless Marxist lectures, no sex, no alcohol – and flew back to Budapest, where he joined his father, now head of the security police. He is frank about the snooping and the brutality, and of course the Soviet representatives were all-powerful.

There were also home-grown Communists, though not many. In October, in Budapest, a pact between the Communists and Social Democrats had been made, for a post-war merger, and on 20 November a clandestine agreement had been struck between László Rajk, for the Communists, and Endre Bajcsy-Zsilinszky, for the liberals and the farmers' party, although Bajcsy-Zsilinszky was betrayed, hunted down and shot. This was the nucleus of a Soviet administration.[4]

On 21 December 1944, in that Calvinist College at Debrecen, 230 delegates assembled, a third of them Communist, from villages and townships liberated by the Red Army, and they elected a new government from all the anti-Fascist parties. Its programme included land reform and confiscation for war criminals, but it was also carefully constructed with the western Allies in mind. To some Communists' disappointment, it made no reference to the dictatorship of the proletariat. It also upheld 'the inviolability of private property', and it used patriotic language, with references to Kossuth and 1848 all around. This was standard Popular Front stuff, accepted by a great many people who were far from being Communist. There was, as in Poland, much grief about what had happened, and a widespread consciousness that old Hungary had reached the end of the story (the same appears with Czesław Miłosz's *Captive Mind*) and the great historian Gyula Szekfű, conservative by disposition but soon to be ambassador in Moscow, wrote that 'a line, a long historical line, had reached the end, ingloriously, shamefully, or if you prefer in a grotesque bloody black farce'.[5] An armistice agreement was signed in Moscow on 20 January 1945. The terms were harsh and promised reparations for Czechoslovakia and Yugoslavia as well as the Soviet Union. The Allies had agreed that, in occupied enemy countries, an Allied Control Commission would be set up, chaired by a nominee of the principal occupying Power (or, in Austria and Germany, with other, shared arrangements). The chairmanship was all-important, since it could decide on the agenda and designate action to be taken, if any. In the west and subsequently in Japan, Soviet representation became just a formal matter, and so it was to be in central-eastern Europe for the western Allies. The Control Commission was set up under the Soviet Marshal Voroshilov, and he had the provisional government at his mercy. It lacked everything: only the Communists had an apparatus, and through it Imre Nagy, who knew something about agriculture, put through a radical land reform. This all occurred against a background of chaos.

Budapest and the country as a whole had to be brought back to life after the two-month siege, with only a pontoon bridge (in place of today's Szabadság Híd, linking the Hotel Gellért with the Csarnok, or main market). The Germans, departing, had taken

214,000 tons of goods, including machinery and food, by barge or railway (32,000 waggons) or lorry (8,000 loads); 70,000 dwellings had been destroyed, and a quarter of the inhabitants were homeless. A million Hungarians had fled with the Germans, civilians and soldiers, and a gold train had taken away the valuables stolen, mainly from Jewish families. (The property stolen from Jewish families and others, and the gold reserve of the National Bank, ended up in mining shafts in Austria.) The Holy Crown of King Saint Stephen I and the crown jewels were also transported west, and later revealed to the Americans. These artefacts were only brought back in 1978, as an acknowledgement of the status quo. The Soviet government was not inclined to forget the desperate resistance that the Red Army faced; as in Berlin, there was an orgy of revenge rape.

Meanwhile there was the matter of Hungarians in Soviet captivity. Apart from prisoners of war, hundreds of thousands were interned in detention centres, the Communists playing a shabby collaborationist part. The civilians who were taken into captivity were made up of different groups. First, there were the Germans – Swabians – who were collectively ordered to work in the Soviet Union. Many did not even speak German, and quotas were filled up with anybody from the street. Secondly, there were ordinary citizens – 100,000 from Budapest alone – who were counted as POWs to give substance to Soviet generals' boasting reports. Thirdly, there were political prisoners (thousands, or even tens of thousands) who were condemned by a special jury in farcical proceedings. They were sent to the gulag, after enduring detention centres and transport by train and ship. Their destinations amounted to death-camps, as dysentery and typhoid fever took their toll.

Deportation of Hungarians to the USSR struck hard in Carpatho-Ruthenia (the Subcarpathian Ukraine), Eastern Slovakia and Northern Transylvania as well. The Soviets admitted that 550,000 Hungarian prisoners reached military-camp destinations in the Soviet Union, and there were also several thousand more in the civilian gulag system as well. Only half of them came back.

Altogether, 900,000 lives had been lost, of which some 500,000 were Jewish.[6] Half of the industrial plant, the railways, the bridges, the livestock, had gone.[7] There was not much help. United Nations parcels did arrive, as in Germany, and the international Jewish organisation, the Joint Distribution Committee, also helped with soup kitchens, but Hungary could not get the official American help that went to countries in the western sphere of influence. And a decisive problem, in what followed, was that Hungary was isolated. At the Yalta conference early in February, no one had spoken up for her. In October 1944, just as Horthy's effort to get out of the war was falling through, Churchill happened to be in Moscow, trying to negotiate terms for Polish–Soviet reconciliation. There was really no hope that Stalin would give up control of Poland, where he distrusted (and earlier had had shot) even the Communists. Churchill, without American support, had a weak hand and gave way, and in return for face-saving devices – the appointment of non-Communist ministers to unimportant posts – he would reluctantly recognise the Soviet-nominated Polish government. In return, he drew up a bargain with Stalin. The essential was that Great Britain would have 90 per cent of the influence over Greece, where the Communist resistance movement might easily have taken over (a civil war went on until 1949), while Stalin could in effect keep the Balkans. Greece and the eastern Mediterranean were a vital British interest, as had been the case in the Crimean War. Hungary was supposed to be shared out, and the British did acquire an enormous embassy, a former bank, in central Budapest. (It did serve its purpose in the 1980s, but has now been given up, partly for reasons of security, and mainly because its upkeep was expensive.) But the expectation that Great Britain would have '50 per cent' influence in Hungary was soon shown to be far-fetched. The Allied Control Council (with offices in Aradi utca, just off the Grand Boulevard) was almost powerless if the Soviet chairman decided that that should be the case. Meanwhile, as far as the future was concerned, a peace treaty would have to be signed. The technical aspects of this took time (until January 1947) to sort out, and meanwhile Hungarians could only hope that the Soviet Union would help as regards the frontiers. Was it possible to retain at least some of the gains of the Vienna Awards of 1938 and 1940?

For a time, that hope held. Many Hungarians of the upper classes did not bother to leave the country. Life as a refugee in Germany was very hard: better stay on, even in a corner of the old manor house, with the chance of rebuilding things, than risk that kind of misery. They expected that at some stage the Red Army would withdraw, and that proper democracy would follow. At this stage of the Cold War the Soviet Union retained the forms of democracy for countries such as Austria, Czechoslovakia, Finland and Hungary. At stake here was the strong possibility that France and Italy (and even Belgium) might go Communist, as the party there was very strong; and Stalin needed support at the new United Nations, where France sat on the Security Council. The biggest prize by far was Germany, and there were even free elections in the Soviet zone, earlier than in the future West Germany. Poland saw no such thing, as Stalin knew perfectly well that free elections there would be a disaster, that a strongly anti-Soviet government would result, and he already regarded Rumania and Bulgaria as his, as part of the bargain with Churchill over Greece. But in Czechoslovakia and Hungary he was careful to keep to the forms. This involved a Popular Front government, all the 'anti-Fascists' included. Besides, there were very few Communists on the ground in Hungary, and the party would have to be created. There were exiles in Moscow who could do this. Gerő was a considerable specialist, but meanwhile the returned Communists were ordered to appear moderate and patriotic, and told that they would have to wait at least ten years for a proper Communist state. An instruction in November 1944 enjoined leaders to keep out of the limelight and to get other parties to do what they wanted. Hence their moderation in Debrecen. The works of Lenin and Stalin were not published in Hungarian; even the phrase 'dictatorship of the proletariat' was not used.

But the Communists could extend their influence, as they did in Czechoslovakia and Poland, through the land reform that had been proclaimed.[8] If peasants wanted land, they would have to get it via the party. In Hungary, by now, almost everyone agreed on land reform; all estates over 1,500 acres were expropriated, while owners of less than that could keep 150 acres if they were landowners in the traditional sense, 300 if they were peasants and 450 if they had been anti-Fascists. Committees dominated by Communists and the National Peasants' Party people carried out the redistribution, usually with political considerations foremost, and within three months 8 million acres had been taken over, some for state farms but the greater part (5 million acres) given to 500,000 new owners, whose votes would no doubt go to the Communists or their rural allies in the National Peasants' Party. The Catholic Church lost 90 per cent of its lands, and 'feudalism' was eliminated. There was therefore much patronage available in Communist hands, and the party looked forward to the municipal and general elections scheduled for October and November. It made an electoral pact with the Social Democrats, expecting to take the working-class districts of Budapest – Csepel, Angyalföld, Újpest, Kőbánya – and it recruited energetically, counting 500,000 members by October. Some of these were former Arrow Cross men, small fry who, quite successfully, escaped prosecution. To a protesting letter from a Jew, Mátyás Rákosi just said that the party needed to build up a good base among the lower classes. But for the moment, patriotism, anti-Fascism and Popular Front were the watchwords.

Other Communists had stayed in Hungary, and had different experiences – prison, clandestinity, non-Jewishness. László Rajk (of Transylvanian German origin) was a student Communist, fomenting builders' strikes, and a veteran of the Spanish Civil War, where he had been political secretary of the Hungarian battalion of the International Brigade. Two of his brothers were Arrow Cross men, and one of them, with some authority in the Arrow Cross government, allegedly spared his life (as Rajk did for him, later). Others of this home-grown type were János Kádár, Géza Losonczy and Ferenc Donáth, all of them working-class, and all to be prominent later on. Kádár, the illegitimate son of a Slovak serving-girl, by a soldier who would not marry her, grew up in poverty, no doubt hating his father's family. Such Communists did not, any more than the Greek Communists, understand Stalin's instructions about refraining from immediate revolution, and Révai had to tell them that the Americans and British would not recognise a Communist government. Gerő also told them that socialism could not be constructed on 'the rubble of defeat'. With Voroshilov's backing, the Communists nevertheless took essential posts. One was the Ministry of the Interior, which went to Ferenc Erdei, leader of the (left-wing) National Peasants' Party and a strong Communist sympathiser. He now controlled the police and created a secret security police force, the Államvédelmi Osztály, or ÁVO. Its headquarters were in the old offices of the Arrow Cross, at 60 Andrássy Avenue, which had once belonged to the Perlmutter family and had been rented, as headquarters, by the Arrow Cross itself (it was known as 'Loyalty House').[9] Its new chief was one Gábor Péter, a torturer, and its initial purpose was to track down war criminals, but it also terrorised Communist opponents, reading letters and listening in on telephone calls. Vladimir Farkas describes how he opened post and listened to recordings of telephone calls. One of the first victims was one Pál Demény, not only a Communist, but one who had arranged forged documents for Gábor Péter when he was in hiding. His crime was to be popular among the workers, as a home-grown rather than Muscovite Communist. People's Courts were set up, issuing severe sentences, including the death penalty for Szálasi, Bárdossy, Imrédy, Sztójay and Baky, who claimed that he had had no idea that the death camps were death camps. Baron Kemény, the Arrow Cross foreign minister, was also condemned, although he could make a plausible claim that he had helped Wallenberg save Jews. The trial was staged in the Music Academy's concert hall.[10] Some were hanged from lampposts on the Oktogon square on the Grand

Boulevard in January 1946, but before being executed they were taken round the ruins of Budapest and shown the disinterred bodies of patients who had been murdered in the Jewish hospital. The People's Courts were arbitrary, and 25,000 people were sentenced as war criminals, with 500 executions, and there were 40,000 further prosecutions.[11] Rajk, as the new Minister of the Interior, purged 50,000 officials, who were condemned at public meetings, and there was nothing that even the non-Communist Prime Minister, Ferenc Nagy, could do.

The Communists were confident that, well organised and capable of delivering food to the capital, they would win the elections, and they even brought famine to their own country in order to export grain. Stalin made a similar mistake in the Soviet zone of Germany: he assumed that the display, in the Second World War, of Soviet strength would convince even Germans to take up the Soviet model. But as Rákosi wrote to Dimitrov, who ran the successor of Comintern, 'the excesses of the Red Army have become the Party's liability [...] mass rape and robbery repeated as each region is liberated [...] Raids are routine, in which workers are taken to camps where they disappear.' Besides, Soviet officials were busy dismantling whole factories as 'reparations'. In a true free election the Communists would not flourish. Finally Cardinal József Mindszenty, a man of cussed courage, fulminated against 'violence and oppression'. In the Budapest municipal elections the Smallholder Party won 121 seats, eighteen more than the Communists and their Social Democrat allies. This happened again nationally in November, where the Smallholders had 57 per cent of the vote and 245 seats, to the Communists' 70 and the (now again separate) Social Democrats' 69. The National Peasants' Party (a Communist front) took 23 seats.

This was a blow to the Soviets, but they had their answer. Voroshilov insisted that the coalition government must go on, and although some adherents wanted to form a purely Smallholder government, Zoltán Tildy and Ferenc Nagy, the chiefs, did not want to oppose the Soviets directly, and were hoping that in return they would have easier terms in the peace treaty to come. Tildy was a Calvinist pastor, and Nagy, from a peasant family, had broken away from Bethlen in 1930, opposed the right-wing governments of the 1930s, had been arrested by the Gestapo, worked underground after their release in October and then joined the Debrecen coalition. But they assumed that the Red Army would withdraw after the peace treaty had been signed, and supposed that good behaviour might result in a milder treaty – an illusion that the Communists fomented. It was not dispelled until early in 1947.

Meanwhile there were problems all around. A process of ethnic cleansing was going ahead, hitting Hungarians. In summer 1945 President Beneš in Prague had decreed savagely against the Hungarians (whom he seems to have hated, even in 1915). Their part in Hitler's dismemberment of Czechoslovakia was not forgotten, and Hungarian rule over the Slovakian areas awarded to Hungary in 1938 had not, of course, been popular with the Slovaks. Beneš now dismissed all state employees without a pension, confiscated property over 100 acres (including the estate of a Count János Esterházy, who had been the only member of the Slovak assembly to vote against anti-Semitic laws) and banned the Hungarian language in any official context. Tens of thousands of Hungarians were expelled, reaching Budapest penniless. In Yugoslavia, a cruel vendetta was carried out by the Communist partisans, on Germans, Italians and Albanians by nationality, and South Slavs by ideology. Around 15–20,000 Hungarians were put to death, sometimes in atrocious circumstances. In Transylvania, the Soviet authorities stopped the Rumanian militias' ethnic cleansing and re-introduced military administration. Ferenc Nagy visited Allied capitals to protest, but it made no difference; and in any case Hungary herself was expelling about 250,000 native Germans, the Swabians, and in fact two-thirds of the total, although they were well on their way to assimilation. (You can see this from the number of German names in Budapest.)

The Hungarians pleaded for a moderate peace treaty, and used old Károlyi as ambassador in Paris. He and his wife, the 'Red Countess', had spent decades in sometimes hard-up exile, could talk to the left and, of course, knew foreign languages. But the other Hungarians' rhetorical style – earnest, lengthy and self-righteous – did not go down well, and the world had lost patience with minority problems. In any case, in Stalin's eyes the Hungarians had been Hitler's last allies. Some people – Domokos Szent-Iványi in the Foreign Ministry, for instance – had seen this coming, but Horthy had not taken the necessary steps in time. There were also men in the State Department who drew up borderlines that were less absurd than those of Trianon, but the Russians were effectively in charge, and they rewarded Rumanians and Czechs. On 10 February 1947 the Foreign Minister, János Gyöngyösi, had to sign a peace treaty in Paris which just confirmed the Trianon borders, with the casual insult that three Hungarian villages opposite Bratislava on a Danube island were annexed by Czechoslovakia. Besides, the Red Army, although in theory withdrawn, was allowed to continue the occupation, allegedly to secure its communications with its zone in Austria. And it had authority to make provisions for its own security, and these could be very widely interpreted. The knock on the door at 3 a.m. would frequently be heard, and informants were all around.

There was also an immense problem with money.[12] The government had no real financial control, and the Soviets were making off not just with industrial machinery but with food as well, since Hungary was required to maintain the large occupying army. Reparations to neighbours were impending, and middle classes with an income to tax, especially the Jews, hardly existed as such. The gold reserve was in Austrian mine shafts. Money was therefore just printed, with predictable effects. This time Hungary produced another world record, for the number of zeros on the notes. When a new currency, the forint, replaced the pengő in August 1946, it was worth $4.6 \times 10$ to the power of 23. Wages went down to a tenth of the level in 1939, and half that even of 1945; barter prevailed, and there was even a sort of official exchange list: a bag of first-class coal cost 14 kg of flour or a litre of cooking oil or 1½ kg of poultry.[13] In 1946 the poet György Faludy was paid 3 trillion pengő for a reprinted work and raced to the market to change it into a chicken, a bottle of olive oil and some vegetables. Inflation of this type is the great engine for radicalisation. There is a good rule: if a country produces 2,000 of its currency on a note, go there, because with a foreign passport you can see the standard minor virtues – thrift, sobriety, chastity etc. – going: the story of post-war Italy or France, beloved of Americans. If it produces 100,000, leave: there will be blood on the streets. People will be so busy just struggling to find food and fuel that they will not have the energy for resistance, as Lenin found in 1918, when he tamed conservative Moscow. Then again, the working people could be brought around by a party that could deliver the basics, and the trade unions were quite soon taken over by it: many Social Democrats followed Árpád Szakasits and György Marosán (later a senior figure, in both the Party and the government, under Kádár) in falling into line. A Supreme Economic Council took major decision-making out of government hands, with Communist nominees, and the Soviets were in vengeful, confiscatory mode. With various devices, from April 1946, they extracted over \$1,000 million up to 1954,[14] quite apart from the forced labour sent to Russia.

It was all too easy to persuade people that 'the rich' were to blame for it all: no doubt black marketeers flourished, and there was no doubt either that people resented the money made by itinerant peasant dealers, but there were not very many 'rich' left in Hungary. Early in 1946, when the Communists brought out their troops, in tens of thousands, to demonstrate on the boulevards against the Smallholder right, it was an early display of what they poetically called 'the organised discontent of the masses'. If you were of the intelligentsia, underfed, longing for proper coffee and cigarettes, darning your socks in dim lighting, the temptation to fall in line was very strong. So it was with the working class, now the darling of the regime. The memoirs of the national poet, György Faludy, are eloquent on the point. Working in a publishing concern, he sees one after another of his colleagues slip off in a Communist direction, snooped on by the office bitch, who makes trouble over filing cabinets and the like. (His marriage broke up when his wife just nagged and nagged, until he walked out, though he had probably given her other reasons for nagging.[15]) Whom do you trust, outside a very narrow religious or social circle?

This was the backdrop to the Communists' infiltration of everything. They insisted on the Ministry of the Interior, with control of the police, and so could spy on or arrest anyone; the security side would make sure to extract confessions, while in other ministries there would be a deputy head in their hands. The Smallholders had already accepted the principle of a coalition government, so their leaders Zoltán Tildy and Ferenc Nagy gave way, becoming respectively President and Prime Minister, and a process of elections continued; on the surface, a proper state was now restored, with, on 1 February 1946, a new constitution, for a republic. The Communist László Rajk was Minister of the Interior.

Now, to understand what happened, Hungary's history has to be seen internationally. Stalin had allowed the British to take over Greece. The Communists there were powerful, having dominated the Resistance movement, and a civil war broke out in March 1946. Stalin gave no support at all, and just told the Communists to join a progressive government, as in France or Italy. Their emissaries in Moscow were received only by a junior official, and it was really only the megalomania of their leader, Nikos Zachariadis, a one-time Istanbul dock worker, that caused them to disobey instructions. By 1949 they had lost. Stalin's quid pro quo was, of course, influence in Hungary and elsewhere, but he had to go carefully, leaving the forms of democracy in existence: parliament, parties, press, law courts. Two obvious tactics could be used: first, the creation of a left bloc, the Communists in effect taking over the more popular Social Democrats; and second, a splitting of the opposition. If the west complained, answers had to be ready and pretexts prepared.

There were openings. The Smallholders had ceased to be a party of small farmers and had broad support from non-Communists. Inevitably there were tensions between Jews and non-Jews, including some intellectuals (as Ágnes Heller remembered in *Biciklizö majom*), and the Communists made a great parade of supposed anti-Semitism. Possibly 250,000 Jews (Tamás Stark's figure) had survived in various ways, most of them in the ghetto, from where black marketeers emerged. Inner-city Budapest – districts VI and VII – was heavily Jewish (35 and 40 per cent respectively) and was kept going by soup kitchens and the 'Joint', the international Jewish agency. Others emerged from hiding with friends, others in the safe houses. And others survived the camps. The results in 1945 were to be seen all around: the future historian György Ránki, a man to whose generosity of temperament many non-Communists were to owe much, emerged from Auschwitz as a fifteen-year-old, of skin and bone. There were fights over property, and some vicious revenge took place. A particularly gruesome case occurred at Gyömrő, a spa town with a castle east of Budapest.[16] Jews returning from labour service found that their families had vanished. They teamed up with veterans of 1919 and even some former Arrow Cross men, forming a local Communist Party. 150 people went missing, of whom 23 men were later identified after their bodies were found[17] by a swimmer in the lake, some of them sexually mutilated. The truly guilty men had probably all fled to Austria in time; these were at most some clerks who had registered deportations, with two clergymen, two 'cock-feather' gendarmes, a Count Révai who taught Classics, and the owner of the castle, a Count Coronini. They had not been accused at all when the People's Judges came round. There was a scandal, which reached parliament, but the case was suppressed as an almighty embarrassment. (It was not forgotten, and references were made to it after the end of Communism.) István Ries, a Minister of Justice and fellow-traveller Social Democrat, announced an amnesty for the perpetrators, but he was subsequently beaten death by Communists.

In 1946 the Party was led by a Jewish quadrumvirate, and six of the eleven members of the Politburo were Jewish, although they had changed their names, including Gerő (born Singer) and Farkas (born Löw), while Vas's father was a rabbi, Weinberger. This was also the case with the top elements of the ÁVO as well, where Jews made up 70 to 80 per cent of the higher elements in 1949, including the administrators of the chief political prison for women, where inmates' teeth fell out through starvation by a sadistic woman governor. The People's Courts, dishing out arbitrary justice, were advised by Jewish lawyers,[18] and sometimes the sentences were unjust. The populace in places rebelled, and, the background being the enormous inflation and black-marketeering, there were pogroms. Peasants in Ózd and, more ominously, workers in Miskolc rioted and lynched. In Kunmadaras on 20 May 1946 a riot broke out against the People's Judges and a Communist leader; two Jews were killed and fifteen wounded after a church ceremony. Bitterness, of course, grew. Fifty thousand Jews wanted to emigrate in 1945, and 35,000 did so; there were 20, 000 in Soviet captivity, and by 1948 there were between 150,000 and 200,000 left in Hungary. Their votes went half-and-half to the left-wing parties, and the Party had half of the vote in the heavily Jewish districts V, VI and VII in November 1945, otherwise flourishing only in the proletarian quarters of Angyalföld and Köbánya.

Anti-Semitism was of course disavowed, and governments said the right things (though there was never much of an attempt at property restitution), but there was an obvious problem. Prominent writers such as László Németh, Mihály Babits, Gyula Illyés and the historian Gyula Szekfű tried to suggest that there was a 'Magyar character' different from Armenians, Germans and Jews – more or less what Horthy had told Hitler in his saloon-bar way, that 'the Hungarian peasant is a gentleman', leaving money matters to these others. Even in 1945 a book on peasants resorted to an old trick and gave in parenthesis the Magyarised Jews' original names – for example, Lukács (Löwinger) – as well as referring to the non-Jewish Commissar of 1919, Sándor Garbai, as 'shabbos goy'. One commentator, István Bibó, attracted national attention when he said that Jews were indeed different and would have to choose accordingly. Bibó himself was progressive-democratic, had a good record and was very knowledgeable, but there were skeletons in his cupboard. His father-in-law was the Calvinist Superintendent (formally 'Bishop', by an odd Habsburg twist) László Ravasz, who voted for the first two anti-Jewish laws, although he opposed the later ones and was resolutely opposed to the deportations, and he had an uncle who, though half-Jewish, was with the 'Awakening Magyar' Pál Prónay, a one-time 'White terrorist' who at the age of seventy set up a recruiting stall at the Pest end of the Elisabeth Bridge to collect other old fools for the siege battles. Bibó said Jews were ethnically alien to peasants and fantasised as to how they stuck together.

Trying to make sense of it all was not easy, and though there have been very spirited efforts, the results are abstract, and in interviews conducted with individuals there is only a story that might have been expected: being a Jew was a nuisance, there was gratitude to the Soviets, Communism was a new identity, it was the wave of the future.[19] George Soros just went to the LSE and then west, to make money, and to this writer's knowledge has said nothing much on the subject of his origins. Besides, as time went by, the issue disappeared. The Communists, despite the origins of Rákosi et al., turned anti-Semitic. After 1948 the word 'Jew' disappeared from the press, almost nothing followed the 300 books on the Holocaust that had been published by then, would-be emigrants to Israel were prevented from leaving, like everyone else, and the religion was persecuted. In 1956 anti-Semitism was the dog that did not bark.

Still, in 1946 the Communists had various weapons to use if they wanted to demolish the democratic majority. At this time there was a great deal of loose talk, of resistance to the Communists. The atmosphere of the era is superbly shown in Boris Kálnoky's *Ahnen-land* (Munich, 2008), which centres on the story of the author's grandfather, Hugo, a Transylvanian nobleman whose career did not much prosper after his military service in the First World War. Eventually he settled as a journalist in Budapest and fondly imagined that he could be part of some Catholic regeneration of Hungary. In March 1944 an arrest warrant was issued for him by the Gestapo, but he managed to hide in the episcopal residence at Győr, where Bishop Apor went far out of his way to rescue anybody and everybody. (He helped to fake conversions of 100,000 Jews.) Hugo Kálnoky had a great row with his pregnant wife as to whether he should stay on in Budapest to fight the Communists, and he let her go to relative safety with relatives in Czechoslovakia. Then, with like-minded people, he talked, and asked Cardinal Mindszenty what he should do. Mindszenty had at first supported the idea of opposition, but said the Communists were worse than the Fascists, because they would stay longer.[20] It was easy enough for the state security to record such things. They netted a heroic figure, Domokos Szent-Iványi, who had been at the centre of opposition to the Nazis and now proposed the same for the Communists. He was arrested late in 1946 and sentenced to ten years' imprisonment.

In March 1946 Voroshilov arrested two deputies who had opposed the proclamation of a republic, and it was easy for the Communists to claim that 'reaction' was gathering under Smallholder protection and to set up a left-wing bloc, with the Social Democrats, the trade unions and the National Peasants' Party, which, with street demonstrations early in 1946, demanded the expulsion of another twenty Smallholder deputies as 'reactionaries'. The Smallholder government might have resisted, but the party was not united, and in any case could hardly resist the Soviet pressure or their own Minister of the Interior. Nagy meekly expelled them, and one of them, Dezső Sulyok, set up a new opposition party (the Freedom Party). The Smallholders also accepted a draconian penalty law against allegedly anti-republican propaganda. Rajk meanwhile, with ineffectual opposition from Nagy, got rid of 60,000 'right-wing elements' from the public service. Planted evidence near the scene of the murder of a Russian officer implicated the Catholic Youth Association, which was dissolved, and over the next few months the same happened even to the Boy Scouts and the Young Farmers' club. The final assault on the Smallholders came early in 1947, when a conspiracy was discovered, in which two ministers and other Smallholders were implicated: by now there were endless displays of 'the organised discontent of the masses' – 400,000 of them, veterans, women's organisations, trade unions etc. in a main square. There was a show trial in January–February, implicating Béla Kovács, the Smallholders' secretary-general. The Smallholder party's left wing – István Dobi and Gyula Ortutay, both of whom made an opportunistic career later on – forced the executive to accept a Communist-influenced programme, and the President and Prime Minister, Zoltán Tildy and Ferenc Nagy, were ultra-cautious. Why provoke the Soviets when conciliation might make them more amenable – the collaborationists' invariable arguments. They did try to make an alliance with the Social Democrats and to merge with the radical National Peasants, but the Communists thwarted this (in the autumn of 1946). There were arrests, with extracted confessions, and the real target was exposed as Béla Kovács, the party's secretary-general and a tough opponent. Nagy advised him to accept interrogation, and he was arrested by the Russians – despite Allied protests – and taken to the Soviet Union, where he 'confessed'. In protest at Kovács's fate, another minister, Zoltán Pfeiffer, led another fifty deputies from the Smallholders, this time as the Independence Party. In other words, the Smallholders' party had been split three ways.

Prime Minister Nagy was the next victim. He was in Switzerland but he had left his small son behind. Rákosi telephoned him and threatened to keep the boy if he did not resign. He resigned, and the boy was allowed to leave the country. A tough priest, Béla Varga, was also pushed out of the chairmanship. Another compliant figure, Lajos Dinnyés, took over (31 May 1947) as Prime Minister, obviously only anxious to do the Communists' bidding. By now there were several parties in competition, including a 'Christian Women's Camp', which had views as to the crucifix on school walls. They were all, of course, powerless in view of the Communists' control of anything that mattered.[21]

These tactics – 'salami', as Rákosi (or maybe Pfeiffer) called them – alerted the west to what was really happening, but it was difficult for the foreign ambassadors to document what they knew.

Now the left bloc pushed through a law that disenfranchised all whom Rajk called Fascist collaborators, all ethnic Hungarians from Slovakia and all Swabians, thus removing 500,000 voters from the roll. A threat of mob violence forced Sulyok to close down his party and flee abroad. Elections were to be held on 31 August 1947, when many people would be on holiday, and Rajk arranged for the printing of excessive numbers of 'blue slips' that enabled voters to vote in other constituencies. Such slips were then issued to bands of Communists going round in lorries and motor bikes to vote in selected places. This accounted for another 300,000 votes. In the election, the Communist share went up to 22.3 per cent, but the Smallholders' went down to 15.4 per cent, while Pfeiffer's Independence Party did well. However, the new law meant that there were national as well as constituency deputies, and this worked out to the left-wing bloc's advantage: it won 271 out of 411 seats. Now came the time for stooges. A pliant Smallholder, Lajos Dinnyés, was allowed to stay on as Prime Minister, but the bloc took most of the cabinet posts. Rákosi now said that there would be trials, and the leaders fled west. The main springs here had nothing to do with Hungary herself, which was merely an iron filing caught in a big magnetic pattern.

The background was the Cold War, now intensifying. By 1947 the Americans were present in force in Europe, and the real question was over the future of Germany, the industrial power house. By the summer of 1947 it was clear that West Germany would soon emerge as an Anglo-American-supported state, and Marshall money was coming to the rescue of the western European economy. Stalin responded by getting his satellite states (including the Finns) to turn down Marshall Aid and setting up a formal Communist bloc. At Szklarska Poręba, in newly annexed Polish Silesia, Stalin's deputy, Zhdanov, from 22 to 27 September 1947 berated the Communist Parties' delegates for their slowness in taking power; a successor to the Comintern would be created, the Cominform, with headquarters in Belgrade. Hungary signed the usual pacts of friendship, with Moscow in February 1948 and with other satellites later. Here was a monolithic bloc pledged to peace and opposition to German rearmament.

This had consequences everywhere: strikes, even bombs on railway lines, in France and Italy amounted almost to civil war, although they also led to a decisive right-wing electoral victory, and France's final adhesion to the American-led bloc. She gave up her resistance to the formation of a West German state, and West Germany was represented at the Marshall Plan office in Paris (by Americans) before she even formally came into existence. In Czechoslovakia the Communists changed their tactics, aiming at a takeover which came in February 1948. In Hungary, in October, the ÁVO moved on the Independence and Catholic Democrat parties and, as a result of confessions obtained through torture or forged, 103 of 106 elected deputies resigned and most fled abroad. Communists replaced them. Then in March 1948 at the Social Democrats' congress, the Communist-influenced left turned out the moderate leadership, including the veteran and very brave Anna Kéthly (who was imprisoned and tortured), and called for a merger with the Communists. It took place on 12 June after a joint congress, and the Magyar Dolgozók Pártja, the Hungarian Workers' Party, was born. Two hundred thousand Social Democrats were expelled or left the party, with several going into exile. The Smallholders and National Peasants stayed on as rump parties, as part of a Hungarian People's Independence Front, set up in 1949. These did as they were told, and, with some competition for the title, the most preposterous stooge of the entire bloc was in the front: István Dobi, an old peasant whose taste for the bottle meant that he threatened no one.

He was even made President of the Republic, after his predecessors had been arrested and locked up, and when he visited Moscow, Molotov took pity on him at a conference table and slid a bottle down in his direction. A new constitution came into force on 20 August, and now the government became the executive instrument of the party (which had also purged 100,000 members). There was a party congress, to which local and institutional delegates were sent, and then a Central Committee of seventy, elected by it, and then the Politburo of twelve, elected by the Central Committee. In effect, the four Communists who had spent the war in Moscow ran the Party, with Rákosi as General Secretary (and subsequently, to the Soviets' annoyance, Prime Minister as well: this was a breach of the rules, and Beria later berated him). The National Assembly was now a rubber stamp, meeting for short sessions two or three times a year. The chairman of its presidium and apparent head of state was a collaborationist Social Democrat, Árpád Szakasits, who had succeeded Tildy as President when Tildy was forced out in July 1948. Then came Dobi. At the same time Stalin proclaimed a blockade of West Berlin, in an attempt to bully the Americans into giving it up; the Red Chinese won the civil war; and in 1949 the Soviet Union successfully tested an atomic bomb. In Hungary tyranny descended.

# CHAPTER 7

# 'A mad old man', 1948–56

One of the great landmarks in the history of the Cold War was the speech that Winston Churchill delivered in March 1946 at Fulton, Missouri, where he had been invited to address President Truman's old school. He said that 'an Iron Curtain' had descended on Europe, 'from Stettin in the Baltic to Trieste in the Adriatic'. There was much objection, then, to his words: there were still many people in the west who admired the Soviet Union for what it had achieved during the war, and there were others still – a great many – who thought that the Soviet planned economy was a model for the future. Even President Truman did not fully endorse what Churchill said. But the old Victorian was right. As he spoke, the first moves were being made in Budapest to split the democratic government, with the arrest of 'reactionaries', and over the next two years an Iron Curtain, of an almost literal kind, did indeed clang down. Hungary was under a puppet government in September 1947; the same had happened in Poland months before; and on 25 February 1948 the Communists took over Czechoslovakia. She had a common border with the American zone in Germany, and people managed to flee across it. It was then sealed, with barbed wire, minefields, watch-towers and guard dogs; and so too were other borders, particularly the Austro-Hungarian, although at the time eastern Austria was a Soviet zone. By 1948 the population was sealed in. Hungary had been lined up to fight Soviet battles in the Cold War.

A powerful totalitarian screw came down over the land. Hungary was regimented, and even the smallest businesses were nationalised; private schools were taken over, including the most famous institutions of Budapest, such as the Fasori Gimnázium; everything was reduced to a grey, uniform level, and huge, hideous statuary went up, particularly an enormous Stalin just off the Museum Square and the City Park. An official press produced unreadable uplift, and a fake democracy was set up in 1949: the Independence Front – the party's dummy coalition device, in which non-Communist collaborators could figure – won 96.27 per cent of the votes, and in 1953 it won 98 per cent of them, in a 98 per cent turnout. The resulting parliament hardly met at all. The party was more active, but power was concentrated there in the Politburo, dominated by Rákosi, who used the secret police to keep an eye on everything, including itself. This was standard Stalinist stuff, for Hungary was to be transformed in the Soviet image. The Soviet presence became more obvious and active in that year, 1947–8. Every ministry had its 'advisers', and 2,000 officers were attached to the ÁVH(atóság) or 'State Defence Authority', as it was renamed in September 1948. The Soviet embassy gave out orders and received information from people high in the party, including, of course, Gerő and possibly Imre Nagy as well, although he was not in favour at that time. In the army there were Soviet advisers down to regimental level. Military service was a way of integrating the young men, of indoctrinating them even, and the army grew to 300,000 men between 1948 and 1951, with three-year conscription starting at the age of eighteen. Old professional officers were sacked and sometimes shot, to be replaced by men of working-class or peasant origin who had been given a rushed training. There were élite troops in ÁVH service, particularly the frontier guards. An enormous security apparatus was now

constructed, with informants everywhere, and when the time came
to control private farming, the police were out in the fields to make
sure that ploughing had been correctly done, and they also pried
around villages to detect whether pigs had been illegally
slaughtered.

The problem with tyranny on this scale was that it required
enormous energy (and expense), and at its head there was endless
mistrust and back-stabbing. A reign of terror then started which
lasted until 1953. Over a million accusations were opened, of which
650,000 reached the courts. Three hundred and ninety thousand
people were put in prison, which works out at 700 cases per day, 400
of them involving prison, after trials that lasted hardly an hour.[1]
And then the regimentation of everything, even to the timing and
nature of applause at party events. A continuous purge in the Hungarian Workers' Party went ahead, mainly against old Social
Democrats, including Szakasits, sentenced to life imprisonment,
and then against native Communists, even Kádár, in 1951. Kádár's
successor as minister, Sándor Zőld, fearing the same fate, killed his
wife and children before committing suicide. Two hundred former
Social Democrats went to prison, and 200 others to quarries in
Récsk or to the internment camp of Gödöllő, where once Empress
Sisi had gallivanted.[2] Intelligent party people kept their heads
down, and there were a great many unintelligent ones – trade-union
war-horses, time-servers of the Dobi class – who simply did as they
were told. They were rewarded in 1950–51, when they acquired villas
and grand flats from people of the old order.[3] These were not people
associated with the Arrow Cross – quite the contrary. Vindictiveness was shown to Szálasi's wife, an innocent fool. She had been his
companion and, like Hitler with Eva Braun, he married her at the
very last moment, on 28 April 1945, in Mattsee in Austria. He had
fled with the castle chef, who organised such festivities as were possible. She was imprisoned for ten years in a woman's internment
camp in Kistarca, together with Anna Kethly, and her teeth fell out
from scurvy; she survived thereafter as a cleaning woman.[4] *Szabad*

*Nép* reported on 7 August 1951 that 21 Horthy ministers, 25 secretaries of state, 190 generals, 1,012 professional officers, 274 police officers, 88 gendarmerie officers, 810 leading civil servants, 172 factory owners, 157 bankers, 391 wholesale traders, 252 large landowners, 9 princes, 163 counts and 121 barons had been evicted from their dwellings and deported to the countryside. This list omitted café owners and the like – in all, in 1950, 5,182 families, and then in 1951 another 1,200. They were given twenty-four hours' notice to vacate the premises. (In Rumania they got no notice, in the middle of the night.[5]) Party nominees moved in, with their sisters and their cousins and their aunts, and the buildings declined drastically.

This was the world of Bulgakov's *Heart of a Dog*: only a truly essential medical professional, or an academician of worldwide renown, such as Zoltán Kodály, could be exempted: they continued to live in the old upper-middle-class style. Countess Mihály Károlyi, *née* Katinka Andrássy, retained a flat in the Károlyi Palace, and the square near by, once named after Apponyi, was renamed 'Liberation' – Felszabadulás (Felszab for short). 'The countryside' meant hard agricultural labour, and the deported families were settled in the houses of peasant farmers who were singled out for discrimination. Pista Pálffy volunteered to 'build socialism' as a manual labourer to escape trouble, was conscripted, started well but was then tried on a pretext, and sentenced to two years in a labour camp, late in 1955, and released by a revolutionary mob in 1956. His mother was deported to an independent peasant's house, lived in the kitchen and worked in the fields. The alternative was some labour camp, and the quarries of Récsk acquired a sinister reputation. The poet György Faludy wound up there, and gradually lost his left-wing sympathies.

There had been much progressive enthusiasm in the post-war years, a will to make education more open, and national figures such as Albert Szent-Györgyi, Gyula Szekfű and Zoltán Kodály oversaw a reform of primary schools. But then came the politicisation of the curriculum under the Communists, and here they encountered serious resistance. The Catholic Church dug its heels in (as it successfully did in Bavaria, to Germany's subsequent profit, over proposals to introduce American comprehensive schools to replace the traditional hierarchy, at the tip of which was the classical Gymnasium). A law was passed for the state to take over 6,500 religious schools, and Cardinal Mindszenty forbade the 18,000 Catholic teachers from becoming state employees. Mindszenty was a pain in the neck, capable of crassness on a grand scale. (He remarked in 1947 that the Communists should not harp on about the Holocaust because now the Jews were doing the same to the Christians: but he himself had been interned by the Germans and the Arrow Cross, and had protected Jews.) In December 1948 he was arrested. There was a show trial in February 1949, and of course it could easily be shown that he had transgressed the laws governing currency: everyone in Budapest used dollars wherever possible, and the Church had access to them. This ended in a sentence of life imprisonment. In 1949–50 a campaign went ahead against religion, including Judaism. (Annie Fischer, who had taken refuge in Sweden, volunteered to give a concert in honour of Wallenberg. She was told, no.[6]) Monasteries were closed and priests arrested. The security police had an office of church affairs, which controlled all religious activity, and there were 'peace priests' who reported on bishops and censored sermons. The Protestants suffered similarly, as the head of a seminary would report which of the students prayed too devoutly. The famous Calvinist Gimnázium closed. Higher education suffered even more as staff and students became proletarianised, Marxism-Leninism became compulsory, and the Academy's Library was purged of 4,000 books. Even the People's Colleges, designed for young peasants, with 10,000 students, were just turned into student dormitories as higher education expanded overnight five times. All of this was accompanied by relentless propaganda, and informants were everywhere.

This went together with a command economy that tended towards chaos. By 1949 the western European countries were recovering, in the context of the Marshall Plan – West Germany managed to export more than Great Britain even in 1951 – and Hungary could have followed that path. The great inflation had come to an end with the introduction of a new currency, the forint, in August 1946, after the Americans returned the gold reserve, taken by the Nazis. The financial situation was quite quickly stabilised. A great national effort had been made for recovery: by 1946 the Szabadság bridge was rebuilt, along with half of others destroyed by the Germans; most of the railway track was restored and the mines, drained, were at 90 per cent capacity. However, the Communists took charge of the economy early on, and Gerő, as Minister for Commerce, handed the USSR a near-monopoly of foreign trade. A Supreme Economic Council under the Communist Zoltán Vas took more and more of the economy under control and reduced the private sector through regulations, and a Reparations Commission bought up two-thirds of output cheaply for the Soviet Union. State purchases accounted for 95 per cent of the output of the Manfred Weiss metallurgical works. From July 1946 heavy industry was taken over by the state, and in 1947 ten banks. By March 1948 all industries employing more than a hundred workers were taken over, and late in 1949 all employing more than ten. By late 1950 the private sector had ceased to exist. And then came the Plan.[7]

Investment in industry and infrastructure had gone up from almost nothing to a fifth of the national income by 1948, and in 1949 industrial production was substantially above the level of 1941. However, there followed a Five-Year Plan, in imitation of the Soviet Union, and this was an act of folly, inflicting much hardship on the people thereafter. Hungary was by now a small country, with excellent agricultural land, and she should have followed an Austrian, or for that matter a Danish, path. Instead, there was mad industrialisation. In part this happened because of Stalin's expectation that war could break out: industry would be needed, and Communists were confident, since Stalin had defeated Hitler, that they had the answer to modernisation. Russia, they claimed (wrongly), had been a backward peasant country in 1914, but a Stalinist wand had been waved, and she had become what was later known as a superpower. Hungarians suffered from a variant of this – sneered at as backward and feudal, not least by themselves. Now Rákosi would show that Hungary too could become an industrial country. The Plan took effect on 1 January 1950. Investment was already high (60,000 million forints) but was increased (to 80,000 million). Heavy industry had priority, with a crash programme for iron and steel, although iron ore and coking coal were lacking. These had to be imported, a distortion of the country's foreign trade. A steel town, Sztalinváros, went up as a showcase, modelled on an American steel town of the 1920s: like Nowa Huta, outside Kraków, it was meant to produce The New Man, with sports stadia rather than churches. Women were involved in the work force in droves, even for manual labour.[8] But insistence on growth in volume, and on meeting impossible targets, meant that factories produced quantities of useless stuff, and from 1952 to 1954 production went up by 12.7 per cent, but unsaleable finished products rose by three-quarters. These, and uncompleted investment projects, accounted for 2 per cent of the national income, and Gerő himself complained in 1951 that 'as far as quality is concerned, the situation is intolerable'. Inspectors or the market rejected 25 per cent of manufactured goods, and to improve the situation regulations multiplied, together with an economic bureaucracy, which halved the ratio of blue-collar to white-collar workers from 9:1 in 1941 to 4:1 by 1953. On paper the Plan did succeed, metallurgical products doubling or, in the case of aluminium, trebling. The industrial workforce grew by 500,000. Communists did not like peasants, indeed regarded them with contempt ('quadrupeds') and wanted them to become proletarians as soon as they could. The German Marxists, in the 1890s, vaguely realised that they should make some effort to get peasants' votes, and their leaders would go round the villages, patiently explaining that if there were free trade in food, then the proletariat's sausages would cost less. True, it was admitted, that would not help peasants, but said peasants could always troop off to the towns. This won no votes except in a weird mountainous tip of southern Bavaria, which had remained violently anticlerical since the sixteenth century. Socialism and the peasant did not make for a happy marriage.

And agriculture turned out disastrously. Here again the example was Soviet: collectivisation, or in other words, elimination of the peasant farm. This had some theoretical economic logic behind it, in that large estates used machinery and fertiliser more effectively, but it was also a political matter. Peasants were generally not Communist, were inclined to follow priests and did not always take kindly to full-time education: it diverted children from farm work. In August 1948 Rákosi announced that mass collectivisation would proceed over the next four years, although a party conference, responding to Imre Nagy's warnings, had resolved that the rural economy was not ready for it. Gerő said that the Five-Year Plan would bring socialism in the villages as well. But there was mass resistance, not least because many peasants had only owned their land since the reform of 1944–5, and it was not easy to break this, even with evictions and terror. By 1953 there were only 5,224 co-operative farms (a euphemism for state control), representing a quarter of the arable land. Persecution of 'kulaks' – farmers with 40 acres – alienated most peasants, and, as in Russia in 1932, peasants just left the land, so that 4,500,000 acres went uncultivated. Those who remained faced penal taxation and compulsory state deliveries at prices that did not match those required for the tools they needed – again a Soviet phenomenon, the Scissors Crisis, when two graphs of prices had a dramatic gap between them. In 1952 drought combined with compulsory deliveries to bring much of the peasantry near to starvation, and production of wheat and wine went down drastically, requiring imports that Hungary could hardly afford. Agronomists who understood things were dismissed, research was not done and there were not enough tractors. This was a dismal period. In the immediate post-war period there had been a modest recovery in the way people lived. Once the plan started, this went

into reverse. Consumption suffered from the enormous invest-
ments, and by 1952 incomes in terms of what could be bought went
down by two-thirds.

In 1951, as part of a deceptive gambit, wages were increased by
20 per cent, but prices went up by 50 per cent or doubled – again a
repetition of Soviet practice, which went together with compulsory
purchase of bonds for the 'Peace Loan', for party journals etc. Urban
housing was very scarce, with the migration, and fell into disrepair.
Factory workers would rise at 4.30 a.m. to cling onto straps in overcrowded trams to be in the workplace in time for the briefing of
what the Party newspaper had said, with more political education
after a day's work, itself more demanding because the workers were
paid for output, not input of hours. Queuing for necessities made
up this dismal picture. This all went together with a series of fake
trials. This acquired an edge of hysteria and paranoia in the summer
of 1948, when a crisis of suspicion grew up in Moscow itself over
Tito's Yugoslavia. A spectre haunted Communist Russia all along,
almost from the very start of the system, in 1903, when a few dozen
exiles had argued in Brussels and then in London. What was the
relationship of the international proletarian revolution to
nationalism? Nationalism could also be revolutionary, and in the
event, ninety years later, brought the system down. Should it be
encouraged or not? This problem came up with the Communist
parties of the satellite states, and many home-grown Communists
were suspected in Moscow of wanting 'a national road' to
Communism, and not the Soviet model. Tito, the boss of Yugoslavia,
incurred Stalin's wrath. Of course, he purported to be a loyal Communist, much like the others, and had even worked in Spain for the
Comintern (and probably also for the NKVD). But Yugoslavia was
not just any old satellite. She had been liberated from within, and
with considerable help from the British; and besides, Tito had been
talking of a Balkan federation, chiefly with Bulgaria. Stalin did not
want a big state, and abusive messages went from Moscow to Belgrade. When Tito did not grovel, Yugoslavia was cast out of the

Cominform in summer 1948, but Tito did not fall. Instead he resumed old connections with the British, and the beginnings of a Balkan alliance came up, with Greece and Turkey. This excited paranoia in Moscow: were any other of the satellite Communist leaders contemplating a Tito-like bid for independence? By 1949 alarms went up in the satellite capitals, and anyone suspected of 'national Communism' felt fear.

Rákosi used this to eliminate any threat to himself. He had been in prison for sixteen years, with only a brief interruption, and later on one of the chief Hungarian negotiators with the International Monetary Fund, János Fekete, told his counterpart, with whom he became friendly, that Rákosi had become 'a mad old man'.[9] He was not in fact very old – he celebrated his sixtieth birthday, or rather it was celebrated for him with orgies of surrealism, in 1952. But who can say how prison affected his brain? The Communists were in any case given to mistrust, and there was always a gulf between those who had served in Moscow throughout the war years and those who had risked all in clandestinity at home. László Rajk was one of the latter group, and besides, he was not Jewish, another potential reason for mistrust, although of course nothing was ever written down. After Zhdanov's harangue at Szklarska Poręba in September 1947, Rajk could have said that he had been right all along, that the Party should have moved faster, been more revolutionary. He was moved because of this from the Interior to Foreign Affairs, a less powerful post, because he could not appoint his own people to important posts in the Party or the state machinery. But he was already suspected of 'Titoism': of a belief that Hungary should take her own road to socialism. There was maybe some truth in this, although there was no evidence for it. He was arrested in May 1949, and Farkas got to work with torture. Some officials were arrested and forced to condemn Rajk as a spy and a Titoist. Despite being tortured, he would not confess, and he collaborated only when his friend and successor János Kádár got him to do so with a promise that his wife would be left alone and that he could go to the Soviet

Union. His trial started on 16 September 1949 under the direction of an NKVD general, Belkin, a specialist in the grotesque choreography of such events. He was then executed, and Kádár witnessed the execution.

Both the Mindszenty and Rajk cases were meant to counterbalance the concurrent trials of Communists in the USA, particularly Alger Hiss, but they were also the tip of an iceberg, with hundreds of lesser trials being staged in an atmosphere of fabricated plots, torture and killing. There was some resistance, but Hungary, mainly flat and bare, was not suitable for guerrilla activity, and much of the adult population had had experience of Soviet captivity. Some groups prepared for the outbreak of a third world war, putting out anti-Communist leaflets or obtaining weaponry; but some were shams set up by the ÁVH to flush out subversives, and draconian sentences were then imposed. A serious effort was made by an organisation of emigrant military officers who cooperated with sabotage cells left behind in the last month of the war, and this organisation – *Magyar Harcosok Bajtársi Közössége*, the Community of Hungarian Fighters – waged a hidden intelligence war against the ÁVH, to some effect (e.g., a white paper on the fate of deportees in the Soviet Union), but it did not get any real support from the western secret services, and was divided along ideological lines. The MHBK suffered a decisive defeat in 1951, when most of their inland agents were caught, and others kidnapped.

In cultural matters 1945 had been a time of some hope, that the country could escape from the stale nationalist rhetoric. The Budapest intelligentsia were a famous phenomenon, some of them, like Arthur Koestler, extraordinarily adaptable. Gyula Illyés and Sándor Márai led a literary revival, in the tradition of the modernist inter-war periodical *Nyugat*. After 1948 the dead hand of censorship descended, and the Party's Writers' Association, with its journal *Irodalmi Ujság*, became a place for second-raters, as in Moscow. Russian literature took over, with socialist realism, and even György Lukács fell under a cloud for being insufficiently respectful of Soviet tomes. The Party worked hard to control leisure, with youth movements to replace the boy scouts; and of course sport was much promoted. Ferenc Puskás became something of a folk hero in England when Hungary won in international football (he later defected). In every village there was now a People's House where lectures were delivered and the right songs sung. But under it all was prodigious resentment and hatred. The Soviet embassy was well aware of this, but under Stalin everyone felt paralysed. And then Stalin died.

The death of Stalin on 5 March 1953 brought about a great silence over all Eurasia, from Vladivostok to Rostock. He had held Eurasia in his grip, with huge statues and portraits, endless avenues and towns named after him, his lifeless works dominating the bookshops, and he ran his satellite system with huge care, even telephoning the Warsaw security police chief in the middle of the night. His suspiciousness of everyone had no bounds, and in the end this was what killed him: he had a stroke, but for hours no one dared break the door down to save him, and in any case no one was competent to look after him because his doctors, almost all Jewish, had been arrested because he had embarked on an anti-Semitic campaign. Two of them had to be dug out of prison, and treated for their wounds. Almost at once a fight for the succession started, and the immediate victor appeared to be Lavrenty Beria, the head of the security services. He had his tentacles in the satellite Parties, including the Hungarian, for even its reformist chief, Imre Nagy, had been an NKVD informer in his Moscow years. Rákosi in Hungary was a mini-Stalin: locally he was unassailable. He had even managed to use Stalin's anti-Semitism to further his own cause. The prisons were crammed full of writers or peasants or 'former people' or simple victims of any malicious informer, but the latest victims were their persecutors: Gábor Péter, head of the ÁVH, and the Minister of Justice, Gyula Décsi, both of them Jews, arrested in parallel with Stalin's own anti-Jewish purge. (They were sentenced to life imprisonment, rather than being killed, only because Stalin had died.)

In May 1953 there was the usual parade election, and Rákosi

took it all seriously at least as a demonstration of his power to mobilise enormous masses of people ostensibly on his side. He failed to spot the warning signs that were coming from Moscow. But there a great row was brewing. Obviously, Stalin's confrontation with the west had been a failure: NATO now existed, West Germany was prospering and moves were made to unite western Europe; the Korean War was a long stalemate; Yugoslavia had survived. At home, the policy of suppressing the nationalities meant that their regions were controlled by Stalinist Russians, and there were plenty of Ukrainian or Baltic equivalents who would manage things with a larger support base. The same was true as regards the 'national Communists' in the satellite countries: did Communism have to mean slavish imitation of anything Soviet, the suppression of native traditions, however harmless, and the incarceration of so many innocents? This was not a matter of idealism. In the Soviet system the only agency that really knew what was happening was the KGB, whose informants were everywhere, and Beria could therefore suggest some liberalisation as a practical way forward. It would also appeal to the west, where the Stalinist confrontation was just not understood. Eisenhower in the USA and Churchill in Great Britain were only waiting for some gesture of *détente*. Hardly had Stalin been immured in the mausoleum than the Korean War was wound down. An approach was soon made, also, to Tito, the leading 'national Communist', and there was even, in the air, an idea that East Germany could be given up, in exchange for a neutral Germany.

It was also necessary to remove some of the Stalinist excrescences in the satellite states. Rákosi was in this position in Hungary. He failed to spot the warning signs, and in June he was summoned to Moscow, and was told to bring with him Imre Nagy. He was not told to bring Farkas or Révai. In Moscow he was berated: Beria told him that the Party must cease to be dominated by Jews. He said, 'We have heard that you have had Turkish Sultans, and Austrian Emperors, but we have not heard that you have had Jewish kings'; he went on, that in the Hungarian Party 'the Jews oppress the non-Jews'.[10] Socialism was now looking for a human face. Imre Nagy seemed to fit the bill. He came from a poor peasant family in Somogy county, on the Croatian border. Born in 1896, he had been taken prisoner by the Russians and fought in the Red Army. He came back to Hungary in 1921, and stirred up trouble among farm labourers in Somogy, for which he was briefly imprisoned. He went to Vienna and then in 1930 to the Soviet Union, where he worked in the Comintern's agrarian section. He did not apply for Soviet citizenship and was even expelled from the Hungarian exile Party in 1936, with another spell in prison – all of this, of course, consistent with the story that he had informed on the Party, to which he was re-admitted in 1940. He became Minister of Agriculture in the Debrecen government, and the Soviets, who did not want to repeat the experience of 1919, promoted him, as non-Jewish. He became Minister of the Interior, but he opposed Rákosi's ideas on collectivisation of the peasantry, which he said was unnecessary and would be calamitous, and this caused him to lose his Politburo seat. Then, after a year teaching in an agricultural college, he was put in charge of compulsory food deliveries from the peasants, which he competently did, and was re-elected to the Politburo in 1951. This all sounds as if he had clandestine Soviet support, and in 1952 he became Deputy Prime Minister with special responsibility for agriculture. The Kremlin meeting of 13–14 June 1953 to which he had been summoned confirmed his rise: Beria told Rákosi to his face to stop trying to be 'the Jewish king of Hungary'. Rákosi had already gone too far in trying to be Prime Minister as well as Party secretary, and he was told to hand the Prime Ministry to Nagy. Two weeks later Rákosi, Gerő, Farkas and Révai made speeches of self-criticism to the Central Committee, which then resolved that industrialisation, collectivisation, neglect of living standards and arbitrary police action (850,000 cases between 1951 and May 1953) had all been mistakes, associated with a cult of personality. Such were the 'June resolutions', rubber-stamped by the assembly in July. Farkas and Révai lost their seats on the Politburo; amnesty was declared, in part or whole; internment camps were closed. Nagy announced this 'New Course' on the radio, and over the next year there was something to show for this.

Two-fifths of the peasants abandoned co-operatives, and a fifth of these closed. Compulsory deliveries were reduced, and arrears cancelled. Investment in heavy industry was cut by two-fifths, and consumer industries did better; artisans were licensed. Less important prisoners were released, and some of the deported families came back from the countryside, though not to their old houses. But Nagy was not really in control. Rákosi still controlled the Party, and on the Politburo Nagy had no supporters; the secretariat consisted of Rákosi nominees, while Gerő ran the Ministry of the Interior and the central economic affairs committee. Nagy did appeal to Moscow, and Rákosi was reprimanded, but he counted on a change in the course of events in Moscow, where he guessed that the Stalinists were only waiting for a comeback, and in a sense he was right. Beria was overthrown in a grimly surreal coup (smuggled out in a carpet after a meeting of the Politburo), and for a time the succession was not clear. At first Georgi Malenkov seemed dominant, but eventually Nikita Khrushchev would emerge.

Nagy created a new organisation, the Patriotic People's Front, naming his son-in-law, a Calvinist pastor, as its head, and this, along with many writers and journalists who had been released under the 1953 amnesty, supported his New Course. He was also able to secure the release of Party people, including János Kádár. But events showed that modest reforms of the Communist system only led to trouble: less work discipline, a black market. On top of everything there was a financial crisis. In 1955 Moscow said that it would cut its deliveries of raw materials by half, as they were needed at home for Khrushchev's own version of a new course. Credit would be needed for replacements, and to improve the worn-out machinery of the industrial plant. The credit might come from the west, given *détente*, but the Politburo vetoed this, and since Hungary was importing armaments from the Communist bloc, her trade balance was very unfavourable. At the end of 1954 Rákosi spent weeks in the Soviet Union, talking to allies, and undermining Nagy. In January 1955 Moscow invited the Hungarian leadership, and this time Malenkov berated Nagy at length for weakening Party control. He would be allowed to stay as Prime Minister but must confess errors. What was really behind this was a temporary alliance of Khrushchev with the old guard who disliked the New Course and its implications. Nagy refused to recant and was attacked in the Central Committee for right-wing deviationism, while Mikhail Suslov of the Politburo arrived in April 1955 to encourage Nagy's expulsion, although he kept his Party card. András Hegedüs, a Rákosi man, took his place, and an 'anti-Party conspiracy' was then unearthed by the ÁVH in eastern Hungary, with hundreds of arrests and six executions. Mihály Farkas had supported Nagy too early and now lost his Politburo seat – he was soon to be imprisoned.

However, Rákosi could not go as far as he no doubt wanted, because the Austrian State Treaty came up in 1955. Here, yet again, the fate of Hungary was to depend on that of Germany. The Soviets were very anxious to neutralise her, not to let her join in the western coalition, and they could offer their zone in East Germany as a reward. An independent, neutral Austria offered a model, and that had implications for Hungary next door. Although Nagy had been sidelined, Rákosi could not turn the clock back. Then Khrushchev visited Tito, with a view to reconciliation there (May 1955). And Tito made no secret of his dislike of Rákosi, who 'has staged false trials, given false information, sentenced innocent men to death'.

Moscow told Rákosi not to persecute the Church, and Mindszenty was released under house arrest. The collectivisation drive was resumed, but it met resistance, and in any case there was already a considerable intellectual ferment going on. Nagy had authorised this, in the sense that he had released writers, and permitted hitherto banned classsics; the literary journal *Irodalmi Ujság* became readable again, and in March 1955 the Communist Youth Organisation (DISZ) set up a debating club, the Petőfi Circle, where there was freedom of at least Communist speech. In September 1955 an issue of the literary magazine was suppressed for criticising the Minister of Culture, and fifty-nine writers, mostly Communist, publicly protested. Many were forced to recant; some refused and were expelled. Nagy himself was then expelled as 'a rallying-point for the enemies of socialism'. He defended himself vigorously in writing, saying that 'No enemy propaganda [...] will destroy more completely the people's faith in socialism than a forced return to the old, mistaken pre-June policy, degenerate Bonapartist authority and dictator.' His sixtieth birthday, on 7 June 1956, saw a stream of figures coming to his villa in Buda, including Illyés and Kodály. Here was real defiance, which would not have happened unless discreetly encouraged by Moscow. Two of the brightest Soviet grandees, Anastas Mikoyan and Yuri Andropov, were directly observing Hungary.

Rákosi could shore up his authority by control of Party posts, but his whole position was under threat. In February 1956, at the Twentieth Party Congress, Khrushchev memorably and, for those present, shockingly denounced Stalin: the killings, the cult of personality, the wartime blunders. Rákosi bent to the new wind, and indicated concessions. These included the rehabilitation of László Rajk, whose fate was blamed on Gábor Péter. But it was too little, and too late. He was heckled at Party gatherings, and a young schoolteacher, György Litván, said to his face, 'The Hungarian people no longer trust you'. Tito lobbied in Moscow for his removal, and the dissolution of the Cominform was another sign that the times were moving against him. János Kádár, one of his victims, managed to blame Rákosi directly for Rajk's fate. Meanwhile the Writers' Association bestirred itself, as did the Petőfi Circle – all of it in Party language – and on 18 June Julia Rajk, the widow, was hugely applauded when she called for justice against the people responsible for so much corruption and destruction. A debate on the press on 27 June was so widely attended that loudspeakers had to broadcast it to an audience outside; the writer Tibor Déry spoke for freedom, and Nagy's reinstatement in the Party was demanded.

There were parallel developments in Poland – riots in Poznań – and and Rákosi pointed to this as a sign of what might happen. He got the Central Committee to vote for the expulsion of Déry and suspension of the Petőfi Circle; on 16 July he wanted the Politburo to have Nagy and his associates arrested, to close down the Writers' Association and suppress the literary journal. But one member at once telephoned the Soviet ambassador, Yuri Andropov, and Mikoyan arrived a day later, to reconvene the Politburo and to tell Rákosi to resign. Rákosi telephoned Khrushchev, saying, 'If I go, everything collapses'. But on 18 July he resigned on health grounds and flew to the Soviet Union, eventually dying in Kirghizia in 1971. Even the return of his remains was problematical and had to be carried out in secrecy. However, his successor was to be Gerő, rather than Nagy, and this did not promise much improvement. On the contrary, a new Five-Year Plan announced more restrictions on consumption, and there were strikes, and the metallurgical works on Csepel Island were paralysed by discontent. In the next three months the gulf between the Party leadership and the people became unbridgeable, and everyone felt that there was something in the air.

Gerő announced that he would combat 'leftist sectarianism' – Rákosi – and 'rightist deviationism' – Nagy. He made concessions: no living Hungarian was to have a street named after him (Rákosi then disappeared), and Farkas senior was removed from Party offices. People's Colleges – the peasant intellectuals – were reinstated, and proceedings against various writers were stopped. But the protests went ahead, and on 15 September the Writers' Association voted against official candidates for its board while electing non-Party people such as Paul Ignotus, a Social Democrat who had been in prison. The literary journal *Irodalmi Ujság* was now the chief vehicle for outspoken articles, and the Petőfi Circle debated away. When, on 6 October, Rajk was re-buried in the Kerepesi Cemetery, there was an enormous silent demonstration, after which students marched along the boulevard to the Batthyány memorial, close to the Parliament, shouting anti-Stalinist slogans without police interference. There were other incidents, and on 21 October news from Poland caused ferment. Khrushchev had tried to bully the Poles with troop movements to stop them from electing Gomułka – in effect, their Nagy – as Party chief; Khrushchev had backed down. The Budapest students then produced their own demands for an end to Soviet domination, pursuit of the Stalinists and multi-party elections; this was widely circulated. On 23 October a demonstration was called for in Petőfi Square, on the Pest Embankment, which was allowed, then forbidden, then allowed again; the students marched over the Margaret Bridge to the statue of Bem, a Polish general who had fought in the 1848–9 war. The students were joined by a large number of workers whose shift had just ended, and there were cries of *Ruszkik haza* ('Russians Go Home') as the crowd swelled to 50,000, and apartment buildings along the route sprouted national flags from which the Communist emblem had been excised. The crowd grew to 200,000 and went to the great square in front of the Parliament, where the cry went up for Nagy, who very reluctantly did appear, and was booed when he started with 'Comrades'.

His appeal for order went down badly, and some of the people marched off to tear down the huge Stalin statue near Heroes' Square. Others went towards the Museum Boulevard to demonstrate outside the radio building, demanding the broadcasting of the students' demands. There matters turned violent. The radio was broadcasting a speech by Gerő in the usual style, 'the yoke of Horthy fascism and German imperialism' etc., while a student delegation was inside the building, negotiating to set up their own broadcast. There was a state security detachment in the building. Tear gas grenades were thrown from it, and the crowd did not disperse; when conscripts were summoned they handed over their weapons and joined the crowd. Shooting began, and an armoured regiment came on the scene. It too went over to the crowd, and at midnight it was joined by young workers who had taken rifles from factory stores. The building was now besieged and was captured, around dawn, and another group moved towards the City Park, to demolish the huge Stalin statue down to its knee-boots; the Party newspaper offices were also attacked. Gerő understood how serious this was and asked the Soviet ambassador for direct assistance. Khrushchev insisted for form's sake that it should be requested by Hegedüs, as Prime Minister, but it came at once. Two mechanised divisions came from Rumania to join the two already in Hungary, and Gerő convened the Central Committee, which agreed to martial law and Soviet intervention. But it also appointed Nagy as Prime Minister and removed six of the old guard, replacing them with reformers, in this case Nagy's associates Géza Losonczy and Ferenc Donáth, though they refused the offer while Gerő stayed.

Nagy was meanwhile more or less kept in custody in the Party building on Akadémia utca for the next three days. He did broadcast on the 24th for calm, and that day Suslov and Mikoyan arrived; Soviet tanks had been in action for some hours. But they were caught in narrow streets, easy targets for Molotov cocktails, and were attacked by ten to fifteen thousand young workers from the poorest districts. The students had now more or less faded from the scene, and in some factories workers' councils had taken over. On 25 October it was known – the radio worked, but there were no newspapers and public transport had stopped – that Gerő had been replaced as Party Secretary by Kádár. Nagy spoke a second time, promising reforms, and that morning a large crowd, some fraternising with the Russians, gathered in Parliament Square. ÁVH men on the roofs opened fire on it, and well over a hundred people died; Soviet tanks also opened fire. At this point an experienced commander, Colonel Pál Maléter, who had fought with the Soviet partisans, defected when ordered to restore discipline at the Kilián barracks and successfully defended them against a tank attack. The revolution was meanwhile spreading beyond the capital, and there was some violence, provoked in Miskolc and elsewhere by the ÁVH. A free radio service came into being. The dictatorship collapsed nearly everywhere, not least in the villages. In most settlements

Communism simply ceased to exist, and self-governing committees emerged to manage local affairs.

Nagy now asserted himself, and on 26 October was established in the Parliament. He was of course a convinced Communist, but he promised the Central Committee new elections and properly equal negotiations with the Soviets: this had been agreed with Mikoyan and Suslov, although they wanted control of the media. On 27 October a new government was announced, containing the old progressives Zoltán Tildy and Ferenc Erdei as well as Béla Kovács, released from his Soviet camp, but most were Communists. Heavy fighting continued in Budapest on the 27th and 28th, with the destruction of many buildings and the burning of tanks. But Communists were at a loss when workers stood against them, as was happening in Miskolc and Győr as well as in Budapest; Gerő and Hegedüs now fled to the Soviet Union, and on the 28th Nagy announced a cease-fire and a Soviet withdrawal, such that on the 29th calm was largely restored. And it seemed that the revolutionaries had won. Nagy said he would return to the coalition principle of 1945 and set up an inner cabinet of that sort.

That evening Moscow Radio broadcast a conciliatory statement, but the background was tangled. There had been much pondering in Moscow. On 23 October there had been an idea of leaving it to the Hungarians to sort out, and this was Mikoyan's opinion. Marshals Voroshilov and Bulganin (now Premier of the government), with Molotov and Suslov, were against this, and Khrushchev himself vacillated. He did not want to appear, before the United Nations, as an 'imperialist'. At that very moment the British and French were, with Israel, attacking Egypt in an effort to re-take the Suez Canal, and Khrushchev supported the Egyptians. He did not want to appear before the United Nations as the invader of Hungary. This accounted for the conciliatory statement. But Nagy's announcement of a return to coalition government caused worry that the example would be infectious in the rest of the Soviet bloc, and the Chinese, at the time present in Moscow, said that Soviet troops should not be withdrawn. Even Tito had second thoughts, perhaps fearing a return of Hungarian irredentism, and Khrushchev, his position somewhat vulnerable after the Stalin speech, needed an appearance of strength. On 31 October he argued for the use of troops, as otherwise the USSR would appear weak, giving away both Egypt and Hungary. Meanwhile the Communist Party in Hungary was in effect dissolving, and Cardinal Mindszenty was freed from prison and spoke on the radio on 3 November. The Presidium resolved that a new government should be installed, under Ferenc Münnich, former ambassador for Rákosi, and János Kádár. The next day Mikoyan, back from Budapest, argued for giving Nagy two weeks' grace, but he was overborne, not least by Marshal Zhukov, and Khrushchev flew to see Tito on his island retreat of Brioni. The new decision was probably prompted by events on 30 October in Budapest, where a lynching occurred of loyal ÁVH troops. The Budapest Party headquarters on what is now John Paul II Square still contained a detachment of them, and at 10 a.m. it was besieged. The troops resisted, firing. Three armoured cars arrived to relieve the building, but on seeing the carnage (which included women who had come to help the wounded) they fired instead at the building. A small delegation offering surrender was shot; and when the ÁVH came out, they were gunned down and lynched.

There was a brief period of euphoria just the same. The Social Democrats elected Anna Kéthly as leader, and the Smallholders Béla Kovács. Mindszenty was released from house arrest and *Irodalmi Ujság* published Gyula Illyés's denunciation of the Stalinist era. Workers' councils took over factory management, and revolutionary councils similarly appeared in ministries and even the Bank. János Kádár even announced the dissolution of the Party, on 1 November, and the setting up of a new one, the *Magyar Szocialista Munkáspárt* (MSzMP), or 'Hungarian Socialist Workers' Party'. But that same day Nagy was informed that there was a huge troop movement across Hungary's eastern borders, with three thousand tanks coming from the Ukraine and Rumania. Andropov denied this was anything other than a standard manoeuvre, but as the reports were confirmed, Nagy convened the cabinet, which resolved that Hungary should leave the Warsaw Pact and declare neutrality. Andropov was told, and Kádár apparently said with much emotion that he knew this was the end of Communism in Hungary but that he would resist any Soviet intervention. Hungary's neutral status was officially announced to the United Nations. But simultaneously the Suez Crisis developed, as on 29 October Israel had invaded Egypt, the United States announced its opposition, and the United Nations met that same day, 1 November. The Americans reassured Moscow that they did not consider the eastern European states as military allies, although Radio Free Europe was less guarded.

By dawn on 2 November the Soviets had taken control of the railway system, placing guards on bridges and cutting the major roads to Budapest. Nagy reshuffled his government and called in the Budapest chief of police, Sándor Kopácsi, who told him that Münnich and Kádár, soon to be the Soviet nominees, were not to be found. The two had been flown to Moscow via the Soviet Embassy on 1 November. Kádár impressed the Soviets because he spoke quite frankly about what had gone wrong, and he was rewarded as the Soviets made him head of the Party. He came back with Soviet troops. In Budapest that evening negotiations continued, and the Hungarians went to Soviet headquarters, where they were just arrested by Ivan Serov, head of the KGB. At dawn on 3 November came an all-out assault on Budapest, and Nagy made his final broadcast to the world, as he took refuge in the Yugoslav Embassy.

There was not much military resistance, as the troops had no orders, although the Kilián barracks did hold out for a day. Shelling did enormous harm to the city centre and damaged the suburbs; machine-gun bullet scars defaced the boulevards for years afterwards. Some armed groups of workers did fight; the Csepel metalworkers fought on until 11 November, and around Pécs the resistance went on for three weeks. But on 4 November Kádár made a broadcast from Szolnok to the effect that he was now Prime Minister, with other anti-Nagy Communists, and he cited the lynchings of the ÁVH troops, and the 'counter-revolution', as his reasons for doing so. He got back to Budapest on 7 November. The new government was sworn in by the great survivor István Dobi, as chairman of the Presidential Council. From 4 November a great wave of refugees clogged the roads to the Austrian and Yugoslav borders, and by mid-December 200,000 had fled, 2,700 people had been killed and 27,000 wounded. The Soviets lost 669 dead and 1,450 of their troops had been wounded. Cardinal Mindszenty took refuge in the American Embassy.

# CHAPTER 8

# Kádár

—

J ános Kádár was born János Csermanek in the then Hungarian Adriatic port city of Fiume in 1912, and his was one of innumerable sad stories familiar in Europe in that time. He was illegitimate. His mother was a servant girl from Slovakia, his father a soldier who would not marry her, although she followed him to Hungary, where János grew up, very poor, in a village south of Lake Balaton. There were charitable agencies in England, such as Dr Barnardo's, which sent such children for adoption in Canada, but in continental Europe their fate was harsh. His mother went to Budapest, with a job first as house cleaner and then as newspaper seller, but the boy at least benefited from the educational system in place at that time: after eight classes he became an apprentice typewriter repair man. He lost the job as the Depression bit and became a young Communist, spending two years in prison because Communist sabotage was thought to be behind a railway disaster in 1931.

These prisons were Marxist universities where young rebels came to understand political-economic dogma, with the added and important element of hatred, and there he got to know Rákosi. When released, he worked again for the Party and was again imprisoned in 1937. Now he counted as a hard-boiled clandestine worker and became a member of the Central Committee, then under László Rajk, in 1942. He took the name Kádár ('Cooper'), rose to run the tiny Budapest Party but dissolved it in 1943, when Stalin, for cosmetic reasons, dissolved the Comintern. (There was a substitute, the International Department of the Soviet Central Committee.) He was again imprisoned after the German occupation in March 1944 but managed – probably with the judges' connivance – to pass himself off as a deserter. He felt guilty because by this time his mother was selling newspapers for a pittance and needed his support. She was soon to get it, as he arrived in a large black car, courtesy of the then arriving Red Army. Kádár was an obvious man for the new Politburo, and thrived, until he was again arrested and imprisoned in 1951, because he had been an associate of Rajk's. The arrest was part of a grimly surreal sequence, as the Stalin-machine sought enemies within. As Rákosi told Stalin, there were still too many Horthy-era policemen, and Kádár's cowardly behaviour when in their hands made him an easy target. Besides, like Rajk, he had planned to bring the ÁVH under ministerial control, and that was forbidden territory. When he emerged again in 1954, he was consumed with hatred against Gábor Péter, Mihály Farkas and especially Farkas's son Vladimir, who had been the chief torturer. Kádár did turn to Rákosi, whom he saw as a father-figure, but soon came to detest that old man as well. From youth onwards he had been a good chess player, and his attitude towards Communist politics was also that of a chess player, with which title he was introduced in a much later *Time* magazine interview. He had a prison face, a look of sadness, not surprisingly for the years he had spent there and in the underground. He resented intellectuals, was aware that he was not highly educated and in that sense got on with Khrushchev, who had learned mathematics in a small Russo-Ukrainian town from a priest, in return for a sack of potatoes. Kádár's loyalty was to the Hungarian Workers' Party, and in 1956 he went to Moscow just to present the Hungarian case: it was the Soviet Politburo that decided he was their man, which indeed he was.

Protected by tanks, the new puppet government moved in through a defeated city and, once installed in the Parliament building on 7 November 1956, the 'Revolutionary Worker-Peasant Government' was an object of derision. They counted as Soviet puppets, and lived for weeks in a deserted Parliament, sleeping on doors that had been detached from their hinges and then padded, while the women used sofas. Workers' councils were still in control of Csepel factories, and even adopted a programme drafted by István Bibó, who by now counted as the wise man of post-war Hungary, and these councils required the return of Nagy. Much was later on made of these councils' alleged revolutionary character, to the effect that they aimed at real revolution. The Soviets tried to persuade Nagy to recant and then go abroad, but he would not and refused from then on: he had been shabbily treated, betrayed, and from the Yugoslav Embassy he sent out a list of reforms, which received support from a council of intellectuals under the chairmanship of Kodály. Kádár used conciliatory language at first, and even said 'we want a multi-party system and free, honest elections' when he spoke to a delegation from the Central Workers' Council on 15 November. But quite soon he would resort to traditional brutal tactics, and in the meantime, operating under the eyes of a formidable Soviet team – Malenkov, Suslov and Aristov – he had to deal with the presence of Imre Nagy. Here a great betrayal took place. Kádár had assured Tito that the safety of Nagy would be guaranteed, but as soon as Nagy and his companions got into a bus, supposedly to their homes, they were abducted by Soviet officers on 22 November, detained in a military academy and taken to house arrest in Rumania, in a resort village north of Bucharest on the 24th. Kádár established a militia to take over from the Soviets, and when, on 8 December, the Central Workers' Council called for a general strike, Kádár felt strong enough to move against it, arresting its members. The 110 protesting intellectuals had a similar fate, and in places the protesters were fired on. There were thousands of arrests. The other Communist leaders – East German, Czechoslovak etc. – were afraid that Kádár might introduce a multi-party system and arrived in Budapest on 1 January 1957 to stiffen his resolve to re-introduce the Communist monopoly of power. When they had gone, on 5 January, he decreed two years of 'systematic repression and revenge'.[1] People's Courts, with faster procedures, were introduced; the police could intern or deport indefinitely and arbitrarily; the Writers' Association was dissolved, and several of the leaders, including Tibor Déry, arrested. Striking earned the death penalty, even for juveniles, who would be kept alive until, at eighteen, they could be legally executed. The repression eased off in 1959 but carried on until 1961, and 341 death sentences were carried out, with 22,000 people put in prison, half of them for five years or more, including a future President, Árpád Göncz, the historian of 1956, György Litván, and István Bibó himself. Thousands more went into internal exile or lost their jobs.

The most eminent victims were Nagy's circle. In March 1957 they were brought back from Rumania and imprisoned in Budapest, but would not co-operate in a show trial. In February 1958 a trial behind closed doors began and was stopped when Moscow feared its effect on the then warming relations with the west. It reopened in June, and all but Donáth and Kopácsi, the police chief of Budapest, who had joined the revolutionaries, were sentenced to death. Nagy made the memorable comment that 'I know that [...] I shall be rehabilitated, and three times as many people will come to my re-interment as went to Rajk's. My only fear is that my executioners will do the re-habilitating.'[2] He knew his Communism: this was, after all, what had already happened to Rajk. He and the others were executed on 16 June 1958, and buried in unmarked graves. The whole thing was a burden on Kádár's conscience, or perhaps it was just that he knew that he had irretrievably ruined his reputation. But he also knew that there was no defying Moscow. He had excellent relations with Khrushchev, who visited him for a week in 1958. He had convinced the Russians that he, not Ferenc Münnich, a war-horse, should be their man. And he also kept Rákosi well away; the ÁVO men, Farkas father and son, were imprisoned, together with Gábor Péter. Gerő was exiled until 1960, when he made an obscure return (as translator), dying in 1980. Révai also escaped to Moscow and returned very obscurely, dying in 1959.

But at the same time Kádár was attempting to win acceptance, and here he was helped by exhaustion and fatalism, carrot and stick. The organised discontent of the masses – or rather, organised semi-contentment – was trundled out again, and several hundred thousand citizens took part in the Mayday 1957 march along Dózsa út, past where the Stalin statue had been: Kádár was relieved, and at least could deal with the crowd in familiar terms, for he spoke reasonably well. He put up wages by 20 per cent and abolished compulsory deliveries from the peasants; small traders were not excessively taxed as before. Forty thousand of the refugees of 1956, promised amnesty, returned, and the senior archbishop, József Grősz of Kalocsa, indicated that the Church would co-operate, even though old Mindszenty was still shut up in the American Embassy. In 1958 the churches accepted state subsidies and were able to organise religious education outside school hours; and by November 1959 the Party had grown in membership from 100,000 in 1956 to 400,000, as ordinary people realised that Communism was there to stay; their jobs and prospects depended on it. But in the Politburo dogmatic Communists did not make the running, and the regimentation was not as severe as before. Khrushchev meanwhile beamed in his stage-peasant way, came in April 1958 for trade agreements and offered approval as such phenomena as a Communist Youth Federation and a Workers' Militia emerged. There was now not much resistance, and at sinister farce elections in November 1958 the newly revived Patriotic People's Front candidates had 99.1 per cent approval in a turnout of 98.5 per cent. At this stage it was still possible to believe that Communism would win in the end, whatever the concomitant crudities, and the Russians solemnly installed a provision in a constitution that they would overtake the United States. In the era of Sputnik, the Russian space shot of 1957, this seemed not implausible.

One area in which the new government was vulnerable in Soviet eyes was agriculture. Collectivisation was a mess – in 1956 it had collapsed, and in 1958 only about a sixth of the arable was under co-operative management. Small farmers grubbed along in the obstinate old way. Elsewhere there was much more – in Rumania, 75 per cent of arable, for instance – and Moscow complained. Khrushchev was now in master-of-the-world megalomaniac mode, brandishing his hydrogen bomb, launching space satellites, spreading revolution to Cuba and browbeating President Eisenhower. He had a vision of a Soviet Union that would overtake the United States, and he foresaw an enormous grain field growing from the Austrian border to the Volga, with cotton further east; Kádár was told by the 21st Congress of the Soviet Party to get a move on. Khrushchev reinforced this when he announced to Budapest that he was keeping Hungary going, and that she should just do as he said.[3] Kádár obeyed, and there were peasant haters on the Politburo who would have pushed collectivisation by main force, on the grounds that peasants were hopelessly backward and hostile. In 1958 and 1959 industrial investment was returning to previous levels – it rose by a third in both years – which would mean vast factories churning out questionable steel, and that in turn meant squeezing farmers, giving very low food prices to them, in order to feed the workers. In 1965 agriculture got less money than the Ministry of Defence – 5 per cent of the national income. Kádár at least avoided the labour-camp method of collectivisation that occurred in Stalin's Russia, and he made a vital concession: collective farmers would have their own small plot – 1.5 acres – with access to tools; they would have pensions (men at seventy, women at sixty-five), and there would be tax concessions. But there would be tax increases for those who stayed out of the collectives, and their children might lose places in secondary education. Party people came in buses from the towns to threaten and cajole, and by 1961, 90 per cent of the arable was in state farms or co-operatives on the Soviet model. This was not particularly successful, because the men often just moved to the towns and left the women to get on with farming; the agricultural population fell by 20 per cent between 1958 and 1961,[4] and the grain-field scheme did not really make much sense.[5] In 1961 grain had even to be imported from Canada as the process of collectivisation did not go smoothly, and there was already something of a problem about how such imports should be paid for. Even in 1956 Hungarian officials had been dealing in Vienna, and with the Bank of International Settlements at Basle, over foreign exchange. There were contacts, now, with the International Monetary Fund about how Hungary's trade deficit could be financed.[6] This was a problem that would grow and grow. The Hungarian debt became a factor in east–west affairs, and prompted some internal change in Hungary.

But in any case Kádár's Hungary was caught up in Khrushchev's de-Stalinisation. He made another speech in 1961, in an obvious attempt to gain popularity at home and abroad, and Stalin was removed from the Mausoleum. Until then Hungary had suffered something of an international boycott, her representative not accepted at the United Nations, but the second wave of de-Stalinisation led to change. In 1960 there was a partial amnesty for political prisoners, including Tildy and Donáth as well as the writers, and the internment camps were closed. The Writers' Association came back to life, and there was some relaxation of censorship. When, at the 22nd Soviet Congress in 1961, Khrushchev denounced Malenkov and Molotov, Kádár could tell that it was safe for him also to remove the remaining Stalinists. The Central Committee condemned the crimes of Rákosi's era, expelled him, Gerő and fourteen ÁVH officers from the Party, and Kádár himself took over the Prime Ministership from Ferenc Münnich, publicly saying that non-Communists might occupy senior positions in the state administration. This had already happened, and even quite early on, with some men brought back from deportation in the countryside when specialist knowledge of finance or railways was involved; there had been some remarkable survivors. But this now became more general. Students of middle-class origin could now again attend university without discrimination, and when the 8th Party Congress opened in November 1961, signs of reconciliation came thick and fast. An extraordinary figure emerged at this time, György Aczél, who managed matters with the intelligentsia. He had been born, as Henrik Appel, in Angyalföld, a part of town where you never saw anyone with an education, in 1917. He lost his father, a carter, early on, and got on badly with his mother and stepfather, who placed him in an orphanage. He remembered with detestation having to wait in the rain for a ceremonial visit from its 'sugar daddy' patron, Archduke József. His mother had some pretensions for, although she worked in a pawnshop, she had optician relatives. A spell with a Jewish psychiatrist for difficult children led Aczél to become interested in Freud and Jung; he read very widely while doing odd jobs, and in the later 1930s fell in with the left-wing intelligentsia who met in the Café Central – the poet Miklós Radnóti, Aladár Schöpflin, the radical agrarian Gyula Ortutay, the Kádár associate Ferenc Donath, and the writer Antal Szerb. He became a Communist in 1935, and changed his name (Aczél, meaning 'steel', has echoes of 'Stalin', but this seems to be coincidental). The second anti-Jewish law, with its 6 per cent *numerus clausus*, caused trouble even on the stage but, like lawyers, actors could go private. Aczél became, and made a living as, a jobbing actor. This helped him as an underground Communist, and when the Germans occupied Hungary in 1944, his role was heroic. Together with Zionists, he had a factory for the manufacture of false papers, and a church in Ullői út in Pest gave certificates of conversion. Aczél himself donned German uniform, and although he did not speak German, could imitate to perfection the sound of a German officer in a rage, and, with a commandeered automobile, saved lives. In the post-war period, as a provincial Party secretary, he had kept good relations with Catholic priests and had been vaguely associated with the national-Communist line. As such, he had fallen foul of Rákosi, and spent five years in prison, and with this curriculum vitae recommended himself to Kádár. In 1957 he became deputy Minister of Culture.

'Deputy' in the circumstances was an ironic description, for he kept an eye on everything, and, being both vain and sociable, he also knew his intelligentsia. In 1960 he made the right concessions, releasing two prominent authors, and came to terms with the Writers' Union. Hungarian publishing then became interesting: not much of the Marx-Lenin incantation that went on elsewhere. There were remarkable historians who were not only good in their own right but went out of their way to help younger scholars who would otherwise have counted as class enemies. György Ránki, born in 1930, had been in Auschwitz, and came back weighing 30 kg. As a favoured historian, he helped young historians, even of an anti-Communist background (such as the future Foreign Minister, Géza Jeszenszky, or the literary historian Mihály Szegedi-Maszák, both from old gentry families), to make a career and to have scholarships abroad. Péter Hanák, born in 1920 and forced into the labour service in Galicia, sympathised with the revolt of 1956; surviving in the Institute of History, he acted similarly. In 1962 there was a certain opening up to the enormous cultural diaspora, with language-course instruction in Debrecen (attended by this writer). Aczél was associated with all of this, and remained very close to Kádár: his wife was Kádár's wife's doctor.

And he provided the regime with the slogan that marked it. *Népszabadság* in January 1962 quoted Kádár to the effect that 'those who are not against us are with us' – the line perhaps first written by Tibor Déry after his release from prison. Kádár appealed to the 'many hundreds of thousands of non-Marxists who respect our Party and our government for having created a legal order and a normal atmosphere'. There would be no need for 'intensification of the class struggle'. The key was, of course, to avoid trouble with the Soviet Union, and at the time, with neutral Austria beginning to flourish, there was no doubt some sense in Moscow that Hungary should not continue as a nasty little counter-example, as East Berlin was for West Berlin. An important part of this would be economic. It was, of course, preposterous for a country such as Hungary to be attempting heavy industry, and to apply the Soviet planning system. But Kádár knew that he must not provoke Moscow – in fact, the Hungarian embassy in Moscow removed a modernist tapestry when Khrushchev, a hater of 'modern art', objected in 1962.[7]

Economists, and bureaucrats in the Finance Ministry, had had a great shock in 1956, when revolutionary mobs gathered outside their buildings and they had to creep home incognito in the dark. The events of 1956 had damaged the economy, but it was a mess anyway. A threatened crisis prompted criticism of the existing system, itself based on Soviet precepts. Such criticism had surfaced under Nagy but had fallen away when he left office in 1955, but it was obvious enough that central planning, in which everything – investment, wages, prices, raw material allocations – was decided at the top for every state enterprise, was quite inappropriate. A one-time Small-holder Party adviser, the economics professor István Várga, reported in 1957 that the system must be overhauled with prices to reflect reality, or even supply and demand. But such arguments always broke down against 'socialist' orthodoxy, and as things turned out, soft loans and credits from the USSR allowed a rapid economic recovery, with production reaching its level of 1955 again. However, the problems indicated by Várga did not go away. In the first place there was foreign debt, both to the Communist trading bloc, COMECON, which attempted to integrate the bloc's economies to the advantage of the USSR, and to other countries. The debt, $1,600 million in 1959, rose because of grain imports to $4,100 million in 1963. Hungarian exports were generally of low quality, and over half of textiles and shoes from some plants were just rejected: 54.5 per cent of the shoes produced in the Divat factory fell apart, and three-fifths of silk exports were turned down.[8] There were attempts to pay for the debt with industrial exports, and the results were comic. There was a Technoimpex for machine tools, and the Milan distributor, a Dr Breviano, said, 'I am not willing to gamble my reputation with the unimaginable quality of your produce'. A French director was even more rude: no notion of spare parts, pieces constructed with endless errors, and packed like a sack of potatoes. The truth was, of course, that the managers, appointed for the wrong reasons and then prevented from organising production on common-sense lines, could not care less. There was prodigious waste of resources, including labour. Once the Stalinists were removed, something could be done, and Rezső Nyers, head of the Central Committee's economic department, was asked to make an overall analysis of the situation. He, a former printer and Social Democrat, had been Minister of Finance, and he believed that market forces could be utilised under socialism. By October 1965 the eleven committees working under him came up with what came to be known as the New Economic Mechanism, which was introduced, with modifications, in January 1968. This was in effect what was to be known as 'the Prague Spring' in 1968, but without the political headlines.

In Czechoslovakia there had also been some liberalisation in 1964, but she differed from Hungary, in the first place because the Czech lands were industrialised – in 1938, on a level with Belgium – and in the second because she had a nationality problem. The Party was dominated by Czech Stalinists, who despised and mistrusted Slovaks, with their peasant, Catholic and Hungarian background. Slovaks responded craftily and produced a reformer with good Soviet contacts, Alexander Dubček. Economists who could see how much was wrong with the prevailing system could criticise, but because of the Czech–Slovak rivalry this burst into politics: Dubček rose through Slovak self-assertion, and had an uneasy alliance with Czech versions of Nyers. But in 1968 this burst over into politics, the slogan being 'socialism with a human face', and, faced with the possible defection of Czechoslovakia, Moscow decided on intervention. Oddly enough, Slovaks took advantage, and subsequently switched much industrial investment to their part of the country. It was an illustration of the national problem that did so much in the end to bring down Communism.

Not so in Hungary. Nyers avoided any political dimension, spring or otherwise, and had the state continuing to own the means of production but not controlling every aspect of what they got up to. Production would be more sensitive to world prices, the Plan would indicate rather than prescribe, and regulators would prevent waste of labour or raw materials. There would be material incentives for improvement. Tax was used for such regulatory purposes, and managers within limits could determine wage levels for rewards and punishments, with a tax penalty on the firm if it bit into its investment fund. There was a three-tier price system. Raw materials, such as oil, were fixed, as were food and children's clothing, but most manufactures and construction also had uncontrolled prices. Co-operative farms were encouraged to move into food processing and had a free hand otherwise (mostly). Constraints on private economic activity would be gradually removed. Lenin had said of this sort of thing that the petty bourgeoisie would reconstitute itself hour by hour, and so in a sense it proved. This was all presented in thickets of impenetrable prose, but the implications were clear enough. In 1968 Kádár had to handle the Czechoslovak crisis. Dubček had started reforms on Hungarian lines and even wanted to set up a West German trading office in Prague; on the other hand, open support for Dubček would weaken Kádár's standing with the Soviets, and he trod very carefully. He argued in Moscow late in May for moderation, and did so again when a bad harvest forced him to ask for Soviet help. But Dubček wandered into political reform, allowing 'factionalism' in the Party, and when the two men met secretly at Komárno, Kádár said at the end, at the railway station, 'Do you really not know the sort of people you are dealing with?' But when, on 21 August, the Soviets invaded, Hungarian troops took part, whereas Rumanian ones did not. Kádár cancelled all engagements for two months. But he knew that in the end everything depended on Moscow.

There was opposition. Nyers sometimes referred to 'democratisation' of economic life, and said, in quite Marxist terms, that 'If you develop the mind of economic man, you develop the mind in general [...] we shall have to develop in connection with the economy our cultural and political institutions as well' (1980). High unemployment and inflation would follow, said some. The bureaucrats of the Plan system feared that they might become redundant, if enterprises were free to make their own decisions. The reformers had to make concessions – the tax on enterprise profits became absurdly high, the limits on wage increases were severe, and more consumer goods got fixed prices. The Politburo resolved in 1969 that 'changes on a large scale must be avoided'. Still, this was a sea-change: the command economy was dismantled. Besides, there was immediate improvement.

In the last two years of the Third Five-Year Plan (1966–70), productivity rose by 6 per cent, and so did the GNP. Consumer goods were more on offer, and the standard of living rose. Agriculture benefited as the permissive approach to private plots and co-operative autonomy caused a great increase, such that by 1978 private plots accounted for 50 per cent of output in horticulture and livestock, although only 18 per cent of the arable land. Hungary once more exported grain, and agriculture accounted for a fifth of exports and more than half of her foreign currency earnings. The co-operative farms were amalgamated, sometimes on the lines of the old great estates, falling from 4,600 in number in 1961 to 1,600 in 1978. They were integrated with the food-processing industries and profited from this, to the extent that Hungary equalled Denmark in terms of meat production per capita. Industry was hampered by constraints and did not flourish as much, quality control showing that only a fifth of the output met world export standards. Already in 1972 Nyers was considering how Hungary could be more exposed to world competition. The later 1960s and early 1970s saw significant advances in the general standard of living, as system-built housing blocks spread, together with ownership of appliances.

However, events in Moscow were not conducive to further efforts. Khrushchev had been ousted in 1964, and the successor regime, under Leonid Brezhnev, was conservative, fearing, not wrongly, that any change would be for the worse, and the other ruling Communists, for instance in East Germany, were suspicious of Kádár's men. Kádár himself cultivated Brezhnev carefully, and as a long-serving satrap was on the whole trusted. But the critics, at the Tenth Congress in 1970, were vocal, in that income inequality was rising: the term 'goulash Communism' was used in disapproval, suggesting a political system made up of contrasting elements, like a Hungarian stew, but Brezhnev was present and allowed Kádár his way. Besides, agricultural incomes rose faster than industrial ones, and when Kádár went to Moscow in 1972, he found a hostile article in *Pravda* saying that nationalism, social problems, petty-bourgeois trends and even Zionism were raising their heads in Hungary. The Politburo criticised him to his face, and when his Prime Minister wanted increased deliveries of Soviet raw materials, Alexey Kosygin, the Premier, curtly refused. In the Party there were grumbles that managers were earning too much, and that peasants were doing better than the working class. Six months later, in November 1972, the Central Committee, at Soviet prompting, restored central planning and state control, and the reform programme was reversed. In 1973 the oil crisis and the general commodity inflation caused the government to abandon experiments, and the setting up of a State Planning Committee in 1973 enabled it to reassert control of the large enterprises, to tax profits more, while subsidies for unprofitable enterprises – such as steel factories in Ózd – plus price supports accounted for one-third of the state budget. In agriculture enterprising managers were eased out over alleged corruption. Livestock on private plots fell dramatically as the proprietors slaughtered sows rather than face a loss on selling the piglets. Nyers lost his place in the Central Committee secretariat in 1974 and was voted off the Politburo in 1975; he retired in effect as a professor at the Academy of Sciences. His ally Jenő Fock lost the Prime Ministership in 1975 to an apparatchik, György Lázár. Brezhnev grumbled also about Aczél, who, with his instinctive guile, sidestepped the problem.

But the old system could not be put back into place. Hungary suffered from the economic crisis of the 1970s. Her oilfields, once important for Hitler's war machine, and later seized by the Communists in a show trial from the American owners, had by now shrunk and met only a small part of demand. The cost of her imports rose by some 70 per cent, whereas exports rose only by half of that, partly because western demand slackened. In 1975 the Soviet government changed the terms on which Hungary got oil – prices no longer fixed for five years, but on a sliding scale, reflecting the rise in world prices. Hungary was the least well-provided state of the bloc in terms of raw materials, as she faced a 50 per cent rise in energy prices as against a rise of 15 per cent for machinery and 28 per cent for agricultural exports. By 1980 she had to export eight times as many buses – a speciality – for a given quantity of oil as in 1970. The only way out was to take on debt, and, the Arab and other OPEC countries being awash with money, it was available. The foreign currency debt rose from $848 million in 1971 to over $7,000 million by 1979. Hungary further owed $3,000 million to COMECON partners, especially the USSR. By 1978 even the reactionaries could see that there was a problem needing to be addressed. There is always the suspicion that the crisis was deliberately worsened so as to arrive at this end, to convince Moscow somehow that action needed to be taken in the direction of independence, of western links. The Poles in the same period produced direct opposition.

Besides, there was a sea-change in European affairs, which affected Hungary's domestic affairs. Kádár himself had by now become respectable. Various problems with the Americans were sorted out – property claims in the first instance, but then also the position of Mindszenty. The Vatican agreed to appoint a deputy for him, and in September 1971 he left Budapest for Rome, there to spend time denouncing the Communists in the old style. (Journalists were rather taken aback by his English, until they realised that he had picked it up from black soldiers in the Embassy.) In 1971 and

1972 the West Germans had made an approach to Moscow called *Ostpolitik*. They would recognise the post-war borders of Poland and Czechoslovakia; they would trade; they would offer credits; they would build pipelines to transport Soviet gas through Austria. (Austria's role in these matters was striking. The later President Kurt Waldheim had a record of such pliancy towards Soviet interests that he may even count as an agent. He closed the Czechoslovak border in 1968 and then, with Soviet backing, became secretary-general of the United Nations, in which capacity he allowed Yasser Arafat to address the body, with a revolver on the stand in November 1974.)

This came together with American embarrassments over Vietnam, and the dollar, in which oil was priced, was weakened by American spending, domestic and overseas. In August 1971 it was no longer backed by a functioning gold exchange, and the Arabs responded eventually by raising prices – using the excuse of an Arab–Israeli war in which, at first, the Israelis suffered a sharp reverse. Now, with German pressure, the Americans accepted a Soviet proposal that had always been on the table. The suggestion of a great pan-European conference to settle borders had been made again and again, and the Soviet Foreign Ministry knew how to handle such events, whereas the west would very likely fall apart in disagreement. The result was the Helsinki agreement of 1975, setting up an international body to guarantee the outcome. One 'basket' concerned human rights, and to begin with the Soviet side was nonplussed. Then it worked out that for every complaint about Soviet dissidents, or about Jews forbidden to emigrate, it could find a Kurd or a South African in response. Human rights then became bureaucratised. In that context Kádár travelled – to Bonn, Paris, Rome – and Hungary received a very favourable press. She also qualified for easy-term loans.

But still, he had acceptance internationally. In 1963, with the release of political prisoners, he was accepted again at the United Nations, and in 1973 diplomatic relations resumed with West

Germany, which became the largest trading partner after the USSR. There was a succession of official visits, and relations with Austria became warm. A settlement was made of western property claims, and in 1978 the Crown was brought back to Hungary and the country was admitted to the IMF and the International Bank of Reconstruction and Development (in Europe), part of the World Bank; the Soviets' permission was not sought, although they were informed. A recent study by the Hungarian Committee of National Remembrance suggests that there may have been a hidden side to this, as various intelligence groups sought to extract Hungarian money by various ingenious devices.[9] Soundings were made in 1982 about a Hungarian link with the European Community – initially for free trade in industrial goods and better access to European markets for agricultural goods. But nothing came of this: at the time less than half of Hungary's trade was with COMECON. Gyula Horn, at the time deputy head of the International Department of the Central Committee, carried on these negotiations in secret, from his own foreign ministry and the foreign trade ministry, which had Soviet agents aplenty. In 1982 these contacts gave Hungary an IMF credit that saved her from debt rescheduling, but the economic performance that followed was not good.

By mid-1978 Kádár had eased out some of the chief opponents of the Mechanism – including even his presumed successor, and deputy, Béla Biszku; there was therefore less opposition to change. In 1978 the government encouraged 'the second economy': i.e., independent second-job activity. And there was an approach to the west for trade and tourism, which meant presenting Hungary as a civilised country. New regulations in 1978 favoured the private plot again, which could be enlarged through long leases of state land. In 1980 came even a sort of miniature Chinese turnaround: radical price reform freed most consumer prices, apart from basic necessities, and also adjusted those of energy and raw materials towards world price levels. Prices were 57 per cent up on 1979 overall (all those cheap railway tickets), and manufacturers had to eliminate waste. Domestic prices also had to reflect export ones, and profits were taxed less. In February 1980 the Politburo recognised that a fifth of half of the workforce's time was spent in the second economy. A high proportion of state-owned shops were now leased out to people who could keep the profits, although they would also face any losses. In factories groups of workers could set up a work co-operative offering maintenance and repair services, renting the factory's own equipment in their own time, profits distributed among the team. By 1986 there were 23,000 of these, using 250,000 workers outside working time. In 1982 private taxis started up. By 1985 private activity accounted for a third of the national income and involved two-thirds of families. This was hailed as market economy within socialism. Andropov allowed it to happen.

The USSR responded to the second oil shock, when prices doubled in 1978–9, by cutting the deliveries it made to Hungary at favourable prices, and requiring dollars. Hungarian reserves of convertible currency then fell from $2,000 million to $500 million in a few months, to March 1982. Growth slowed to 2 per cent, and many major industrial firms, by now antiquated, were enormous, and could not be allowed to go bankrupt for fear of unemployment. And yet the factory workforce, engaged semi-privately, hardly worked on their formal job, whereas the countryside at the weekend was the scene of frenetic activity. In 1983 there was a sense of impasse in government circles, and things kept going through more and more debt: $8,800 million in 1984, $10,700 by 1987 and $20,000 million by 1989.

It helped that the Hungarians in the west were clever people. János Fekete, the main negotiator, was ideal: cultivated enough to exchange well-chosen recordings of classical music – Hungary had outstanding pianists – with his opposite numbers in the IMF, he also had a past in the country's bad time: a Jew, in a labour battalion, he had escaped, across the frozen Don, to Russian internment, where he learned the language and became an interpreter. He had a background in banking, as his father had been a stock exchange clerk, had lost the job in the Depression and had retired to the provinces. His son, bright, could not go to university because of the *numerus clausus* and therefore worked as a clerk until the labour service took him in – from which he deserted. He and others in his Ministry had had a great shock in 1956, when crowds gathered, denouncing Communism, and he took up the cause of reform. Only he did not do so directly: he dealt with the west over debt, gradually winning confidence.

In the early 1960s imports of western consumer goods and of grain went ahead, without much coverage,[10] and there were initial contacts with the IMF. At the time the Soviet Union itself fell into embarrassments and had to import from the USA, with President Kennedy's blessing. Bright people – Communism sharpened the brain, and gave people intuition as to who could be trusted and to what was happening – could see that if bread seemed slightly darker in colour, this meant that the wheat extraction rate was increasing: i.e., that there was less grain.[11] Hungary needed to import, and needed links with the IMF, so that the increasing debts were a millstone round Moscow's neck. A paradox of the Soviet empire was that the 'colonies' were richer than the metropolis.

One thing for Hungary did stand out. There was formidable emigration, probably the most formidable in world history. Two hundred thousand Hungarians had gone abroad in 1956, but there had been many, many before then, and they generally did well, sometimes extraordinarily so.[12] Famously in Britain there were Thomas Balogh, Peter Bauer and Nicholas Káldor, all of them lords, advising on economic affairs. In music, Hungarians had swept all before them, particularly Sir George Solti. In the later 1970s officials of the Kádár régime were making contact with prominent émigrés, and an extraordinary figure emerged, George Soros, who had made a fortune in speculation, and now proposed to use his money to extend links between Hungary and the west. In the decade ahead, Communism was in effect to be hollowed out.

Of all the countries in 'the Bloc', Hungary was most attractive.

Living standards were not too bad – every third family owned a car, though not a reliable one, and every second family had a country retreat, usually very modest. Although allowed only $5 for a foreign journey once a year, there were sufficient foreign contacts for Hungarians to travel to the west – in 1980, 5 million (to all countries). There was every appearance of the rule of law, and there was even some tinkering with democracy in 1972, but all candidates were vetted by the single Party and this was just make-work for opportunists. However, pensions for all – at sixty for men and fifty-five for women – were brought in in the 1970s, and maternity leave was improved, perhaps in view of the demographic crisis that was impending. Hungarian healthcare was of a high level, although it had to deal with a population addicted to bad habits. Education continued to be old-fashioned and efficient. People knew the national classics, and played their instruments.

But life was still hard. There was a chronic housing shortage, and the young lived with their parents until after ten years they got a badly built, two-room municipal flat. Private building did go ahead but was too expensive. The brown-envelope culture was widespread, and from this came the problems: a low birth rate, a high rate of divorce and a suicide rate of 0.065 per cent (60–70 per 100,000 people). Suicide was not uncommon among late teenagers, and alcoholism was also a problem, with 850,000 registered alcoholics, nearly 10 per cent of the population. A third of the population counted as obese. Life-expectancy for a man fell to sixty-five (for women, seventy-three). Mental illness was also a problem, doubling between 1970 and 1980, and then doubling again in the 1980s. Disposable income had grown by 3.5 per cent annually in the 1970s but grew hardly at all in the 1980s; after 1985 it fell, as taxes such as VAT were suddenly imposed. The rapidly growing gypsy population was integrated by force, and most worked as unskilled labourers, but the régime did not really know what to do with them. Some were given old houses in the inner parts of cities, which turned into ghettos, while others lived in gypsy enclaves on the edges of villages. Racial hatred was stigmatised, but the police themselves used the term 'gypsy-crime' (*cigánybűnözés*). The Kádár consensus was over.

On 10 November 1982 came another decisive Soviet death: that of Brezhnev. He and Kádár had been friendly. (They were both heavy smokers. Brezhnev's doctors tried to limit his smoking by giving him a machine that automatically gave him a cigarette once an hour. Brezhnev had a second machine made in order to double his ration.) He had been ill for some time, although that illness had been concealed from the public. Now he died, and Soviet affairs went into convulsion. A Hungarian, François Fejtő, had observed of 1956 that the oppression would go on until, finally, it exploded at the head. Now it did, in Moscow.

# CHAPTER 9

# The 1980s and Beyond

U ntil just before it happened, very few people foresaw the end of Communism. There had been a book, in 1976, called *The Final Fall* (*La chute finale*), by a very young French anthropologist, Emmanuel Todd, who, it happens, is of Hungarian origin (the name Todd being an adaptation of Tóth). He had guessed, from listening to rock music – the siren song of the west – in a student flat in Budapest that the system was collapsing, but of course found more concrete evidence. The book was endorsed by the veteran Raymond Aron, but otherwise had few takers. Even the most pitiless analyst of the subject, Alain Besançon, did not think that the Soviet Union would go, although he did write, in 1976, to the effect that in Poland and Hungary Communism was disintegrating and that another Soviet armed intervention might occur.[1] In any case, at the time, the west appeared to be in worse shape. Its commercial and financial system had broken down, and it lost Iran in 1978–9 as the Shah fell and the ayatollahs took over; the second oil shock – a doubling of prices – came with heavy unemployment, 20 per cent inflation in the USA, strikes in Britain, troubles in Italy and virtual civil war in Turkey. The bookshops sported titles such as *The Crisis of Capitalism*, and Kádár's Hungary generally had a good press. Visitors were persuaded of the virtues of 'goulash Communism' or 'feasible socialism'. There was no unemployment. Unlike in Rumania, there was decent food in the markets, private enterprise brought good little restaurants into existence, central Budapest looked impressive, and the secret police and its network of informers, though omnipresent, were not obvious. People could travel west (although 100,000 were quietly refused permission, even in the mid-1980s[2]). If you had a foreign passport, Hungary was a most interesting place. The dreadful dullness of politics made people concentrate on other matters. The intelligentsia were very good, with excellent English, and were well read, with that special bleak and sardonic Hungarian humour. The country produced good films (*Mephisto*, about Nazis, *Angi Vera*, about Communists), and the pianists – Tamás Vásáry, András Schiff, Zoltán Kocsis – had worldwide reputations; the historians did not bludgeon you with Marxism. The television was closer to Austria's than to Czechoslovakia's,[3] and its magazine, *168 óra*, was comparable to the BBC's *Listener*. Who would have guessed that Hungary, within a few years, was to have a leading role in bringing down the entire system?

In concrete terms, the Cold War had begun in November 1945, when the Soviet Union stopped co-operating over the proposed new trade and financial arrangements for the post-war world. These, after a multinational conference at Bretton Woods in New Hampshire, established the International Monetary Fund and the World Bank, and Stalin declared non-co-operation. Hungary at the time had no peace treaty at all, and did not have the option of candidacy. In a small but significant move, in May 1982 she did join the IMF, while 'the Second Cold War' was at its height. The Politburo under old Brezhnev had decided to invade Afghanistan late in 1979 to install a puppet, and Moscow got stuck, fighting fanatics. The USA retaliated by refusing to ratify a nuclear arms limitation treaty, and sought to match Soviet medium-range missiles in western Europe. Part of the governing German Social Democratic Party objected, and its Chancellor, Helmut Schmidt, lost office. It was at this moment that the Hungarians surreptitiously declared demi-semi-independence. Hungarian finances were by now in parlous condition. Without much to sell in western markets, Hungary was nevertheless importing a great deal from West Germany especially, and if that stopped, the standard of living would fall. The Russians were not much help, as they sold their oil for high prices in the west. Hungary's answer was debt, and it was on offer, from the huge surpluses that oil producers built up.

But by the later 1970s, as interest payments went up, the debt became difficult to service, and the negotiator János Fekete was driven to sleight of hand – taking a loan of $500 million from the Japanese and using it at 9 a.m. the next day to pay off an earlier debt.[4] Fekete told Kádár the only answer would be to join the IMF and have Hungary's debts underwritten, but he said no one must know about the approach, especially the Foreign Ministry. In the event, using the excuse that the Russians had originally, in 1944, accepted the Bretton Woods arrangements, the approach was surreptitiously made by Fekete in Washington and Kádár went to the Crimea to tell Brezhnev. This was grudgingly accepted, but on his return to Budapest, Kádár got a letter saying that Soviet oil deliveries would be cut from 6.5 million tons to 1.5 million. In April 1982 Hungary needed an immediate $600 million from the European end of the IMF (the Bank of International Settlements in Basle), and that was not easy: only Helmut Schmidt could arrange it quickly, and he was very busy indeed, given that he was fighting for his political life, in a three-cornered contest between American missiles, the German left and unreliable coalition allies. He gave Fekete ten minutes late at night, grumbling, and agreed to help stave off Hungary's declaration of bankruptcy. With this, Hungary was effectively already in the west, and the IMF was entitled to insist on economic changes.[5] János Fekete understood foreign-exchange markets and the endless complications involved in translating barter-deal token money and other devices used by COMECON, the Soviet bloc's answer to the European Common

Market. It was not very successful: its entire foreign trade amounted to less than Belgium's. He was good company, and a cultivated man; besides, his past could only elicit sympathy. By 1962 he was already in contact with officials of the World Bank. In private, he let it be known that he regarded the Soviet planning system as absurd, and he was among the makers of the reform of 1968.

But no one now in authority had much belief in Communism, and the only real question was what to do. Minds were concentrated by 'the second Cold War'. By 1981 a western counter-attack was under way, with Ronald Reagan, and he had a thought-through programme of challenging the Soviet Union. His understanding with the Chinese, now making their first steps in the direction of economic liberalisation, was part of this. Margaret Thatcher in Britain, in office since 1979, was a staunch ally (taking advice from Vladimir Bukovsky, as it happened) and had already displayed considerable courage in reversing the national decline. All of this occurred in a context of economic and moral recovery in the west. 'Capitalism' was not collapsing – far from it: the Chinese version of it was creating a vast potential rival for the Soviet Union. And the Soviet economy had declined. As Bukovsky said, it was always based on pillaging and now it pillaged itself: it ran out of agricultural land, then raw materials and finally even labour. When world oil prices went down, there was trouble as the USSR relied on that money, and the armed forces were obviously outpaced by the Americans. There was also constant trouble in Poland, where a powerful anti-Communist trade union movement, Solidarność, controlled by the Church, was contained only by the proclamation of martial law late in 1981. In the vast confusion of Moscow's governance, the KGB was the only institution where reality could be faced, and where facts were known, and its head, Yuri Andropov, became Party chief when Brezhnev died in 1982. He himself died in 1983. Then, after a black-farce interlude, came a new face, that of his protégé, Mikhail Gorbachev, who took over in 1985. He promised 'New Thinking', dismissed many of the Brezhnevite old guard, gave up the tactic of appealing to the European left and cultivated the victorious right instead. He had very good relations with Margaret Thatcher, an important way into Washington, but he particularly aimed at Germany, because western European unification had greatly advanced with the Single European Act (1985) and Germany would clearly dominate affairs. But that would mean a general facelift for the Soviet bloc, and improvement in central Europe in particular, and here Hungary came in. Gorbachev went to see Kádár in June 1986 (he knew Hungary well enough, having studied her agriculture before he became head of the Party), and Kádár had forebodings: how would he get on, with his talk of liberalisation?

Hungary had her uses for Moscow, as she could be used as a bridge and even as a showcase. Kádár's relations with the west were good, with Austria especially, and for Germany Vienna was a good post-box. This again had long origins: even in 1952 Stalin had given signals that he might allow German unification – the abolition of the Soviet-zone 'German Democratic Republic' – if the new Germany were formally neutral and not part of NATO. Something of this sort had happened with Austria: in 1955, as a temptation for the West Germans, the Russians gave up their zone in eastern Austria in return for a declaration of neutrality. At that time the Germans were not tempted, but they opened an embassy in Moscow and trade got under way. By 1986 there were more radical ideas. Bright people in Gorbachev's entourage appreciated that East Germany was a liability, a place of pollution and oppression, and the Berlin Wall, designed to stop East Germans from taking refuge in West Berlin, was no advertisement for Communism. Andropov, then head of the KGB, could see that German unification (after the 'Prague Spring') was on the cards, and told the Politburo in 1974 that the Americans had smart weapons with which the USSR could not compete. This was no doubt behind a strange ghoulish episode when, at dead of night, he had Hitler's presumed remains dug up (from a car park in Magdeburg: they had been mixed up with other remains) and thrown into a nearby river: best to avoid some sort of future shrine. Kádár's 'goulash Communism' was anyway a product of Khrushchev's détente, and Hungary might as well just be allowed to become a sort of showcase.

When Mikhail Gorbachev came on the scene, János Kádár responded with gestures, even a provision for multiple constituency candidates in 1985, and though the candidates all said the same thing, the outcome was a small independent political presence. There was already a dissident movement in Hungary. It did not have Polish dimensions, the main reason being that the Catholic Church was not involved to anything like the same extent as in Poland: there was not the fervour that brought a million people, some proceeding on their knees, from Warsaw to Częstochowa in 1979, when the recently elected Polish Pope John Paul II said Mass at the shrine of the Black Madonna. The Church in Hungary had by and large come to terms with the regime – partly because of problems from the Holy See, where Hungarian security had penetrated – and Cardinal Mindszenty had become something of an embarrassment: priests' salaries were paid, religious instruction could be given after school hours, and the Vatican already had its own *Ostpolitik*. The Protestant churches, particularly the Lutheran, did offer some resistance, but the Calvinists had been infiltrated. Hungary was just not a very religious country. The nearest Hungarians came to such sentiments was nationalism, and that could be excited by any reminder of the troubles faced by Hungarians across the borders. These were real enough, especially in Transylvania, where thorough-going Rumanisation went ahead, and travellers from Hungary were body-searched for Hungarian books. There was a plan already under way for the destruction of Hungarian villages and historic buildings. There was a further difference with Poland in that the Hungarian economy worked after its fashion, whereas in Poland there was a first-class crisis, the shops empty, the money funny. The trade unions in Hungary remained part of the system, although the unnecessary jobs and propped-up living standards did make for longer-term problems. After 1977 the effects of western 'stagflation' were felt, and the country in effect lived on credit, which caused a reformation of the New Economic Mechanism and a dismissal of old Party war-horses. Real wages were declining (by 17 per cent between 1977 and 1988), and people (mainly men) were exhausting themselves in second jobs. The difficulty was not mass dissidence; it was apathy, demoralisation, shown in morning drinking and very fatty food. Many urban Hungarians were ludicrously obese and the suicide rate was infamously high.

The intelligentsia were, however, to the fore. Writers, as in France, had a sense of their own importance, and when in 1979 István Bibó was buried, there was a great demonstration of the readership – he was one of the last links with the pre-Communist system, and had been in Nagy's government. A memorial book was forbidden by the Party, but it circulated privately; and so, soon, did a journal, *Beszélő*, edited by János Kis, Miklós Haraszti and László Rajk. They were occasionally harassed by the secret police but not too seriously, as Aczél had their measure. (He lost his place on the Secretariat in 1982 but retained his influence over Kádár, who was also not perturbed by them.) There were three groupings: a partly Jewish one, often with Communist parents, who read *Beszélő* and were concerned with democracy and rights; a populist one, more nationalist in tone, with the poet Gyula Illyés well to the fore; and a Marxist one, in which reform Communists were prominent, including Nagy's one-time associate Ferenc Donáth. In 1985 after the elections representatives of these three groups, a sort of shadow Popular Front, met at Monor, south-east of Budapest, to discuss the social crisis emerging from the decline in living standards and the resulting demoralisation. Already there had been manifestations of dissent: underground religious movements, rock and roll culture and demonstrations on 15 March from 1972 to 1974.

But in any event people were voting with their feet. The relaxation of Hungary's relations with the west had been proceeding for several years and had gone ahead even under the 'second Cold War', which had supposedly started in 1979. Hungarian relations with the west did not suffer – on the contrary, there was a constant flow of visitors to Budapest, and Kádár now counted as an elder statesman. The Soviets grumblingly permitted this to happen, because even the Hungarian Central Committee's economic commission accepted that the economy was 'clinically dead' and Moscow might have to pick up the bill. The reason was that Hungary had built up a considerable debt – it rose from \$8,000 million in 1984 to \$20,000 million by 1989, the highest per capita in the Soviet bloc, and paying the interest (150 per cent of exports) was a strain. By 1985 the 'leadership' was just ignoring the debt, but the economy grew at a torpid 0.3 per cent and a loss was even made on construction projects with Libya, because cement was bought corruptly in the wrong, expensive, places.[6] Fekete was extremely agile in extracting loans from the west, and there is always something of a suspicion that he was deliberately building them up.[7] At least Hungary, unlike East Germany or Rumania, did not conceal the facts.[8] Whatever the case, western leaders were keen to know more, and exchanged visits with Kádár. The Germans were most important, here, and Helmut Schmidt found much common ground with Kádár, but the British also made a spirited effort, sending one of their most astute diplomats, Bryan Cartledge, who had been Margaret Thatcher's principal adviser on foreign affairs, as ambassador. There was an enormous embassy in central Pest, a building that had once been a bank, and the British had taken it over after the war as a sign that they meant to be a presence. Now the huge building justified its costs, as Budapest became a place where, beneath the tensions, deals could be done. Cartledge's own memoirs of this period appear in his excellent history, *The Will to Survive*.

There was another useful western lever: Austria. She had had her own version of *Ostpolitik*, the headline process of which had been West German recognition of the post-war eastern borders, and the acceptance of East Germany as a quasi-legitimate state. Austria had even taken the lead, surreptitiously, in negotiating the delivery, by Soviet pipeline, of natural gas to Germany (the pipeline engineering was German) via Czechoslovakia. Some aspects of this were downright grubby. The extraordinary Bruno Kreisky, by origin a Jew, headed an Austrian government that relied on the sometime Nazi voters of the non-Socialist and non-Catholic party, and he cultivated good relations with the Arab oil producers, the head-quarters of whose cartel were in Vienna. On occasion that meant taking issue with Israel. Kreisky was also the first western leader to make an official visit to the East German state, in 1978, and in 1980 Erich Honecker was welcomed to Vienna. This was maybe a neces-sary swallowing of toads, but Kreisky had something of a tadpole toad in the shape of his lieutenant, one Kurt Waldheim, who had been a very junior intelligence officer attached to the army group that occupied Yugoslavia, and he had of course added his signature to documents that needed verifying, some of them to do with war crimes. Helmut Schmidt had been a captain in the German army on the eastern front, and freely admitted it. Waldheim lied about it, crept up the Foreign Ministry ladder, was fingered by the Yugoslavs and thereafter at important moments acted as a Soviet puppet. As Foreign Minister in 1968, when the Soviets occupied Prague, he ordered the closure of the border (and told the Austrian ambassa-dor not to admit refugees, an order that was disobeyed). His reward came when, with Soviet backing, he became General Secretary of the United Nations, which office he used to promote the PLO. At around the same time Budapest was host to the PLO-related ter-rorist 'Carlos', a sinister Venezuelan. Another weird visit came from David Irving, famous for denying that Hitler knew what was hap-pening to the Jews. He was given access to archives concerning 1956, and wrote a book playing up the Jewish dimension.[9]

In 1956 the Austrians had been very helpful towards people fleeing the Soviet repression in Budapest, and they organised buses for tourists to be taken to Rust, on the Burgenland border, where they would be shown the Iron Curtain in all its glory – watch-tow-ers, binocular-brandishing guards, barbed wire and the rest, the very symbol of the Communist prison world. Relations with Hungary were frosty. Then in 1964 change started, with a sorting out of Austrian property claims, and in October of that year Kreisky, as Foreign Minister, paid an official visit. Kádár himself had his first visit to a western country in 1976, when he went to Austria, and in 1983 the Austrian Chancellor, Fred Sinowatz (who came from the once Hungarian Burgenland: his name showed Croat origins), broke with the tradition that Switzerland would be a Chancellor's first call, and made it Hungary instead. Formally, visa requirements between the two countries had been abolished in 1979, and trade had multiplied tenfold between 1965 and 1984.[10] Hungarians could already travel, though with strict limits to the amount of hard currency they could get, and only with authorisation from their employers' personnel department and from the Party and state security, which of course kept records of who said what to whom. But there was a huge Hungarian diaspora, many people of which had prospered, and they helped their relatives. Even in the later 1970s there had been a sizeable Hungarian presence in Vienna, and astute Hungarians could load up their small and puffing cars with boxes of electronic goods, acquired mainly in the Mariahilferstrasse. By November 1988, in a single day, 100,000 Hungarians visited the Burgenland, causing great traffic jams; by now they did not need to go to Vienna, as vast shopping malls were put up at Parndorf and elsewhere on the shores of the Neusiedler See. A papal Mass there in 1988 was attended by 130,000 souls, 60,000 of them Hungarian. The Iron Curtain was still, formally, there, but it was already almost a museum piece. (The German poet-commentator Hans Martin Enzensberger managed to write a sparkling but, in the manner of poets, wrong-headed essay about the Berlin Wall's becoming just a tourist spot in a world in which there were two German states. Honecker and his Politburo were not learning from Kádár, far from it, and were still executing young hotheads who tried to flee over that Wall.) It was soon to give Hungary, yet again, global significance.

Meanwhile there was an atmospheric change. The more Hungarians travelled west, the more they saw how they had become poor cousins. The sociologist Elemér Hankiss pondered: what does it do to a country when people realise that they produce nothing that anyone wants? Such matters of national morale went together with a growing material problem. More and more people worked in the 'second economy', known elsewhere as 'black', in that everything was done for unrecorded cash. Already in the 1970s private property in the sense of house-owning had emerged, and people could work freely in construction, even using tools taken from their alleged main occupation, and in the countryside even food processing was semi-private. The New Economic Mechanism people returned to positions of influence, particularly Rezső Nyers, and the Central Committee tacitly admitted gross mismanagement of the economy when it transferred responsibility for it to the government, rather than the Party. In Hungary there was another factor of vast importance. George Soros had survived the Arrow Cross and the siege of Budapest with false papers, had gone to London and then on to New York, where he made a fortune on Wall Street. Even before Gorbachev's emergence, he was negotiating with the Hungarians for an opening. His Open Society Foundation got recognition in 1984, and gave scholarships to the west: among the students at Oxford were Viktor Orbán and Zsolt Németh, now head of the Parliament Commission on Foreign Affairs (he turned down the Washington embassy). The deal with Soros was complex. Scholarships were primarily made available in the applied and natural sciences, but in exchange members of the liberal oppositon could go as well. In other words, a new Hungary was taking shape, and Soros's dollars were beguiling.

A decisive moment came with the Twenty-Seventh Soviet Party Congress, in February 1986. At the time the significance was not widely noticed, but in those acres of wooden language there were signs that the initiated could read, and anyway the replacement as Foreign Minister of the Cold War-horse Andrei Gromyko by Eduard Shevardnadze in 1985 had marked an unmistakable shift. (Shevardnadze agreed at the outset to settle the large debt that had been owed since 1918 to the British, which the USSR had always refused to discuss.) Gorbachev would not necessarily support the old guard of satellite leaders, his behaviour recognisably following the tactics of Khrushchev in 1956. In September 1985 Gorbachev saw Kádár and told him tactfully that, at seventy-three, he should be preparing a successor. Kádár asked him in return whether he did not fear being overthrown in a palace coup, as had happened with Khrushchev, and was told, 'I am not stupider than Khrushchev'. There were wobbles in the Hungarian Party, but for the moment Kádár stuck it out and even promoted an old faithful, János Berecz, as head of the international department. Berecz wrote a heroically mistimed book about how the Communist takeover had been impeccably democratic. (The most heroically mistimed such book was J. Arch Getty's, on the Stalin purges, which asserted that only about 3,000 people were killed, mainly through administrative error.)

In 1987 the rising popular discontent prompted further action, and even, in *Beszélő*, calls for Kádár to go, while young Party economists also protested the need for profound reform, including democratisation. The star of the hour was Imre Pozsgay. Here was a characteristic Kádár appointment, an iron in the fire balancing the old opponents of change, such as Berecz. On form, he was an outstanding orator, and a professional English-speaker; he became Minister of Culture in 1976, where he had uneasy relations with Aczél, and then Minister of Education, but was not promoted to the Politburo and had the lesser job of secretary in the Patriotic Front, the umbrella organisation that managed elections, dummy parties and all. Already in 1985, after the first (embryonic) real election, when the opposition figures met at Monor, he was among the reform Communists, including some of Imre Nagy's old associates, who discussed the social and economic crisis that all could feel. Reform Communism, calling for human-face socialism, had always had something of a presence, but this time there was perhaps more: the brighter Party members, who of course included

Pozsgay, could sense that they should look for the exit. There was a tussle with 'hard-liners' and Kádár, trying to hold a key mid-position, ousted the long-serving Prime Minister, György Lázár, and replaced him in 1987 with the less wooden Károly Grósz, who had been involved with media management and then became Party secretary in Budapest, an important position. He was obviously Moscow's man, and it was a sign of Kádár's slipping authority that he had to give Grósz some independence in the matter of personnel and appointments, and there was a further sign with the formation of a forthright reformist wing in the Party. Pozsgay and Rezső Nyers, who had no illusions as to what was going wrong, were present in September 1987 at another important meeting, this time at Lakitelek, a little place on the River Tisza. Pozsgay took centre-stage in discussions with non-Communists. With patriotic language he formed alliances far beyond Communist ranks that were to matter greatly for the future. He was clearly bidding for leadership, but for the moment Grósz was in charge and the Germans also backed him, with a loan of 1,000 million Marks, on condition that reform went through – price rises, privatisation, proper taxation. In any case by now Kádár, at seventy-five, was clearly in bad shape, as his heavy smoking caught up with him. In May 1988 a special con-ference of the Hungarian Party had been convened, as he attempted to stay on. He did manage a last victory, expelling reformist econo-mists and getting the Politburo formally to reprimand Pozsgay and Nyers (for setting up a separate reformist group). But then (on 10 May) the Central Committee rejected Kádár's own suggestions for modest personnel changes – always, in the Party, the key element in power struggles. He accepted that it was time to go, in return for an honorific appointment and assurances that he would not be prose-cuted. Moscow sent him a special emissary, Vladimir Kryuchkov, head of the KGB, an old accomplice of 1956, to persuade him to go (Kryuchkov had been in Budapest as a diplomat in 1956, and spoke the language), and on 19 May there was a farewell telephone conversation with Gorbachev, as Kádár agreed to take the honorary position; he was not even in the Politburo. In June 1988, at the 19th Party Congress, Gorbachev formally renounced Brezhnev's way of intervening in satellite countries, and later said he was withdrawing 10,000 troops from Hungary. This was a sign that no one could ignore.

Moscow allowed Grósz to become Kádár's successor, but already a non-Communist proto-government was forming: it was almost as if the salami of 1946–7 was being unsliced. The Lakitelek meeting in September 1987, with the 150 intellectuals and Pozsgay present, had set up a 'Hungarian Democratic Forum' (MDF). This became the first opposition party, dominated by József Antall, soon to be Prime Minister, and his son-in-law Géza Jeszenszky, soon to be Foreign Minister. Both were in a sense products of Kádár's Hungary, in that they were recognisably from pre-war days but had modestly prospered by avoiding any open challenge, and were not even present at the Lakitelek meeting. Antall's father had been the civil servant dealing with refugees during the war, and he had been notably humane as regards the Poles, including Polish Jews, who had fled from Hitler, many to join the British army. He had been prominent in the post-war Smallholders' Party, the chiefs of which generally met in his grand flat near the Károlyi Palace; when the Communist takeover happened, he remained in the rump Small-holders' Party as part of the Patriotic Front, and therefore survived, with connections strong enough for him to get his son out of prison in 1956. József Antall then became a very proficient archivist and librarian, eventually director of the Medical History Museum in Vadász utca, where once, in the 'glass house' at No. 29, the Swiss diplomat Carl Lutz had protected hundreds of Jews. With excellent languages and manners, Antall imposed: like his son-in-law, he could 'talk European' and would be the ideal candidate if ever Hungary were to take the Austrian road. And now, helter-skelter, came political change and economic reforms. Prices and wages were freed. State enterprises could become private companies, but this was a device for the managers to make fortunes from the unregulated sale of state assets, which went for absurdly low sums of money in a closed circle of Party members. A stock exchange came into existence. By January 1989 the greatest price increase since 1946 was under way – medicine 80 per cent, water 200 per cent, milk 40 per cent, and 2 million people, a fifth of the population, lived on or below the poverty line. Occupants of low-rent state flats could now buy them very cheaply. One of the ministers said, 'Our aim is to prolong the acceleration of the deterioration'.[11] But political life was now free. Censorship came to an end, and a new party of youth, FIDESZ, emerged in March 1988: its star speaker was Viktor Orbán. The *Beszélő* people, who went their own way, set up the Network of Free Initiatives, aiming to incorporate all opposition under one umbrella. When they realised this did not work, they set up their own Free Democratic Alliance (SzDSz). These were the 'dissidents' whom western journalists had known all along – fluent in English, well read, talking the language of the free market, human rights, democracy. The flowers were impressive, but the roots proved to be shallow.

The Party, at the end of 1988, still looked formidable – huge assets, 800,000 members. Grósz obviously expected to have a good central position, given that the opposition was divided. But he took on too much, heading both Party and government, was permanently exhausted, was clumsy and was being outmanoeuvred, as Pozsgay bid for the nationalist vote; when Grósz tried to compete, visiting Ceauşescu in Arad to plead for concessions in Transylvania, he allowed himself to be browbeaten by this preposterous Balkan mountebank, with his food tasters. In January 1989 in a radio interview Pozsgay took what, in the circumstances, was a decisive step. He said that 1956 had been a legitimate uprising, not a counter-revolution, thus disavowing decades of propaganda. Again Grósz could only unwillingly compete, agreeing that Imre Nagy should be rehabilitated, with a state funeral (which allowed Grósz's enemies a field day). But Pozsgay's nerve failed him, as Gorbachev's chief adviser, Alexander Yakovlev, stressed that Grósz had Moscow's support, and at a would-be reformist gathering in Kecskemét in April 1989 he delivered a temporising speech, did not set up a breakaway Party and thereby left the running to others, who wanted a break with Communism or, as Viktor Orbán said at the Nagy funeral, 'Asia'.

Grósz relinquished the government to a technocratic economist, Miklos Németh, and concentrated on the Party, but by now, in March 1989, an independent lawyers' forum came up with the notion of an opposition round table, bringing together all opposition groups to initiate negotiations with the government as to fundamental change. In Poland such an institution had appeared, and the mass support in Hungary was obvious. On 15 March, the national day, celebrating 1848, 100,000 people had demonstrated on the opposition side, with demands that echoed 1956; and the Party reformists met in Szeged in May, with Nyers and Pozsgay, although again there was no formal breakaway. Still, the Party was in disarray. Thousands of its members were tearing up their Party cards, the Youth Organisation (KISZ) was dissolved in April, and in May Kádár was removed as chairman, deprived of his membership of the Central Committee. He burst in on the Congress Hall and, nearly overcome with illness, spoke incoherently about his own misdeeds. The Party lost its right to veto non-party appointments and handed over its militia to the Ministry of Defence. The Prime Minister, Miklós Németh, himself abolished the informer-ridden Office of Church Affairs and set in motion the reburial of Nagy. In the spring the dictatorship suffered another defeat after environmentalist protests against a new dual power plant on the Danube, being built in collaboration with Czechoslovakia. After demonstrations, Németh ordered a stop to the construction. On 26 June 1989 came a great symbolic moment, when the Iron Curtain with Austria was dismantled, and Grósz, as Party leader, agreed to hold a Party conference, to negotiate with the round table. He probably calculated – like Moscow's other men elsewhere – that the opposition would fall apart and would allow him to continue to lead the country even after an election in 1990, provided he kept the shrunken but rich Party together.

The reburial of Nagy in the Rákoskeresztúr cemetery on 16 June 1989 was a huge demonstration of how wrong Grósz was. There were five coffins – Nagy and his fellow victims – and a sixth representing all the other dead of 1956. Two hundred and fifty thousand people came and listened to speeches contemptuous of Communism – the outstanding one being given by the young Viktor Orbán, of FIDESZ. He made biting points that after the Rajk reburial the Party had promised never to repeat a judicial murder, but had then gone on to execute hundreds. 'We are not satisfied with the promises of Communist politicians that commit them to nothing. We must see to it that the ruling party can never use force against us again.' Meanwhile, on 13 June, negotiations had started at the round table, which was in fact triangular (the third side was taken by the 'organisations' – women, veterans etc. – which had once been stage props for the 'Organised Discontent of the Masses' of 1946 and were now again trundled out, but in the opposite direction), with an overall determination that there should be no violence. There were arguments about property, about whether to have a presidential election or a general election first, and both the SzDSz and FIDESZ refused to sign the final accord. But the MDF was strong enough, and had its alliance with Pozsgay, for a deal to be done. Kádár died with some symbolism on 6 July, just as Nagy was reburied. The parallel with Rajk escaped no one's notice: Kádár's principal victims were given pride of place as Rajk's son almost presided over the huge ceremony. The bodies had been buried in unmarked graves, in the prison cemetery, but the families were invited to the exhuming and identification, and the twin museums on Heroes' Square were swathed in black, as powerful speeches were made. Young Viktor Orbán was speaking for his generation. 'Europe' was a universally used word: the writer Péter Esterházy suggested people should pay the state a forint each time they used it, and thus pay off the debt. Posters showed the back of a thick Russian military neck and head, marked 'Comrades, it's over' (*tovarishchi konets*), in Russian.

But while the round table had gone ahead, there had been an earthquake at Lake Balaton. The Iron Curtain in Hungary was 243 kilometres in length, and it still looked formidable – two rows of barbed wire (which had to be imported from the west, as it otherwise rusted), then three landmined metres, then five more rows of wire, with watch-towers and alarm systems. By the 1980s it was becoming dilapidated, and there were many false alarms; already in February 1989 the Politburo had resolved to dismantle it, and it was common gossip in East Germany that you should take your holiday in western Hungary.[12] On 27 June, at the suggestion of either Alois Mock, the Austrian Foreign Minister, or Gyula Horn, his Hungarian opposite number, a little ceremony was held in which the two men solemnly snipped a chunk of rusty wire. (The section of barbed wire had to be reconstituted for the cameras.) Until May, East Germans trying to escape had been sent back (1,088 of them in 1988), and one of them was even shot. On 19 August, with Austro-Hungarian blessing, a 'pan-European picnic' at Sopron in the Hungarian Burgenland, planned by the Debrecen MDF partly for the Rumanians fleeing their insane dictator, had allowed hundreds of East Germans just to walk into Austria, and thousands more besieged the West German embassy in Budapest. Thousands and thousands more waited in Hungary. Gyula Horn, the one-time Soviet puppet workers' militia man of 1956, asked Moscow what to do and was told, it is your choice. He then negotiated an agreement with Helmut Kohl and the German Foreign Minister, Hans-Dietrich Genscher, to allow these East Germans to proceed to Austria, and on 10 September all East Germans who wanted to do so were allowed to travel west. By mid-September 23,000 had done so – superb television, and the greatest possible demonstration that East Germany was a fake place. The Hungarians were frank, to the effect that they wanted to be paid. A credit of 500 trillion Marks was offered, though, out of propriety, the deal was settled when

Lothar Späth, Prime Minister of Baden-Württemberg, turned up in Budapest. To be on the safe side, Kohl telephoned Gorbachev in Moscow and was reassured: there would be no shooting. An exodus then happened, with crowds of East Germans camping out in the embassy grounds in Prague or even Warsaw, until finally, on 9 November, the Berlin Wall itself was breached. Gyula Horn (whose career had begun when he helped Kádár crush the revolutionaries of 1956) now has a street named after him in Baden. By the end of the year even Ceaușescu in Rumania had gone – done to death by a kangaroo court, together with his wife, whose last words were, 'How can you do this to an honorary doctor of Imperial College, London?'

There was not much room left for the Hungarian Party. During the six weeks following Nagy's funeral the old Parliament still functioned and passed the new laws – the most important, a re-editing of the constitution, adopted on 23 October. Dead-eyed, fat-faced men voted themselves out of existence, but no doubt with considerable consolation. Many of them, sensing the privatisation to come, were entrenching themselves, and were to prosper. On 6 October the Communists re-branded themselves as the Hungarian Socialist Party (MSzP), led by Nyers and Pozsgay, who had hopes of becoming President. But the liberal Budapest SzDSz and FIDESZ (sneered at as 'the Yuppie party') contested this, and in a referendum over some results of the round table (mainly concerning Party property) they managed to stop an early presidential election that Pozsgay would probably have won. As things worked out, the President was chosen by a new parliament, after elections on 25 March 1990. Pozsgay was cheated of his ambition. The new President was a veteran of 1956, Árpád Göncz, who had been imprisoned for six years but had used the time to acquire English, to the extent that he could translate part of *The Lord of the Rings*. He was associated with SzDSz, not with the MDF.

The electoral turnout was low, at 45 per cent in the second round, as so many voters were tired of politics (under Communism there had been endless elections, with compulsory voting), and now, with proper democracy, could find other things to do. Twenty-eight parties, some re-formed from the old days, emerged, and the right, in which the MDF was easily predominant, won a large majority, despite western help to SzDSz. József Antall was an imposing figure, much respected abroad, and he aimed for national consensus. The main element in opposition was the liberal SzDSz, dominated by dissident intellectuals who were not obviously in sympathy with the traditional-minded moderate nationalists (some of them immoderate) of the MDF, but Antall did a deal with them, which enabled him, if needed, to obtain two-thirds majorities to change the constitution. He himself was optimistic, thinking that in ten years Hungary would be on Austria's level, and he had studied the writings of the German political economist Wilhelm Röpke, one of the chief architects of the German 'economic miracle'. On the face of it, Hungary, an old part of Europe with a very well-educated population, should have managed this. There was a formula, more or less, which had its origins in the later 1940s, when Germany recovered, in the 1950s, when France did, and the 1960s, when Italy did; a variant of it had applied to post-Franco Spain and even post-Colonels Greece. In the era of the Marshall Plan (1948) the Americans had spent a huge sum on European recovery, encouraged democracy and insisted on European union; with NATO they had defended it. Hungary was associated with the European Union in 1991, and joined NATO in 1994. In 2004 she became a full member of the EU, with complete freedom of movement for her citizens within the Schengen area (and Great Britain as well). The overall results were not, however, those that the formula was expected to produce.

In part this was because the point of departure was utterly different from that of West Germany in 1950. There had been millions of refugees in Germany, many of them highly skilled, whereas a main problem in Hungary was that enterprising people would go abroad (in 2018, probably 800,000, mainly in Austria, Britain and

Germany). In 1947 the Americans were omnipresent in western Europe, able to veto any wrong moves, and it was they, through Marshall money, who pushed through European integration. And in that era heavy industry was the basis of prosperity (the old flag of the European Union shows this – black for coal, blue for steel). Thanks to the Communists, Hungary had acquired heavy industry. It was usually badly managed, overmanned, and it kept going through captured markets, but in 1990 much of it was obsolete, as Brazil or India offered competition, and the go-ahead economy had moved on. Hungary should really have been a sort of Denmark, with highly sophisticated agriculture and ingenious light industry. Even in political terms there was no real comparison possible between the world of 1947 and that of 1990. The West German constitution, a considerable success, was the work of some sixty men in 1948–9, and is quite short. The Hungarian round table had needed 1,300 people, and human rights, as the concept had developed, meant endless paragraphs. Hungary was being invited to join a European Union that was much more invasive and demanding than had been that of 1958, when its ancestor got going. Post-Franco Spain, true, had joined in 1986, when there was already a bulky passage of requirements, but there was not, beyond empty generality, any comparison between Franco's Spain and post-Kádár Hungary. In any case, by the time Hungary became a member-state, the *Acquis Communautaire* rulebook contained 50 million words covering everything from electrical plugs to minority rights, an enormously rich field for lawyers and 'non-governmental organisations' to interfere in. 'Europe' had ceased to be a magic wand, and became something of a cudgel.

The initial euphoria brought the Antall coalition to office, but it had no political experience, the (bloated) Kádárite civil service was not sympathetic, and Antall himself was seriously ill (he died in 1993). The debt was enormous, and if Hungary, profiting from the great good will in Austria and Germany, had asked for it to be cancelled, this would greatly have helped. As things were, the

Europeans drove a hard bargain. Hungary did not make much that western Europeans wanted, and their own weird arrangements as regards agriculture and viticulture caused them to discriminate against Hungarian produce. Their main contribution was therefore government-to-government aid which the outstanding economist Lord (Peter) Bauer described as a method by which the poor in rich countries pay for the rich in poor countries. Spain, especially, resented the competition. The trade balance, already unfavourable, worsened. However, investment ($8,000 million) did come in, whether for urban property or because of the promised privatisation, which by 1994 affected 60 per cent of state enterprises; half a million jobs then disappeared, but limited companies mushroomed (to 79,000). The picture was worsened because there was an immediate economic crisis as the eastern bloc disintegrated and the export of buses, food and pharmaceuticals stopped, while petrol prices rose by two-thirds (which caused a strike by taxi drivers, whose prices were controlled). By 1993 GDP had fallen by almost a fifth from 1989, and there was also price inflation of 35 per cent in 1991 and 20 per cent thereafter. In general, people were worse off by 15 per cent compared with 1989, and pensioners particularly suffered, most noticeably in Budapest because the demographic crisis caused a preponderance of old people. Antall, a poor public speaker, and himself concerned with a European image, ruled a party that had a nationalist wing which eventually split off altogether (under a playwright, István Csurka). After Antall's death there were elections, and the post-Communist Socialists won over half the vote. Gyula Horn, who had long experience of government and who had a good relationship with the Germans, used the resources of the Communist Party to effect, and had a network of media allies. He now became Prime Minister, and did a deal with the SzDSz, who had won a (poor) second place. They had good European links and supplied a finance minister, whose prescriptions would inevitably be unpopular. Their support was useful to Horn, and there was not much of an opposition left. However, FIDESZ, thumbing its nose, managed to clear the electoral hurdle, and began to make waves as its leader, Viktor Orbán, matured and did his political homework.

He was helped by the obvious problem faced by any government: that it would have to do unpopular things. Debt charges took one-third of the budget, but there were other items in health and social insurance that were hugely expensive and impossible to change, given the bureaucracies involved (who got the backing of two big bankers, for reasons of their own). Horn was cunning and masterful, and let his SzDSz finance ministers (he had five in four years) take the blame, and in the event it was pensioners who, through infla-tion, suffered (a fall of 25 per cent in real terms). In March 1995 the formula of what was known as 'the Washington consensus' (i.e., the IMF and the Europeans) was imposed by Lajos Bokros, the SzDSz finance minister: devaluation of the forint to help exports, reduc-tions of government spending, a salary freeze and accelerated privatisation. It worked, in its way, and Hungary had $18,000 million of foreign investment, more than any other former People's Democ-racy; the debt fell from $33,000 million to $27,000 million in 1996, and it cost Bokros his job, as similar programmes cost his succes-sors. He went to the World Bank, as the last Communist Prime Minister, Miklos Németh, found solace with the European Bank of Reconstruction and Development. Somehow the European tech-nical bureaucrats found more common ground with men of this stamp than with the forthright anti-Communists, often hairy, sen-tentious and deficient in English. European money had a smell attached to it, and is associated with some nasty structures, perhaps designed to show off 'capitalism' – in Budapest, a glass office box and an ugly hotel on a square containing the classical central Cal-vinist Church and close to the National Museum; a McDonald's next to the historic Astoria Hotel; and a would-be shopping mall, West End, which comes across not as a Harrods but as a huge Woolworths. There were well-founded rumours of corruption. At the same time French and, especially, German chain stores moved in, with the British taking an interest in the property market, or (in the case of Tesco) buying land, in the hope of building up a vertical production-to-sale structure, complete with computerisation – not a senseless plan but dependent on the vagaries of the post-Communist bureaucracy and the post-baroque Common Agricultural Policy. This, before its reform, caused a cow to be more expensive than a student. After its reform ('set aside'), a non-cow cost more than a student. Gypsies took over the emptying villages of the Great Plain and in eastern Hungary accounted for 20 per cent of the population – which stimulated some vicious reactions. In Communist times they had taken over much of the property in the old Palace Quarter of Budapest, District VIII, and since professional-class parents did not want their children educated in the same schools, property prices there remained astonishingly low. Foreigners arrived, and many veterans of 1956, who stood out because their Hungarian was sometimes semi-forgotten, and they showed often enough that they knew better than the poor old natives. (This writer remembers from that time that, speaking halting Hungarian, he sometimes got sour looks.) This had much to do with the emergence of Csurka's splinter group. Horn himself was often arrogant, failing to back his subordinates, and the SzDSz was broken by its association with him (although it is also true that the world had moved away from dissident intelligentsias, given to be prima donnas). In the elections of 1998 the Socialists took 35 per cent of the votes, but the associated SzDSz collapsed, some of its stalwarts finding an escape in the Central European University, which George Soros opened in Budapest around this time. It became a celebrated institution, pledged to what was called 'the Open Society', and it was well organised, with an excellent library, and a respected place among scholarly institutions. However, the Open Society was a popular cause with the Budapest intelligentsia and the media in general, not altogether with the voters.

A government of the right followed, this time dominated by FIDESZ. Its leader, Viktor Orbán, was an excellent speaker, in English (he was very well read) as well as in Hungarian – he understood the rhetorical differences – and had moved the party to the right. He now spoke for Christianity, the nation and the family in a style far removed from the rhetoric he had used in his twenties, when he had been irreverent and his relations with the elders of the MDF frosty. But Orbán reckoned that the MDF had lost because Antall did not play politics properly, did not cultivate businessmen and did not have a friendly newspaper. He was also no absolutist devotee of the free market, which, paradoxically, had been a cause of the failure of the socialist-liberal government. But he had few allies among the intelligentsia, and narrowly lost an election in 2002, after a campaign of media contempt and even hatred that he did not forgive; he returned to office in 2010, determined that this would not happen again. After more worldwide vilification he is still there, still demonstrably in charge, and perhaps the best-known European leader, beyond the Franco-German axis. The heart of this is the failure of the left in Hungary. The Horn government had pursued privatisation, and its successor, in office from 2002 until 2010, discredited itself for ever, to the point at which (in 2016) its headquarters were sold . There was one scandal of corruption after another, as clever former Communists helped each other, using 'Europe' as an excuse. Its leader, Ferenc Gyurcsány, was in some ways deserving, growing up in poverty, the child of a single mother and emerging in the Kádárite world as a youth leader. He married (for the third time) into a Communist dynasty, his mother-in-law a very successful businesswoman who had been Horn's chief of staff, and the background is imposing villas in smart parts of Buda. He did have an idea that he could be Hungary's Tony Blair, modernising the party to free it from dependence on welfarism and trade unions, but the task was beyond him, because the old Communist bulwarks were still there, preventing the deep structural reforms that post-Communism needed. In 2006, at a Party meeting on Lake Balaton, he was recorded as telling the faithful, 'we have been lying morning, noon and night' and that the government had done 'nothing'. When mass protests followed, he let the police behave brutally: on the fiftieth anniversary of 1956 there was a Communist prime minister and blood on the streets. The financial crisis of 2008 found Hungary very badly exposed, and in 2009 Gyurcsány, with a budget deficit of 10 per cent of GDP, and with support from the IMF amounting to three times as much as all privatisation had brought in, resigned. This was what brought Viktor Orbán to office again in 2010, this time with a majority large enough to draft a truly new constitution, clearly with a view to shortening the isotopic half-life of Communism.

All in all, it is a moment of hope, not a normal feature of Hungarian history, and it is symbolised by the re-emergence of Budapest as a sparkling European metropolis, the great architectural monuments being restored. There is not much doubt that the transition to post-Communism has been mismanaged, and that the Europeans have a good part of the blame. Antall's dream, of reaching the Austrian level in ten years, has not been realised, and in agriculture this is all too obvious as you cross the old Burgenland border. But a shadowy version of the old Habsburg unity is coming about, and Hungarians learn.

# Notes

___

## Chapter 1: The Setting

1. L. Siklóssy, *Hogyan épült Budapest* (Budapest, 1930; repr. 1985), p. 574.
2. Indro Montanelli, *L'Italia del Seicento* (Milan, 1998), p. 276.
3. Jenő Zoványi, *Magyarországi protestantismus története* (Budapest, 2004), vol. 1, p. 32.
4. See Graeme Murdock, *Calvinism on the Frontier, 1600–1660* (Oxford, 2000), pp. 153ff.
5. Bronisław Geremek, *Poverty* (Hoboken, NJ, 1994), p. 231.
6. Zoványi, *Magyarországi protestantismus története*, vol. 1, pp. 152–64, and Murdock, *Calvinism on the Frontier*, pp. 164ff.
7. Zoványi, *Magyarországi protestantismus története*, vol. 1, pp. 221ff., and Béla Köpeczi (ed.), *Erdély története* (Budapest, 1986), vol. 2, pp. 763ff.
8. Louis Eisenmann, *Le compromis austro-hongrois de 1867* (repr., Paris, 1969), p. 14.
9. Géza Bárczi, *A magyar nyelv életrajza* (Budapest, 1963), pp. 290 ff.
10. See Balázs Ablonczy, *Keletre Magyar!* (Budapest, 2016), p. 26.
11. See James Buchan's excellent book on eighteenth-century Edinburgh, *Capital of the Mind* (2007), pp. 128–9.
12. Paget was one of those endlessly self-confident Victorian polymaths: a geologist, a good linguist, interested in what he saw, carefully taking notes on everything from Roman ruins to gypsy folklore. His wife was Hungarian, and he lived in Hungary, advising on cattle-raising.
13. L.-F. Céline, *Semmelweis* (repr. Paris, 1999), the oddest medical thesis ever written.

## Chapter 2: Absolutism and Compromise

1. To an originally Jewish woman, according to Géza Komoróczy, *A zsidók története Magyarországon*, 2 vols (Pozsony [*sic*], 2012), vol. 2, p. 19.
2. Ignác Romsics, *Magyarország története a XX században* (Budapest, 2010), p. 475.
3. Eisenmann, *Le compromis*, p. 193.
4. Academy of Sciences, *Magyarország története*, vol. 6, part 1 (Budapest, 1979), p. 458.

5. *Magyarország története*, vol. 6, part 1, p. 469.
6. *Magyarország története*, vol. 6, part 1, pp. 553, 581.
7. Austrian Academy of Sciences, *Die Habsburgermonarchie 1848 bis 1918*, 7 vols (Vienna, 1973–2000), vol. 1, pp. 325ff.
8. Slovene and Czech have much in common, and the Slovene lands were run from the Bohemian chancellery. This accounts for Shakespeare's 'coast of Bohemia' in *A Winter's Tale*.

## Chapter 3: Dualism, 1867–1914

1. See Béla Bede, *225 Highlights of Hungarian Art Nouveau Architecture* (Budapest, 2012), pp. 287ff.
2. László Siklóssy, *Hogyan épült Budapest* (Budapest, 1985), pp. 75ff.
3. A. Gerő, *Az elsöprő kisebbség* (Budapest, 2017), p. 250.
4. Judit Frigyesi, *Béla Bartók and Turn-of-the-Century Budapest* (Berkeley, CA, 1998).
5. Norman Lebrecht, *Why Mahler?* (London, 2011), pp. 51–64.
6. Gerő, *Az elsöprő kisebbség*, p. 153, says that the going rate was 200,000 Crowns.
7. Komoróczy, *A zsidók története Magyarországon*, vol. 2, pp. 210ff.
8. Komoróczy, *A zsidók története Magyarországon*, vol. 2, pp. 185ff.
9. István Hargittai, *Martians* (Oxford, 2006).
10. H. W. Steed, *The Habsburg Monarchy* (London, 1914), pp. 145–81.
11. Montanelli, *L'Italia dei notabili* (Milan, 1973), p. 484.
12. See Bernard Wasserstein, *The Secret Lives of Trebitsch Lincoln* (1988), and Tom Bower, *Maxwell: The Outsider* (1987).
13. Balint Varga, *The Monumental Nation: Magyar Nationalism and Symbolic Politics in Fin-de-Siècle Hungary* (New York, 2016), pp. 31–2.
14. Romsics, *Magyarország története a XX században*, p. 228.
15. Köpeczi (ed.), *Erdély Története*, vol. 3, pp. 1637ff.
16. Peter Broucek (ed.), *Ein General im Zwielicht* (Vienna, 1988), p. 31.
17. Gabor Vermes, *István Tisza* (New York, 1985), pp. 436–7.
18. Tim Butcher, *The Trigger* (London, 2014).
19. Ottokar Czernin, *In the World War* (1920), p. 38.

## Chapter 4: War and Revolution

1. E. Iványi, *Magyar minisztertanácsi jegyzőkönyvek az első világháború korából* (Budapest, 1960), p. 61.
2. Max Hastings, *Catastrophe* (London, 2014), is the best recent account.
3. G. Wavro, *A Mad Catastrophe* (New York, 1914).
4. Szurmay was interned by the first post-war government – Károlyi's – for 'lengthening the war by winning'.
5. See Aleksandr Solzhenitsyn, *Rossiya v obvale* (1998), pp. 75ff.

6. Komoróczy, *A zsidók története Magyarországon*, vol. 2, pp. 346ff.
7. *Magyarország története*, vol. 8, part 1 (1976), 1, pp. 103ff.
8. *Magyarország története*, vol. 8, part 1, p. 84.
9. *Magyarország története*, vol. 8, part 1, pp. 127–8 and 239ff.
10. Komoróczy, *A zsidók története Magyarországon*, vol. 2, p. 359.
11. Romsics, *Magyarország története*, vol. 8, part 1, pp. 395ff., on the 'White terror'.

## Chapter 5: Admiral Horthy

1. *Magyarország története*, vol. 8, part 1, pp. 395ff., and Komoróczy, *A zsidók története Magyarországon*, vol. 2, pp. 382ff., for the Jewish aspect of this.
2. *Magyarország története*, vol. 8, part 1, p. 154.
3. See János Gyurgyák, *A zsidókérdés Magyarországon* (Budapest, 2001), pp. 295–8.
4. He arrived there with not much English, talked his way in and started making money by betting on horses. In this he was knowledgeable, his father being the best-known bookie in Budapest.
5. *Magyarország története*, vol. 8, part 1, pp. 440ff.
6. The Hungarian word *sugárhajtómü* is an example of what can happen to a language when an ultra-thin-skinned academy tries to avoid foreign words: it means 'stream-propellent-engine'. For years the patriotic word for 'football' was a similar *labdarúgó* – very roughly, 'leg grab' – but it now seems to be going out of use.
7. *Magyarország története*, vol. 8, part 1, p. 167.
8. From a speech quoted in Cartledge, *The Will to Survive*, p. 371.
9. In Holland, on New Year's Day 1945, the Jewish Council held a little celebration, congratulating themselves that they had kept the community together. Ninety per cent of the Dutch Jews had gone by then; there had been six SS officers in all Amsterdam, and after the war these council members were put on trial for collaboration (see Jacob Presser, *Ashes in the Wind* (London, 1968)). By contrast, 90 per cent of Belgian Jews survived, although this was partly owing to the connivance of the German Military Governor, Falkenhausen.
10. See Alexander Waugh, *The House of Wittgenstein* (London, 2009). According to Waugh, the silly old women handed almost everything to the Nazis in 1939, and went on holding Friday concerts, as in days of yore, in their palace on the Schwarzspaniergasse until a bomb fell on it in 1945.
11. Komoróczy, *A zsidók története Magyarországon*, vol. 2, p. 73.
12. Stephen Pálffy, *The First Thousand Years* (Budapest, 2008), p. 149.
13. Krisztián Ungváry, *Battle for Budapest* (London, 2007), p. 49.

## Chapter 6: Communist Take-Over

1. Their archives are in Moscow, and were used by Anthony Beevor for his *The Spanish Civil War* (London 2006), the best book on the subject.
2. Thanks to his background in the Caucasus; see Stephen Kotkin, *Stalin: Paradoxes of Power, 1878–1928* (London, 2014).
3. Vlagyimir Farkas, *Nincs mentség* (Budapest, 1990).
4. A remarkably long-lasting book is Hugh Seton-Watson's *The East European Revolution* (London, 1950; repr. 1961), pp. 190ff. of which are a summary of what happened, based on the author's earlier *The Pattern of Communist Revolution*. Its judgements are astonishingly durable.
5. See Elek Karsai and László Karsai (eds), *A Szálasi-per* (Budapest, 1988), p. v.
6. György Gyarmati in I. G. Tóth (ed.), *Millenium Magyar történet* (Budapest, 2002), is a good summary.
7. Attila Mong, *A Kádár hitele* (Budapest, 2012), pp. 26ff.
8. György Gyarmati, *A Rákosi-korszák* (Budapest, 2012), pp. 50ff.
9. Izsák Perlmutter, the original owner, was a noted painter and had an adopted daughter, taken from an orphanage and maybe of Jewish origin, who married the Persian military attaché and was known as Princess Ahmed Yusuf Mirza. The house was bequeathed to the Jewish religious community, with a lifetime interest for the princess. The Arrow Cross failed to pay rent, as did the ÁVO. With vast courage, she took its head, Gábor Péter, to court, and won; she was then exiled to a poor village in 1951 when the property was nationalised, and lived long enough to be awarded compensation.
10. See Karsai and Karsai (eds), *A Szálasi-per*.
11. Jörg K. Hoensch, *A History of Modern Hungary* (1988), p. 178.
12. See Gyarmati, *A Rákosi-korszak*, pp. 79ff.
13. Gyarmati, *A Rákosi-korszak*, pp. 79ff.
14. Hoensch, *A History of Modern Hungary*, pp. 176–7.
15. György Faludy, *My Happy Days in Hell* (London, 1962).
16. Róbert Szabó Györi, *A kommunista párt és a zsidóság* (Budapest, 1997), pp. 126ff.; Maria Palasik, *Félelembe zárt múlt: Politikai gyilkosságok Gyömrön és környékén 1945-ben* (Budapest, 2010).
17. See Palasik, *Félelembe zárt múlt: Politikai gyilkosságok Gyömrön és környékén 1945-ben*.
18. Györi, *A kommunista párt és a zsidóság*, p. 135.
19. For example, Viktor Karady, *Túlélők és újrakezdők* (Budapest, 2002), pp. 40ff, interviews with Jews from 1945–53.
20. Boris Kálnoky, *Ahnenland* (Munich, 2011), pp. 404–8.
21. Gyarmati, *A Rákosi-korszak*, pp. 102ff.

## Chapter 7: 'A mad old man', 1948–56

1. Gyarmati, *A Rákosi-korszak*, p. 268.

2. Gyarmati, *A Rákosi-korszak*, pp. 161ff.
3. Gyarmati, *A Rákosi-korszak*, pp. 249ff., and Komoróczy, *A zsidók története Magyarországon*, vol. 2, p. 1002.
4. See Krisztián Ungváry, *Tettesek vagy áldozatok?* (Budapest, 2104), pp. 34–46.
5. See Jaap Scholten, *Comrade Baron* (Reno, NV, 2016), passim.
6. Komoróczy, *A zsidók története Magyarországon*, vol. 2, p. 961.
7. Gyarmati, *A Rákosi-korszak*, p. 167.
8. See Gyarmati, *A Rákosi-korszak*, p. 175, with surreal illustrations.
9. Mong, *A Kádár hitele*, p. 35.
10. Gyarmati, *A Rákosi-korszak*, pp. 323–30.

## Chapter 8: Kádár

1. See Roger Gough, *A Good Comrade* (London, 2006), pp. 113ff.
2. Sándor Kopácsi, *Az 1956-os forradalom és a Nagy Imre-per* (1980).
3. Mong, *A Kádár hitele*, p. 58.
4. Gough, *A Good Comrade*, p. 132.
5. Imre Körösi, *A lóvá tett ország* (Budapest, 2011), makes the point that small plots could easily produce fruit trees whereas the soil was not appropriate for grain.
6. See Mong, *A Kádár hitele*, pp. 75ff.
7. Sándor Révész, *Aczél és korunk* (Budapest, 1997), p. 207.
8. Mong, *A Kádár hitele* p. 92.
9. Zsuzsa Borvendég, *Az impexek kora* (Budapest, 2017).
10. Mong, *A Kádár hitele*, pp. 50ff.
11. Mong, *A Kádár hitele*, pp. 73ff.
12. See Gyula Borbándi, *A magyar émigráció életrajza 1945–1985*, 2 vols (Bern, 1985).

## Chapter 9: The 1980s and Beyond

1. Alain Besançon, *Présent soviétique et passé russe* (Paris, 1981), p. 253.
2. György Dalos, *Der Vorhang geht auf* (Munich, 2009), p. 164.
3. Dalos, *Der Vorhang geht auf*, pp. 60ff.
4. György Moldova, *Kádár János*, 2 vols (Budapest, 2006), vol. 2, pp. 57ff. Bryan Cartledge refers to the context of this episode, *The Will to Survive*, p. 477.
5. Mong, *A Kádár hitele*, passim.
6. Mong, *A Kádár hitele*, p. 253.
7. Mong, *A Kádár hitele*, pp. 250ff.
8. Dalos, *Der Vorhang geht auf*, p. 66.
9. András Mint, 'A David-Irving kalandja 1956-al', *Beszélő*, 7–8 (2002).
10. Maximilian Graf et al. (ed.), *Das Burgenland als internationale Grenzregion* (Vienna, 2012), pp. 150ff.
11. Dalos, *Der Vorhang geht auf*, p. 76.
12. Dalos, *Der Vorhang geht auf*, pp. 92ff.

# Select Bibliography

A great deal of Hungarian history has been and is being written, and this short list is designed for the English-language readership, as a guide. I have, however, also noted my own principal sources in other languages.

Of larger-scale histories, Bryan Cartledge's *The Will to Survive* (London, 2011) is the best in English, readable and reliable. There have been many attempts at a short history, and two of the older ones stand out. Denis Sinor's *History of Hungary* (New York, 1959) is very good on the medieval period, and Paul Ignotus's *Hungary* (London, 1972) on the modern. (Ignotus was a journalist and knew how to present difficult information, but he had a powerful literary background and gives an excellent introduction to linguistic and literary themes.)

There are some classics which may just count as part of English literature. Miklós Bánffy's *The Transylvanian Trilogy*, translated, superbly, by Patrick Thursfield and Katalin Bánffy-Jelen (3 vols, New York, 2013), has been compared to *War and Peace*. Outstanding memoirs are György Faludy's *My Happy Days in Hell* (London, 2010), by a major poet who spent years in exile from the Nazis and then in Communist camps, and Arthur Koestler's *Arrow in the Blue* (London, 1952) and *The Invisible Writing* (London, 2005), describing an extaordinary international life. Bernard Wasserstein's *The Secret Lives of Trebitsch Lincoln* (London, 1988) records the doings of a world-class confidence trickster. Patrick Leigh Fermor's *Between the Woods and the Water* (London, 1986) is the record of an epic journey in Hungary and Transylvania in 1933–4. Michael O'Sullivan has usefully expanded on it, showing where and with which members of the Hungarian nobility Leigh Fermor stayed (*Noble Encounters*, Budapest, 2018). I would also include in this section John Lukacs's *Budapest 1900* (London, 1988). A very recent and superb guidebook is Annabel Howell's *Budapest*, in the Blue Guide series (London, 2018).

Of British historians knowing Hungarian, the outstanding modern one is C. A. Macartney's *October Fifteenth: A History of Modern Hungary, 1929–1945* (2 vols, Edinburgh, 1963), which is a first-class historical record in itself, ending with the overthrow of Horthy and based on personal reminiscences. *The Magyars in the Ninth Century* (Cambridge, 1930) and *Hungary and Her Successors: The Treaty of Trianon and Its Consequences* (Oxford, 1937) are Macartney's two other notable books. His others are pedestrian. Hugh Seton-Watson's *The Pattern of Communist Revolution: An Historical Analysis* (London, 1953) simply says about the

Communist takeover what subsequent work fifty years later has confirmed. A. J. P. Taylor's *The Habsburg Monarchy, 1809–1918* (London, 1948) is a timeless essay. though best appreciated after some bread-and-butter preparation. He had lived in Vienna for two years as Austrian democracy was collapsing in the early 1930s.

In Hungarian, the bibliography in Ignác Romsics, *Magyarország története a XX században* (Budapest, 2010), is excellent, and includes film. As regards my own sources, there is a useful series of short books, *Magyar História*, published by Gondolat at a time when not even lip-service needed to be paid to Marxism. Of these I would pick out Klára Hegyi, *Egy világbirodalom végvidékén*, about Ottoman Hungary (1976), János Barta, *A kétfejű sas árnyékában* on the eighteenth century (Budapest, 1984), Éva Somogyi, *Absolutizmus és kiegyezés 1849–1867* (Budapest, 1981), and Ferenc Pölöskei, *Tisza István* (Budapest, 1985). I have also used *Magyarország története* (10 double vols, Budapest 1976–88), Béla Köpeczi (ed.), *Erdély története* (3 vols, Budapest, 1986), and *Millenium Magyar történet* (Budapest, 2002), with particular attention to Ignác Romsics for the period 1914–44/45 and György Gyarmati for 1944/45–2000. Two family histories can be singled out: Boris Kálnoky's *Ahnenland* (Munich, 2011) is ingeniously written, with flashbacks, around the story of his grandfather, and Stephen Pálffy's *The First Thousand Years* (Budapest, 2008) is endearingly addressed to his grandchildren in New Zealand. For Jewish matters, see János Gyurgyák, *A zsidókérdés Magyarországon* (Budapest, 2001), and Géza Komoróczy, *A zsidók története Magyarországon* (2 vols, Pozsony [sic], 2012). Protestantism is surveyed in Jenő Zoványi, *Magyarországi protestantismus története* (2 vols, Budapest, 2004). Books that pick out interesting Hungarians of all sorts are Domokos Kosáry's introduction to Árpád Rácz's edition *Famous Hungarians* (Budapest, 2002) and Krisztián Nyáry's *Eminent Hungarians* (Budapest, 2017). Of course there is no escaping the fact that Hungary was part of the Habsburg Monarchy, and the Austrian Academy of Sciences' *Die Habsburgermonarchie 1848 bis 1918* (7 vols, some of them double, Vienna, 1973–2000), with various editors, starting with Adam Wandruszka, has huge amounts of information on all aspects.

Otherwise, I have made use of the following:

Béla Bede, *225 Highlights of Hungarian Art Nouveau Architecture* (Budapest, 2012)
Zsuzsanna Borvendég, *Az 'impexek' kora* (Budapest, 2017)
Ingrid Carlberg, *Raoul Wallenberg*, trans. Ebba Segerberg (London, 2015)
Louis-Ferdinand Céline, *Semmelweis* (Paris, 1999)
Kenneth Chalmers, *Béla Bartók* (London, 1995)
Samu Csinta, *Aristokraták honfoglalása* (Budapest, 2016)
György Dalos, *Der Vorhang geht auf* (Munich, 2009)
István Deák, *The Lawful Revolution: Louis Kossuth and the Hungarians, 1848–1849* (New York, 1979)
——, *Beyond Nationalism: A Social and Political History of the Habsburg Officer Corps, 1848–1918* (Oxford, 1990)

Louis Eisenmann, *Le compromis austro-hongrois de 1867* (repr., Paris, 1969). The grand classic.

Judit Frigyesi, *Béla Bartók and Turn-of-the-Century Budapest* (London, 1998)

Frank Füredi, *Célkereszthen: Magyarország* (Budapest, 2017)

András Gerő, *The Mirage of Power: The Hungarian Parliament 1867–1918* (Boulder, CO, 1997)

Roger Gough, *A Good Comrade* (London, 2006)

Alexander Grossmann, *Nur das Gewissen: Carl Lutz und seine Budapester Aktion. Geschichte und Porträt* (Wald, 1986)

György Gyarmati, *A Rákosi-korszák* (Budapest, 2011)

Péter Hanák, *The Garden and the Workshop* (Princeton, 1998)

András Hegedüs, *Im Schatten einer Idee* (Zurich, 1986)

Jörg K. Hoensch, *A History of Modern Hungary* (London, 1988)

Catherine Horel, *Horthy*, trans. Magda Ferch (Budapest, 2017)

Gyula Horn, *Freiheit, die ich meine* (Hamburg, 2001)

Zoltán Horváth, *Die Jahrhundertwende in Ungarn* (Budapest, 1966)

Igor Janke, *Forward: The Story of Viktor Orbán* (Budapest, 2015)

Andrew C. Janos, *The Politics of Backwardness in Hungary* (Princeton, 1982)

P. M. Judson, *Exclusive Revolutionaries: Liberal Politics, Social Experience, and National Identity, 1848–1914* (Ann Arbor, MI, 1996)

——, *The Habsburg Empire* (Cambridge, MA, 2016)

Sándor M. Kiss, *Frigyes Káhler: Kinek a forradalma?* (Budapest, 1997)

——, *Rendszerváltás 1989* (Lakitelek, 2014)

Domokos Kosáry, *Culture and Society in Eighteenth Century Hungary* (Budapest, 1987)

György Kövér and Gábor Gyáni, *Social History of Hungary* (New York, 2004)

David Mandler, *Vámbéry and the British Empire* (Lanham, MD, 2016)

Sándor Marai, *Memoir of Hungary, 1944–48* (Budapest, 2002)

Henrik Marczali, *Hungary in the Eighteenth Century* (Cambridge, 1910; repr. n.d.) (This has a lengthy introduction by the then classic historian H. W. Temperley which is still very useful as regards the sweep of Hungarian history.)

William C. McCagg, *Jewish Nobles and Geniuses in Modern Hungary* (New York, 1986)

Zsuzsa Mikó, *A terror hétköznapjai* (Budapest, 2016)

Graeme Murdock, *Calvinism on the Frontier, 1600–1660* (Oxford, 2000)

Robert Nemes, *Another Hungary* (Stanford, CA, 2016), collective biographies

Edit Olthay, *Fidesz and the Reinvention of the Hungarian Center-Right* (Budapest, 2012)

John Paget, *Hungary and Transylvania* (Cambridge, MA, 1839) (A landmark, Paget being an agricultural specialist, with a Hungarian wife.)

Mária Palasik, *Chess Game for Democracy: Hungary between East and West, 1944–1947* (Toronto, 2011)

György Pálóczi-Horváth, *The Undefeated* (London, 1959)

David Pryce-Jones, *The War That Never Was* (London, 1995)

Árpád Pünkösti, *Rákosi, Sztálin legjobb tanítványa* (Budapest, 2004)

Zoltán Ripp, *Rendszerváltás Magyarországon 1987–1990* (Budapest, 2006)

Mátyás Sárközi, *The Life of Ferenc Molnár* (London, 2004)

Maria Schmidt, *Diktatúrák ördögszekerén* (Budapest, 1998)

——, *Battle of Wits* (Budapest, 2007)

Jaap Scholten, *Comrade Baron* (Reno, NV, 2016)

George Schöpflin, *Politics in Eastern Europe* (Hoboken, NJ, 1993)

Victor Sebestyén, *Twelve Days: How the Hungarians Tried to Topple Their Soviet Masters* (London, 2006)

Alan Sked, *The Survival of the Habsburg Empire: Radetzky, the Imperial Army and the Class War, 1848* (London, 1979)

——, *Metternich and Austria* (Basingstoke, 2008)

Nigel Swain, *Hungary: The Rise and Fall of Feasible Socialism* (London, 1992)

László Tőkéczki, *Történelmi arcképek – politikus portrék a dualizmus korából* (Budapest, 2002)

Rudolf L. Tőkés, *Hungary's Negotiated Revolution* (Cambridge, 1996)

Theo Tschuy, *Carl Lutz und die Juden von Budapest* (Zurich, 1995)

Krisztián Ungváry, *Battle for Budapest* (London, 2004)

Gábor Vermes, *Hungarian Culture and Politics in the Habsburg Monarchy, 1711–1848* (Budapest, 2014)

# Index